D0500531

GREAT SHAKESPEARE ACTORS

Great Shakespeare Actors

BURBAGE TO BRANAGH

STANLEY WELLS

OXFORD
UNIVERSITY PRESS

OXFORD
UNIVERSITY PRESS

Great Clarendon Street, Oxford, OX2 6DP,
United Kingdom

Oxford University Press is a department of the University of Oxford.
It furthers the University's objective of excellence in research, scholarship,
and education by publishing worldwide. Oxford is a registered trade mark of
Oxford University Press in the UK and in certain other countries

© Stanley Wells 2015

The moral rights of the author have been asserted

First Edition published in 2015

Impression: 1

All rights reserved. No part of this publication may be reproduced, stored in
a retrieval system, or transmitted, in any form or by any means, without the
prior permission in writing of Oxford University Press, or as expressly permitted
by law, by licence or under terms agreed with the appropriate reprographics
rights organization. Enquiries concerning reproduction outside the scope of the
above should be sent to the Rights Department, Oxford University Press, at the
address above

You must not circulate this work in any other form
and you must impose this same condition on any acquirer

Published in the United States of America by Oxford University Press
198 Madison Avenue, New York, NY 10016, United States of America

British Library Cataloguing in Publication Data
Data available

Library of Congress Control Number: 2014952415

ISBN 978–0–19–870329–7

Printed in Italy by L.E.G.O. S.p.A.

Links to third party websites are provided by Oxford in good faith and
for information only. Oxford disclaims any responsibility for the materials
contained in any third party website referenced in this work.

To all the great Shakespeare actors not included in this book

Preface and Acknowledgements

This book draws on a lifelong interest in the history of theatre and of Shakespeare's place in it, as well as on close on seventy years of playgoing. An early stimulus to write it came from an invitation from Alistair Smith, editor of *The Stage*, to contribute to a feature about great Shakespeare actors.

I am grateful for assistance from the library staff of the Shakespeare Birthplace Trust, especially Madeleine Cox, Victoria Swanston, and Helen Hargest; to Kate Welch of the Shakespeare Institute; and to Roger Howells and Paul Edmondson for encouragement and for helpful comments on drafts. Jacqueline Baker, of Oxford University Press, has been an exemplary editor, and I have benefited greatly from the expertise of the production staff at the Press. I owe especial thanks to Nick de Somogyi for the care and expertise with which he has compiled the index.

The order in which the actors are discussed is roughly chronological by date of birth, but in a few cases I have departed from this principle in the interests of continuity.

Stanley Wells

January 2015

Contents

List of Illustrations

Introduction

In this book I offer a series of short essays on my personal selection of the greatest Shakespeare actors from his time to ours. In making my choices I have looked for that degree of special illumination, originality, and communicative power that distinguishes the great from the good, or even from the excellent. I have chosen actors primarily for their greatness as performers rather than for qualities such as entrepreneurship or the ability to run theatres. For all the actors since Edith Evans onwards I have been able to draw upon my own theatregoing experience.

The process of selection has not been easy and I am conscious that many great names of both past and present are not represented here. All but one of the actors I write about are from the English-speaking world. The exception is Tommaso Salvini (Chapter 19), who performed extensively in England and America, interacting with English-speaking colleagues and audiences while speaking in his native Italian. I have limited myself to writing about stage performance rather than film, where the actor has less autonomy, though some actors of recent times have shone equally in both media. Laurence Olivier, great as both stage and film actor, nevertheless wrote, 'film is the director's medium, television the writer's, but the theatre is the actor's'.[1] No one acting in a Shakespeare play performs in a vacuum, but my focus is on individuals rather than on the productions in which they appear or the directors who contribute, often to a great but (to audiences) unidentifiable extent, to their performances.

★

Actors who appeared in the earliest performances of Shakespeare's plays, such as Richard Burbage, Will Kemp, and Robert Armin, achieved star status, as contemporary accounts show, and ever since then his plays have been valued partly because of the wide range of opportunities and challenges that they offer to leading players. For young men—or men able to impersonate youth, because actors need not be of the same age as the characters they play—Berowne in *Love's Labour's Lost*, Richard II, Romeo, Prince Hal (sometimes leading directly to his portrayal as Henry V), and above all Hamlet are, as Max Beerbohm wrote of the last named, hoops 'through which every very eminent actor must, sooner or later, jump'.[2] For male actors more mature in years—or able to impersonate men older than themselves— there are opportunities for greatness in such diverse roles as Richard III, Oberon, Shylock, Iago, Othello, Macbeth, Leontes in *The Winter's Tale*, Coriolanus, Prospero in *The Tempest*, and—the final summit of ambition—King Lear. Actors with a special gift for comedy can revel in Lance in *The Two Gentlemen of Verona*, Bottom, Benedick or (very differently) Dogberry in *Much Ado About Nothing*, Malvolio, three different Falstaffs in three separate plays, and (if they can sing) Autolycus in *The Winter's Tale*.

Great opportunities for young women are provided by Juliet, Titania in *A Midsummer Night's Dream*, both Viola and Olivia in *Twelfth Night*, Rosalind in *As You Like It*, Isabella in *Measure for Measure*, Helen in *All's Well That Ends Well*, Cressida, and Imogen in *Cymbeline*.

Because originally women were played by boys, roles for older women are fewer but they include Queen Margaret in the early history plays, the Nurse in *Romeo and Juliet*, Mistress Quickly in the Falstaff plays, Lady Macbeth, the Countess in *All's Well That Ends Well*, Volumnia in *Coriolanus*, and—another summit—Cleopatra. And, as with men, the actual age of the actor need not be identical with the presumed age of the character: apparently youthful women such as Beatrice in *Much About Nothing*, Katherine the shrew, and Titania have been successfully played by actresses of mature years, such as Helen Faucit, Peggy Ashcroft, and Judi Dench, and Ashcroft played Margaret from young beauty to old crone in an adaptation of the early history plays (see Chapter 27).

In modern times a revival (with variations) of the cross-gender casting of Shakespeare's time, when it was confined to female roles, has increased opportunities for women. As early as the late eighteenth century, Sarah Siddons became the first of many women to play Hamlet. Half a century later the American Charlotte Cushman was an acclaimed Romeo and played other male roles. All-female Shake-speare companies, both amateur and professional, have come into being from time to time. Grown men have played female roles, as in so-called 'original practices' productions at Shakespeare's Globe (inauthentic in that they do not cast boys in women's roles), and in the work of Edward Hall's Propeller Company. And the introduction of colour-blind casting has broadened the palette of roles available to both male and female actors of colour. The fact that reversals of conventional expectation such as these are far more common in Sha-kespeare than in plays by other dramatists, both classic and modern, is perhaps a reflection of the heightened style and tone associated with poetic drama (as with opera): putting it simply, if audiences can accept the unreality of people on stage talking in verse, they may also be able to accept men as women, women as men, black actors as kings of England, and other apparent anomalies.

The great roles are there for the asking, and they invite greatness of performance. How can we define this? What makes a great, as distinct from a good or a merely competent, actor? Some basic qualities are essential, whatever the role. To put it simplistically, actors manipulate their bodies—their limbs, hands and feet, their facial muscles, their eyes, their voices—in order to manipulate the reactions of people who come to see them. This necessary reliance on the body means that there is inevitably at least a subliminal sexual relationship between actors and those who watch them—what Michael Billington, in a chapter of his book *The Modern Actor* (London: Hamish Hamilton, 1973) headed 'Sex and Acting', calls 'the androgynous, bisexual quality that invariably underpins great acting'. Some actors exploit this quality to the full, flirting covertly or even blatantly with their audiences, drawing on their sexual appeal to involve those who watch them with the inner natures of the characters they are playing.

At the most basic level, actors need to be able to inhabit a theatrical space with confidence, to move easily and to stand still in the presence of an audience. Shakespeare knew that stillness, the ability to listen and to react in silence, can command attention and convey emotion as effectively as loud speech or violent action. The direction '*Holds her by the hand silent*' as Coriolanus undergoes the inner struggle that will result in his death, can, as Olivier showed (Chapter 26), enable the actor to hold the audience in silent, awed suspense. 'Silence is the perfectest herald of joy', says Claudio in *Much Ado About Nothing* at the moment of his betrothal (2.1.287).[3] And in the final scene of *The Winter's Tale* Hermione is required to sustain a pose of motionless silence for several minutes.

An actor's physical presence may be modified or enhanced by various means. Some roles clearly call for physical transformation. An obvious example is Richard III, whose deformity is made much of in the text. Olivier is conspicuous for his delight in seeking to find a visual correlative for his characters' inner natures, ageing himself by forty or so years when, at the age of 37, he played Justice Shallow. Of his Macbeth he wrote, 'I had a huge false face on: a nose that went down straight from the forehead, a false chin and a putty forehead with vast eyebrows. The idea was to make something real through a highly poetic and unreal approach.'[4] Vivien Leigh said acerbically, 'Larry's make-up comes on, then Banquo comes on, then Larry comes on.'[5] Costume can assist characterization, helping to indicate social class, for instance, or occupation, or moral attitudes: a Doll Tearsheet will dress very differently from an Isabella, a Dogberry from an Orsino, a Shylock from an Angelo. Most actors need to bulk themselves out to play Falstaff (though it helps if they are fat to start with), and Donald Sinden has described how as Malvolio he felt a need to wear 'black, only relieved by very narrow plain, white collar and cuffs', complemented by 'a period hat like a black flower pot', and gold chain of office (see Chapter 30).

Props may play their part. Antony Sher supplemented Richard III's back deformity with a pair of elbow-crutches which he wielded to devastating effect (see Chapter 37). Attitudes to facial make-up have varied greatly over the centuries, influenced in part by the size of theatres and the nature of the stage lighting—whether natural daylight, gaslight, or electric light.

Actors may be required to interact physically with colleagues, to dance or to fight or to appear to make love on stage. Illustrative or emphatic gesture may be a valuable tool. The Restoration actor Thomas Betterton and his wife, Mary Saunderson, used to practise their movements in front of a mirror (see Chapter 4). But, as Hamlet advises the players, gesture can be overused: 'do not saw the air too much with your hand, thus, but use all gently; for in the very torrent, tempest, and as I may say the whirlwind of your passion, you must acquire and beget a temperance that may give it smoothness' (3.2.48). In my essay on Macready (Chapter 12) I describe how, following advice from Mrs Siddons, he disciplined himself to beget such 'temperance'. He

> would lie down on the floor, or stand straight against a wall, or get my arms within a bandage, and, so pinioned, or confined, repeat the most violent passages of Othello, Lear, Hamlet, Macbeth, or whatever would require most energy and emotion. I would speak the most passionate bursts of rage under the supposed constraints of whispering them in the ear of him or her to whom they were addressed, thus keeping both voice and gesture in subjection to the real impulse of feeling.

Like Betterton, he would use looking glasses, too, to help him to 'keep the features, perhaps I should say the muscles of the face, undisturbed, whilst intense passion would speak from the eye alone'.[6] It is almost as if he were foreseeing the advent of film and television: but Macready played in some of the biggest theatres London has known.

Memory, and confidence in it, play an essential role: Shakespeare writes in Sonnet 23 of an 'imperfect actor'—that is, one whose memory and self-confidence fail him—'who with his fear is put besides his part'. Stage fright has afflicted great actors, such as Laurence Olivier and Ian Holm, for long periods of time, even driving them off the stage. Though actors need to identify with the emotions that their characters feel, they need also to maintain an emotional distance from their roles. Needing at once to be in control of themselves and their audience, they may exist in a schizophrenic state, actor and character held in perfect equipoise, as Donald Sinden wrote of his performance of Malvolio (see Chapter 30). Excessive identification with the fictional situation may result in memory loss: Coriolanus, overwhelmed by emotion as his mother, wife, and child come to plead with him on behalf both of themselves and of Rome, loses self-control like a poor actor who identifies too closely with the role he is playing:

> Like a dull actor now
> I have forgot my part, and I am out
> Even to a full disgrace.   (*Coriolanus*, 5.3.40–2)

Vocal prowess is no less important. At the most basic level, actors must make themselves heard, sometimes in large spaces with difficult acoustics. They may be required to shout, to sing, to speak in dialect or in chorus. In *A Midsummer Night's Dream* Shakespeare shows Bottom's awareness that an actor may need sometimes to speak in 'a monstrous

little voice' and at others to 'roar' in such a way that it 'will do any
man's heart good to hear' him (1.2.48, 66–7). Voice can be manipulated in various ways. Actors may adopt regional, national, or class-
related accents to aid characterization, most obviously for a Shylock or
a Hotspur (who is said to 'speak thick'—Olivier famously gave him a
stammer on the letter 'w' and died trying to say 'worms'), or the Welsh
Fluellen, or Portia's Moorish suitor. Olivier is said to have spent six
months lowering his voice by an octave for Othello (see Chapter 26).
Many actors, from Betterton onwards and including Helen Faucit,
John Gielgud, and Kenneth Branagh, have won praise for vocal beauty;
others, such as George Frederick Cooke and Henry Irving, have
triumphed in spite of serious vocal limitations.

Facial expression plays an important part. 'Your face, my thane, is as
a book where men | May read strange matters' says Lady Macbeth to
her tempted husband. And she advises him to 'look like the innocent
flower, | But be the serpent under't' (*Macbeth*, 1.5.61–2, 64–5). Actors
must be able to control their facial muscles so that they can register
changes of expression, sometimes in large spaces, conveying through
physical means a sense of what is going on in the character's mind.
Writing of Charles Laughton in Chapter 22, I quote John Mason
Brown's observation that his face was 'one of the most expressive
masks that I have ever seen in the theatre. . . . He does not say the
lines, he thinks them. They can be seen gathering like clouds in the
eyes. He can be cross with peppery violence, carnal with a grossness
that is repellent, merry with the expansiveness of Falstaff, cruel with a
hideousness that is sickening and afraid with a whimpering terror that
is almost unendurable'. In my essay on David Garrick (Chapter 6),
I quote Diderot's astonished observation that the actor could 'put his
head between two folding doors, and in the course of five or six
seconds his expression will change successively from wild delight to
temperate pleasure, from this to tranquillity, from tranquillity to surprise, from surprise to blank astonishment, from that to sorrow, from
sorrow to the air of one overwhelmed, from that to fright, from fright
to horror, from horror to despair, and thence he will go up again to the
point from which he started'. And we read of Macready as Benedick
that 'In the celebrated soliloquy in the second act, after he has overheard in the arbour that Beatrice loves him, the complex expression of
his face as he advanced drew roars from the house before he uttered a
word. One might read there the sense of amazement, of gratification,

and of perplexity as to the way of reconciling his newly-revealed passion for Beatrice with his late raillery at her and all women' (see Chapter 12).

Eyes can be variously expressive. Again Shakespeare shows awareness of this weapon in the actor's armoury. 'Disdain and scorn ride sparkling in her eyes', says Hero of Beatrice in *Much Ado About Nothing* (3.1.51), and in *Love's Labour's Lost* Boyet knows that 'the heart's still rhetoric' may be 'disclosèd with eyes'. In *Hamlet* Polonius expresses astonishment that the First Player 'has turned his colour, and has tears in's eyes' (2.2.521–2). G. F. Cooke's eyes were described as 'fiery, dark, and at times terribly expressive, with prominent lids and flexible brows'.[7] Actors may need to call up tears at will, whether through imaginative identification with their characters' suffering, or by a willed control over their tear ducts, or by a combination of the two. John Gielgud, along with other members of the Terry dynasty, was famously tearful.

Playing in Shakespeare may call upon skills beyond those that form a routine part of the training of actors to perform in modern plays. Ability to respond to the varying demands of Shakespeare's verse is basic. Long verse paragraphs such as Juliet's or Berowne's soliloquies call for the kind of breath control for which Ellen Terry and Ian Richardson, among others, were famous. The great director John Barton lays emphasis on the importance of drawing attention by vocal shading to the antitheses that characterize much of Shakespeare's writing in both verse and prose. Judi Dench (Chapter 33) stresses the need for legato in speaking lyrical verse. The wide range of styles that Shakespeare deploys makes diverse demands on the actor, and few can achieve greatness in all of them. Some actors, like Edwin Booth or John Gielgud, or Ellen Terry or Judi Dench, may excel at the lyricism of a Romeo or a Richard II, a Juliet or a Viola. Others, like Donald Wolfit or Laurence Olivier, or Charlotte Cushman or Sybil Thorndike, may more easily summon up the resonance and vocal power called for by more heroic or passionate roles such as Henry V or Coriolanus, or Constance (in *King John*) or Volumnia. Other actors, such as Henry Irving or Antony Sher, or Sarah Siddons or Peggy Ashcroft, may excel in roles of psychological complexity, such as Hamlet or Macbeth, Isabella or Cleopatra. Some, such as Ian McKellen or Olivier again, have an ability to signal irony or emotional detachment or cruelty which makes them particularly good as villains such as Richard III or

Iago. And others, like Garrick, Ellen Terry, Donald Sinden, and Ian
Richardson have special talents for comedy—irony is important here
too, and charm, and the ability to time a comic quip with delicate
precision.

In both tragedy and comedy Shakespeare's prose is often no less self-
consciously constructed and artistically patterned than his verse, and
most of the great roles demand fine prose speaking, with no less
attention to rhythm and verbal patterning than in verse. Hamlet and
Lear, Cleopatra and Rosalind express themselves no less eloquently in
both. And the prose spoken by predominantly but diversely comic
characters such as Lance (in *The Two Gentlemen of Verona*), Dogberry (in
Much Ado About Nothing), Malvolio (in *Twelfth Night*), and Autolycus
(in *The Winter's Tale*) has its own diverse challenges.

Technical acting skills can be acquired through training and the
application of intelligence, but there is an extra dimension to great
acting which transcends and can even defy technique. It calls for an
exercise of imagination, an ability to see beneath the surface of Shakespeare's language, to encompass and weld together the diverse elements
of a role—what the character says, what other people say about it, how
it behaves, how it interacts with others, how it changes or develops
during the course of the play—and it calls for the ability to project this
understanding in performance after performance and often in a wide
variety of physical circumstances. It calls in short for genius, a quality
that we may recognize more easily than we may define.

Genius may reveal itself in handling of language, as Herbert Farjeon
recognized when he wrote of Edith Evans that she 'quickens every
syllable, recognizes in a choice epithet something as three-dimensional
as a living being, reveals new wonders unsuspected and never to be
forgotten' (see Chapter 20). It may illuminate individual moments of a
play's action: it was there when, for, instance, Judi Dench, playing
Viola, spoke 'I am all the daughters of my father's house—, and all the
brothers too' with an inflection of the word 'brothers' that took us
movingly from the fictional situation of Viola speaking equivocally to
conceal her own disguise to the reality of the situation in which she
genuinely believed she had lost her own brother. It can reveal itself in
stage business, as when Edmund Kean as Hamlet, at the end of the
nunnery scene, came back from the side of the stage 'from a pang of
parting tenderness to press his lips to Ophelia's hand' with, wrote
William Hazlitt, 'an electrical effect on the house' (see Chapter 11). It

can be there in moments of silence, as it was, T. C. Worsley wrote, when Peggy Ashcroft, playing Cordelia to Michael Redgrave's Lear in 1950, showed her 'power of touching us simply by her posture and the atmosphere she distils' (see Chapter 27). It is there when an actor achieves not just physical but imaginative transformation such as was described by a young student watching Edith Evans from the wings as she prepared to go on stage as Rosalind:

I used to watch her waiting for her cue, night after night, dressed in her shirt and knee-breeches, transforming herself in a matter of seconds into a sparkling, adorable young creature. Her chin would go up, her eyes begin to shine, her body became spring-like and resilient, and full of confidence in her beauty and gaiety, she would sweep on to the stage to meet her dear love with such lightness that I used sometimes to wonder if her feet actually touched the stage at all.[8]

Genius is there when an actor appears to be possessed by the character, as Mrs Siddons was when, as Volumnia, she 'towered above all around, and rolled, and almost reeled across the stage; her very soul, as it were, dilating, and rioting in its exultation; until her action lost all grace, and, yet, became so true to nature, so picturesque, and so descriptive, that pit and gallery sprang to their feet electrified by the transcendent execution of an original conception' (see Chapter 7). And genius can break rules. Henry Irving was notorious for the eccentricity of his vocal delivery (Chapter 17), Charles Laughton's pronunciation offended some listeners (Chapter 22), and John Gielgud never ceased being embarrassed by his legs, especially if he had to wear tights (Chapter 25).

Performances are inevitably affected by the physical conditions under which they are given. In every period and every country actors have had to adjust the scale and style of their acting to a wide range of playing spaces and to varying expectations from audiences. This was true of Shakespeare's time, when the public playhouses of London, open to the elements, made different demands from private playhouses such as the Blackfriars, in which the King's Men operated from 1609, and from the inn yards, the great halls of aristocratic houses, the town halls, and even the churches in which companies performed when on tour. In later ages too the size and design of theatres has fluctuated, encompassing proscenium arch theatres, playhouses with thrust stages, theatre in the round, studio theatres, and open-air spaces. In London from the Restoration onwards theatres gradually increased in capacity because of the demands of a growing population until in the Romantic period plays could legally be given only in the large Theatres Royal at Covent Garden and Drury Lane, with the Theatre Royal in the Haymarket in use as a summer playhouse from 1766. This severely stretched the demands made on the powers of those who played in them to project their voices and to make visual effects that would register in the furthest reaches of the auditoria (Chapter 7). In more recent times, too, actors have had to scale up or down according to the spaces in which they are playing. It is a far cry from the vast spaces of Drury Lane and Covent Garden to the village halls in Welsh mining villages in which Sybil Thorndike and Lewis Casson played during the Second World War (see Chapter 21), and in recent years the National Theatre has played Shakespeare both in the large spaces of the Olivier auditorium and in the much smaller Cottesloe, just as the Royal Shakespeare Company's spaces have ranged from their main house through the Swan to The Other Place. Transfers from one to the other don't always work. Trevor Nunn's production of *Macbeth* with Ian McKellen and Judi Dench was immensely successful in the small space of The Other Place in Stratford-upon-Avon, for which it was created, but fell notoriously flat when it moved to the main auditorium of the Royal Shakespeare Theatre. I vividly remember the atmosphere of depression backstage at the end of its first perform-ance there.

In writing this book I have come increasingly to feel that acting is a creative art. The playwright provides performers with their raw mater-ial, which may well have its own kind of greatness. But these scripts have unwritten dimensions which come to reality only when they are performed, and which achieve a different kind of reality in each performance. There is, we might say, no such thing as a play: there are only scripts which come to life in different ways each time they are performed. The creative power of the actor was well described by James Agate reviewing Edith Evans's performance of Margery Eyre in Thomas Dekker's comedy *The Shoemaker's Holiday*. 'Miss Evans', he wrote, 'has this characteristic of all good acting—that is she takes hold of her dramatist's conception, absorbs it, and then gives it out again re-created in terms of her own personality and delighted imagination, so that you get the two-fold joy of one fine talent superimposed upon another'.[9] It is because of this necessary interaction between actor and role that we can go on seeing *Hamlet* or *King Lear, A Midsummer Night's Dream* or *Twelfth Night* with pleasure in innumerable productions. Each of them is and is not the same play, a text made flesh by the actors who perform it, a catalyst that can release the creative powers of great actors such as those I write about in the pages that follow.

Figure 1. Putative oil painting of Shakespeare by an anonymous artist, 1610.

PRELUDE

William Shakespeare

Born in Stratford-upon-Avon, 23(?) April 1564, died 23 April 1616. Founder member of the Lord Chamberlain's Men, 1594; from 1603 this company became the King's Men. *Shakespeare roles*: none certainly identified.

Who was the first great Shakespeare actor? Could it have been Shakespeare himself? The First Folio edition of his plays, printed in 1623, seven years after he died, includes a list of 'the names of the principal actors in all these plays'. Shakespeare's name comes first; it has been suggested that this may 'imply that he had been a leading performer in every single play included in the Folio'.[1] It is a bold claim. The heading to the list does not necessarily imply that all the actors named in it had appeared in all the Folio's thirty-six plays. Indeed that is impossible. One of the actors named is Nathan Field, who was not born until 1587, and so would have been an infant when Shakespeare started writing. And another actor in the list, Laurence Fletcher, didn't join the company until 1603.

Still, there is no doubt that Shakespeare was an actor. He, along with Richard Burbage and the great comedian William Kemp, received payments for plays performed before the Queen in December 1594. This shows that he belonged to an acting company, and almost certainly that acting was part of his duty. He is named unequivocally as an actor in the printed list of 'The principal comedians' for Ben Jonson's comedy *Every Man in his Humour* (acted in 1598) and of 'the principal tragedians' in Jonson's tragedy *Sejanus* (which bombed heavily when it was acted in 1603). I think 'comedians' and 'tragedians' in these lists simply mean that the actors named were playing in a comedy and a tragedy, not that they were specially known for one kind of acting rather than another. Also, in a document (known as 'the York Herald's Complaint') of 1602 a sketch of his family's arms is annotated 'Shakespeare the player'. This is usually taken to be a slur, implying that no mere actor could be worthy of bearing arms, but it could be a straightforward statement of fact. A poem by John Davies of Hereford published in 1610 begins 'Some say, good Will, which I in sport do sing, | Hadst thou not played some kingly parts in sport | Thou hadst been a companion to a king...'. This clearly refers to his acting, but it is headed 'To Our English Terence Mr Will. Shakespeare', where the reference to the Latin dramatist no less clearly relates to him as a playwright. So there is documentary evidence that he acted, at least from time to time, from 1594 until the performance of *Sejanus* in 1603. Davies's poem shows that he was still thought of as an actor in 1610 though not necessarily that he went on acting till then.

There are also some early anecdotes. In 1699, long after he had died, a fictional character said he 'was a much better poet than player'.[2] On the other hand the gossipy John Aubrey, writing in the mid-seventeenth century, says that Shakespeare, 'inclined naturally to poetry and acting, came to London, I guess, about 18: and was an actor at one of the play-houses, and did act exceedingly well'.[3] A bit later, in the first attempt at a biography of Shakespeare, published in 1709, Nicholas Rowe said that after he 'was received' into an acting company 'his admirable wit, and the natural turn of it to the stage, soon distinguished him, if not as an extraordinary actor, yet as an excellent writer'.[4] So the balance of evidence suggests that he was a decent but not outstanding actor.

What parts did he play? There is no hard evidence, just a few late rumours. Rowe said, 'I could never meet with any further account of him this way than that the top of his performance was the ghost in his own *Hamlet*.'[5] (Bernard Shaw suggested that he might have played the part because it is 'one of the wonders of the play' and he would trust no one else with it.[6]) Somewhat later the antiquary William Oldys (1696–1761) claimed to have heard that 'one of Shakespeare's younger brothers, who lived to a good old age' said that he had seen Shakespeare play a role which is clearly that of Adam in *As You Like It*.[7] This anecdote is highly suspect because none of Shakespeare's brothers lived to an old age.

Since *As You Like It* and *Hamlet* had been written by the date of *Sejanus*, the anecdotal evidence does nothing to extend Shakespeare's likely acting career beyond 1603, and Jonathan Bate, in his book *Soul of the Age*, deduces from that that he 'stopped acting around the time of the 1603–4 plague outbreak'.[8] He supports this by citing some inconclusive annotations to an early copy of the First Folio and, more significantly, with the fact that 'a recently discovered list of "Players of interludes" in the records of the royal household', dated 1607, lists Burbage and other members of the King's Men but not Shakespeare. 'If he was still acting,' says Bate, 'he would unquestionably have acted at court.'[9]

That is only negative evidence. Another writer, Katherine Duncan-Jones, more positively, cites a late annotation in a 1590 edition of William Camden's *Britannia* which refers (in Latin) to 'William Shakespeare, manifestly our Roscius'.[10] The annotator was born about 1596. Roscius was the great actor of ancient Rome, so it does look here as if Shakespeare were being recalled primarily as an actor and that it could refer to late in his career. More significantly, Duncan-Jones draws attention to the first line of the elegy by William Basse on the death of Shakespeare which is 'Sleep, rare tragedian Shakespeare, sleep alone.' The word 'tragedian' could mean a tragic playwright, but as Duncan-Jones says there is ample evidence that it could also mean an actor—not necessarily even a tragic actor.[11] Shakespeare himself uses it in this sense in *Hamlet* ('the tragedians of the city', 2.2.330) and elsewhere.

To my mind then there is good presumptive evidence that Shakespeare was still thought of as an actor at the time of his death, and therefore that he continued to act after 1603, probably till close to the end of his career. But did he regularly take major roles in his plays or in those of other men? In other words, was he a star actor? The two greatest luminaries of the tragic stage in his time were Edward Alleyn, who worked for the rival company, the Lord Admiral's Men, and is not known to have acted in any Shakespeare plays, and Richard Burbage. We know quite a bit about them. In the case of Alleyn, this is mainly because of the survival of the papers of the theatre manager Philip Henslowe. We know a number of the roles that Burbage played, partly because of an epitaph which names many. We have no such evidence for Shakespeare. Admittedly whether evidence survives is a matter of chance. But we cannot with certainty name a single role that Shakespeare played, and my guess is that he continued to act through most of his career but that he was not a star actor and did not necessarily take roles even in all of his own plays. So Burbage remains on his throne.

Richard Burbage

Figure 1.1. Anonymous oil painting traditionally regarded as a self-portrait of Richard Burbage. By permission of the Trustees of Dulwich Picture Gallery, London

1568–1619. Member of the Lord Chamberlain's, later King's, Men from 1594 to his death. *Shakespeare roles*: Richard III, Hamlet, Othello, King Lear, Pericles, and many others not certainly identified.

If Shakespeare himself was not the first great Shakespeare actor, who was? The answer must be Richard Burbage.

We know all too little about the actors of Shakespeare's company, but Burbage was among the founder members of the Lord Chamberlain's Men in 1594 and stayed with the company through its transition into the King's Men and right to the end of his career, with his death in 1619, three years after Shakespeare himself had died.

Born in 1568, four years after Shakespeare, Burbage came from a theatrical family. His father James was both an actor and a joiner who built the first major English theatre, called simply that—The Theatre—in 1576. This is likely to be the London playhouse where Shakespeare's early plays were given. Remains of it were uncovered in 2012. The family's lease on it expired in April 1597, and by the end of that year the Theatre, now unfrequented, stood empty. A young Cambridge-educated poet, Everard Guilpin, wrote:

> But see yonder,
> One like the unfrequented Theatre
> Walks in dark silence and vast solitude.[1]

Though the Burbages tried hard to renew the lease, the landlord, Giles Allen, decided to pull the building down and 'to use the timbers for a better purpose'.[2] But the original lease had specified that under certain conditions Burbage could 'take down and carry away' the structure, and this his heirs—he himself died early in 1597—proceeded to do. Around Christmas 1598 they, along with around a dozen supporters and workmen, began to dismantle it with the intention of rebuilding it elsewhere.

Shakespeare probably wrote many of his greatest roles with Burbage in mind; indeed their long collaboration makes it likely that Burbage starred in all Shakespeare's plays, and the fact that he belonged for so long to a single company means that he would have gone on playing roles long after they were first created. An anecdote written down by a law student—John Manningham—of the Middle Temple in 1602 shows clearly that Burbage played Richard III some years after the play was written, and may throw light on both his and Shakespeare's private life:

Upon a time, when Burbage played Richard III, there was a citizen grew so far in liking with him that before she went from the play she appointed him to come that night unto her by the name of Richard the Third. Shakespeare, overhearing their conclusion, went before, was entertained, and at his game ere Burbage came. Then, message being brought that Richard the Third was at the door, Shakespeare caused return to be made that William the Conqueror was before Richard the Third.[3]

Burbage's versatility is illustrated by the roles mentioned in obituary verses that circulated after he died:

> He's gone, and with him what a world are dead,
> Which he revived, to be revivèd so
> No more. Young Hamlet, old Hieronimo,
> Kind Lear, the grievèd Moor, and more beside,
> That lived in him have now for ever died.[4]

(An even pithier, though apocryphal, epitaph was 'Exit Burbage'.)

The contrast between 'young' Hamlet and 'old' Hieronimo—in Thomas Kyd's *The Spanish Tragedy*, written around 1588—emphasizes the actor's ability to portray characters of widely differing ages; and he was still under 40 when he first played the octogenarian Lear. By and large we have to deduce his characteristics as an actor from the demands made by the roles that he played. We must assume that he could encompass the irony of Richard III, the lyricism of Romeo, the inwardness of Hamlet, the passion of Othello, and the pathos of Pericles, but the emphasis in his epitaph on the kindness—rather than, for instance, the irascibility—of Lear and on Othello's grief suggests that he had an outstanding ability to arouse sympathy for the characters he played. He was clearly an expert swordsman; on the other hand, none of the parts we know he played requires him to sing. Although he was most famous as a tragedian he played comic roles, too, including, it is said, some written by Jonson—Volpone, and Subtle in *The Alchemist*.

The nearest we get to an eyewitness account of Burbage's acting is in notes written by the physician and astrologer Simon Forman when he saw *Macbeth* at the Globe in 1611. He wrote that Macbeth 'fell into a great passion of fear and fury' on seeing Banquo's ghost.[5] This sounds like a subliminal recollection of the character's description of life as 'a walking shadow'—the word was used for an actor—'a poor player | That struts and frets his hour upon the stage, | And then is heard no more', a tale 'Told by an idiot, full of sound and fury, | Signifying nothing' (5.5.23–7). Forman's description seems to suggest that far from acting in a stylized manner, as is often supposed, Burbage actually seemed to be experiencing the fluctuating emotions of the characters he portrayed.

Burbage was a painter as well as an actor. He may himself have painted the portrait, now in Dulwich Picture Gallery, that is said to represent him. And at the very end of Shakespeare's writing career, on 31 March 1613, the Earl of Rutland's steward recorded a payment of 44 shillings 'To Mr Shakespeare in gold, about my lord's impresa', and of the same amount, also in gold, 'To Richard Burbage for painting and making it'.[6]

Three months later, on 29 June, the Globe playhouse burnt down during a performance of *Henry VIII*—or *All is True*, as it was first called. Burbage seems to have been one of the actors: a ballad written shortly afterward includes the lines

> Out run the knights, out run the lords,
>   And there was great ado;
> Some lost their hats and some their swords;
>   Then out run Burbage too.[7]

He is one of the three actors mentioned in Shakespeare's will of 1616 (the others are John Heminges and Henry Condell, both stalwarts of the company)—all three received a legacy of 26 shillings and 8 pence to buy mourning rings—a common formula for bequests to friends.

Burbage died suddenly, on 12 March 1619, at a time when the theatres were closed because Queen Anne, too, had died a few days earlier. Two months later the Earl of Pembroke, who with his brother was to be a dedicatee of the First Folio edition of Shakespeare's plays, was still so distressed that he could not bring himself to join in the after-dinner festivities at a great banquet which was to be followed by a performance of *Pericles*, in which Burbage had probably created the leading role; the Earl wrote that 'I being tender-hearted, could not endure to see [the play] so soon after the loss of my old acquaintance Burbage'.[8]

And his reputation endured: long after he died Sir Richard Baker wrote, in his *Chronicles of the Kings of England* of 1643, that Burbage and Edward Alleyn, the leader of the rival company, the Lord Admiral's Men, were 'two such actors, as no age must ever look to see the like'.[9]

Will Kemp

Figure 2.1. Woodcut of Will Kemp dancing his way from London to Norwich, accompanied by his drummer, Thomas Sly. Image Asset Management Ltd./Alamy

First heard of, 1585; died 1603? *Shakespeare roles*: Dogberry, Peter (*Romeo and Juliet*), Lance?, Falstaff?, Clown (*Titus Andronicus*)?, Costard (*Love's Labour's Lost*), Bottom?

The greatest comic actor of Shakespeare's company during the 1590s, and one of the few of whom we can say that Shakespeare clearly had him in mind as he wrote certain roles, was Will Kemp, born probably around the same time as Shakespeare. He is first heard of as a performer in 1585. Contemporaries thought of him as the natural successor to the famous clown Richard (Dick) Tarlton; indeed the first printed reference to Kemp, in Thomas Nashe's tract *Almond for a Parrot* published in 1590, two years after Tarlton died, refers to 'that most comical and conceited'—i. e. witty—'Cavalier Monsieur du Kemp, jest-monger and vice-gerent general to the Ghost of Dick Tarlton'.[1] And his reputation as an entertainer to all levels of society endured. Some twenty years after Nashe paid his tribute, and some ten years after Kemp's death, the prolific playwright, actor, and poet Thomas Heywood (*c.*1573–1641), in his *Apology for Actors*, published in 1612, says that Kemp 'succeeded' Tarlton 'as well in the favour of her Majesty as in the opinion and good thoughts of the general audience'.[2]

Like Tarlton, Kemp was a freelance entertainer before joining a theatre company, but unlike Tarlton he worked much on the Continent, travelling in the entourage of the Earl of Leicester to the Netherlands in 1585 both as a member of the Earl's fifteen-strong acting company and as a solo entertainer; in the following year he, along with his 'boy'—presumably an apprentice who may also have acted as a stooge—was one of a group of five English musicians and tumblers who worked for three months at the court of Elsinore. Two other members of this group—George Bryan and Thomas Pope—like Kemp, were to join the Lord Chamberlain's Men; Shakespeare—who so far as we know never travelled overseas—could easily have talked with them about the Danish court before he wrote *Hamlet*.

Also like Tarlton, Kemp achieved fame as what Hamlet calls a 'jig-maker' (3.2.119). These short entertainments, normally a mixture of song, dance, and satirical verse, were frequently performed as afterpieces in the theatres of Shakespeare's time. Texts of four written by Kemp survive, two of them in German translation—an indication of his renown on the Continent. An example is *Singing Simpkin*, printed in 1595 as 'a ballad called Kemp's new jig betwixt a soldier and a miser and Sim the Clown'. Using the age-old comic theme of cuckoldry, and based on an episode from Boccaccio's *Decameron*, it dramatizes a simple tale of a wife who, in her aged husband's absence, seduces a servant, Bluster, who seeks to hide in a chest in case the husband interrupts their lovemaking; but Simpkin is there before him, and keeps up a bawdy running commentary from his hiding place:

> BLUSTER: Within this chest I'll hide myself,
>   If it chance he should come.
> WIFE: O no, my love, that cannot be—
> SIMPKIN: I have bespoke the room.
> WIFE: I have a place behind here,
>   Which yet is known to no man.
> SIMPKIN: She has a place before, too,
>   But that is all too common.

The husband is heard offstage:

> OLD MAN: Wife, wherefore is the door thus barred?
>   What mean you, pray, by this?
> WIFE: Alas, it is my husband!

SIMPKIN: I laugh now till I piss.
BLUSTER: Open the chest, I'll into it;
           My life else it may cost.
WIFE: Alas, I cannot open it.
SIMPKIN: I believe the key is lost. (ll. 65–80)

In Shakespeare's *The Merry Wives of Windsor*, written a couple of years later, in 1597, Falstaff too—who may have been played by Kemp—hides, this time in a clothes basket, to escape detection by a jealous husband; but he is genuinely—if comically—fearful of discovery. The fame of Kemp's jigs as bawdy entertainments is clear from a remark in Everard Guilpin's no less bawdy collection of satirical verses *Skialethia*, of 1598: 'Whores, beadles, bawds, and sergeants filthily | Chant Kemp's Jig . . .'.[3]

Kemp may have acted in some of Shakespeare's plays before the founding of the Lord Chamberlain's Men in 1594. Lance, in *The Two Gentlemen of Verona*, probably written before then, seems an obvious role for him. But his known links with Shakespeare date from his founder-membership of the Lord Chamberlain's Men; on 15 March 1595 he along with Shakespeare and Burbage received payment for two performances given at court during the previous Christmas season, suggesting that, like Shakespeare, as well as being a performer he took partial responsibility for the company's business affairs.

It is difficult to assess Kemp's qualities as a company actor. Only two of his roles can be certainly identified. His name occurs in some of the speech prefixes for the character of the comic constable Dogberry in the First Quarto of *Much Ado About Nothing*, printed from Shakespeare's manuscript in 1600, indicating that Shakespeare had him, and no doubt his specific talents as an actor, in mind as he wrote. The role demands an ability in its interpreters to deliver their dogberryisms with comic but unconscious conviction. If it is to be funny it must be played from the character's own point of view, with no hint of caricature. Kemp's name also appears in early printings of *Romeo and Juliet* in place of Peter, the Nurse's servant. This is a comparatively minor character, but since individual actors often had to play several roles in a single performance, that does not argue against the identification. It does however raise the question of the extent to which the comedians, or clowns, in plays of the period might have been in the habit of fattening their parts with improvisation. Does Hamlet's injunction that 'those that play your clowns speak no more than is set down for them' (3.2.38–9) imply that actors in Shakespeare's own company were accustomed to do this? Is this even an implied criticism of Kemp himself? The question has implications for modern performance. In recent years it has become quite common for the actor playing the Porter in *Macbeth*— written after Kemp had left the company—to interpolate topicalities. But the Porter's principal speech is tightly written. Shakespeare leaves no obvious gaps in it or in comic speeches in any other of his plays; there is no sign that he expected or desired his comic actors to improvise, except possibly in post-performance jigs which he did not script.

Other roles that have been suggested for Kemp include the Clown in *Titus Andronicus*, Costard in *Love's Labour's Lost*, Bottom in *A Midsummer Night's Dream*, and, less confidently, Falstaff in both Parts of *Henry IV* and in *The Merry Wives of Windsor*. As a company member, Kemp is likely to have been expected to play roles other than those that call for the specific talents of a clown; and he was clearly a versatile and intelligent man who may well have achieved success in a wide range of roles. In February 1599 he bought a share in the Chamberlain's Men to help to finance the building of the Globe, but later that year, for whatever reason, he sold his interest in the company and resumed his freelance career.

Kemp's national celebrity is evident from his account of his most famous exploit, the morris dance from London to Norwich which he undertook partly, no doubt, as a publicity stunt, partly to raise money, and partly for fun. He set off early in the morning of the first day of Lent, 11 February 1600, amidst a throng of onlookers at the Lord Mayor of London's house. He was accompanied by his servant, William Bee, a drummer, Thomas Sly, and a minder named George Sprat, whose duty it was to ensure that Kemp didn't cheat—that he 'should take no other ease but [his] prescribed order'. They seem to have taken a horse with them. The nine days of their journey of around 110 miles (or 180 kilometres) were spread over a month, and by Kemp's lively account it attracted as much attention as a modern marathon. Kemp and his companions were royally received when they reached Norwich, the citizens paid all their expenses, and the Mayor awarded him an annuity of 40 shillings. Kemp publicized his exploit after the event in a pamphlet taking the form of a letter addressed to the Queen's Maid of Honour, Anne Fitton, who, he knows, would expect to see nothing 'but blunt mirth in a morris dancer, especially such a one as Will Kemp, that hath spent his life in mad jigs and merry jests'.[4] The title of his little book, *Kemp's Nine Days' Wonder*, draws on an already proverbial expression, roughly equivalent to 'a flash in the pan'. But when in *As You Like It*—assuming that, as seems probable, it was first acted shortly after Kemp's exploit—Rosalind says she is already 'seven days out of the wonder' (3.2.170), Shakespeare must have expected his audience to remember Kemp who, if he had stayed with the company, might well have been playing Touchstone.

In the following year Kemp visited Italy and Germany. His meeting in Rome in 1601 with the English traveller Sir Anthony Shirley is dramatized in a comic episode in a curious play, *The Travels of the Three English Brothers*, by William Rowley, John Day, and George Wilkins, of 1607, several years after Kemp died. In it Kemp has a mildly bawdy conversation with an Italian Harlequin and his wife; Thomas Nashe, in *Almond for a Parrot*, also associates Kemp with Harlequin, suggesting that contemporaries, like scholars later, saw affinities between the techniques of English clowns and the Italian *commedia dell'arte*. By March 1602 Kemp had become a senior member of Worcester's Men; he is mentioned in a payment for a costume in Henslowe's papers in September 1602, and he may be the 'Kemp, a man' buried in St Saviour's Southwark at a time of plague on 2 November 1603.

Robert Armin

Figure 3.1. Robert Armin: a wood-cut from the title-page of his play *The Two Maids of More-clacke*, 1609. Mary Evans Picture Library/Alamy

c.1563–1615. *Shakespeare roles*: Feste?, Touchstone, Lear's Fool?

The other great comic actor of Shakespeare's company was Robert Armin. Kemp's departure had left a gap that had to be filled, though his successor would not necessarily have taken over all his roles: redistribution among several different actors is likely. Armin probably joined the company in 1599. Born around 1563—one year before Shakespeare—he was apprenticed in 1581 to a distinguished goldsmith. According to an anecdote in the anonymously written *Tarlton's Jests* of 1600, Tarlton, recognizing Armin's talents, adopted him (although they were of around the same age), prophesying that he would inherit his clown's costume. Armin would have served his full term as an apprentice goldsmith by 1592, and by the mid-1590s he had joined a provincial acting company, Lord Chandos's Men. But like many actors of the period he maintained at least a nominal alternative allegiance: he became a freeman of the Goldsmiths' Company as late as 1604, when he was already well established as an actor. His popularity is witnessed by a verse tribute headed 'To honest-gamesome Robin Armin, | That tickles the spleen like an harmless vermin.' Written by John Davies of Hereford (who also wrote about Shakespeare), it was printed in his collection of satires *The Scourge of Folly* (1611) and praises Armin in terms that link him with the wise fools of Shakespeare's later comedies. Armin, he says, thou

> with harmless mirth
> Dost please the world, and so amongst [enjoy'st?] the earth,
> That others but possess with care that stings;
> So, mak'st thy life more happy far than kings.

And Davies looks forward to the eternal rewards that Armin will reap:

> So, play thy part, be honest still, with mirth;
> Then, when thou'rt in the tiring-house of Earth,
> Thou, being His servant whom all kings do serve,
> Mayst, for thy part well played, like praise deserve:
> For in that tiring-house when either be,
> You're one man's men, and equal in degree.
> So thou, in sport, the happiest men dost school
> To do as thou dost: wisely play the fool.[1]

Whereas Kemp seems to have specialized in extrovert roles of robust comic humour, Armin, probably slighter in build, was more intellectual. Like Kemp—and unlike any other actor of Shakespeare's company—he had an independent career and reputation as a writer. He was not a jig-maker, but wrote ballads, a collection of tales called *Fool upon Fool* (1600, reprinted in 1605 and, as *A Nest of Ninnies*, in 1609), and an intricately plotted full-length play, *The Two Maids of More-clacke*, printed in 1609. With his recruitment Shakespeare began to create clowns who are more wistful, introverted, and musical: semi-choric commentators on the action rather than active participants.

At least, this is the general view. But Touchstone, in *As You Like It*, of around 1600, just after Kemp's departure, is not all that different in style from the earlier clowns. He has no songs (unless he sings the few lines beginning 'O sweet Oliver...' (3.3.89–95)); indeed, none of the characters Shakespeare is most likely to have created for Kemp has any songs worth speaking of (Bottom's 'The ousel cock' scarcely counts), whereas the two roles most confidently associated with Armin, the wise fools Feste in *Twelfth Night* and the Fool in *King Lear*, are among the most musical in the canon. It must be said, however, that the evidence that Armin played these roles has to be inferred, mainly from the associated facts that these are the roles most likely to have been played by the company's leading comic actor, and that the company's leading comic actor during this period was Armin. Other roles written after Armin joined the company which seem likely to have been played by the company clown, even if they were not tailor-made for Armin, include the First Gravedigger in *Hamlet*, Lavatch or even Paroles in *All's Well That Ends Well*, Thersites—or possibly Pandarus—in *Troilus and Cressida*, the Porter in *Macbeth*, and, most musically, Autolycus in *The Winter's Tale*. Armin died late in 1615, a few months before Shakespeare.

Thomas Betterton

Born *c.*1635; died 1710. Member, later leader, of Sir William Davenant's Duke of York's Company and its successors from 1661 till his death. *Principal Shakespeare roles*: Hamlet, Sir Toby Belch, Mercutio, Hotspur, Othello, Macbeth, Henry VIII, Pericles.

The King's Men went on performing plays by Shakespeare and other dramatists, still always using only male actors, at the rebuilt Globe and the indoor Blackfriars playhouse until London's theatres were compulsorily closed in 1642. But during these years no new major actors came to the fore.

Figure 4.1. An engraving of Thomas Betterton (left) as Hamlet in the 'closet scene'; from Nicholas Rowe's edition of *The Works of Mr William Shakespear*, volume, 1709. Reproduced by permission of the Shakespeare Birthplace Trust

Only surreptitious performances took place during the Commonwealth. But with the coming to the throne of King Charles II in 1660, royal patronage resulted in the founding of two new companies. Thomas Killigrew headed the King's Company, and Sir William Davenant the Duke of York's, which from 1663 played in Covent Garden, giving that area a prominence in theatrical affairs that it still retains. The right to perform Shakespeare's plays was divided between the companies.

As Poet Laureate under King Charles I Davenant had collaborated with the great artist and designer Inigo Jones in the production of masques for the royal court. This experience helped to shape radically new styles of performance at the Restoration. Now plays were given entirely in covered playhouses, very different from the open-air theatres of the earlier period. Perspective scenery set behind proscenium arches such as had been used in the masques became the norm. Audiences were more exclusive. Whereas in Shakespeare's time the players had gone to the court, now the court, including its royal leaders, came to the public playhouses. These were relatively small, so admission prices became more expensive. Biggest change of all, women started to appear onstage, and within a few months were playing all the female roles. As a result, the old plays came to seem old-fashioned, and were either abandoned altogether or heavily adapted to suit the new conditions. The principal adapter of Shakespeare was Davenant himself. He claimed to be not only Shakespeare's godson but also his bastard; and he can be accused of bastardizing his plays.

A new star actor rapidly emerged in the figure of Thomas Betterton, who for well over half a century was to be the acknowledged leader of his profession. His mentor was Davenant, who had been an actor before the theatres closed and had links with men who had acted for Shakespeare. In spite of the changes, there was not a total break in continuity of the acting tradition. When Betterton first played Henry VIII in a spectacular production of the play by Shakespeare and Fletcher, the prompter John Downes noted, 'The part of the king was so right and justly done by Mr. Betterton, he being instructed in it by Sir William, who had it from old Mr Lowin that had his instructions from Mr Shakespeare himself.'[1] Lowin had acted in Shakespeare's company from 1603. Similar stories were told about the theatrical genealogy of Betterton's first great role—which, astonishingly, he was to play to continuing acclaim till he was well over 70—Hamlet.

Luckily for historians of the theatre and of society in general, Samuel Pepys started to keep a diary in the very year, 1660, that the theatres reopened. He was a great playgoer—partly because he liked mixing with aristocrats and the royals—with a roving eye for pretty women both onstage and in the auditorium, and he idolized Betterton. On 24

August 1661 he wrote 'To the opera and there saw *Hamlet Prince of Denmark* done with scenes very well. But above all, Betterton did the prince's part beyond imagination.' Later that year Pepys wrote that he and his wife thought Betterton 'the best actor in the world'.[2] But Betterton let himself down in Pepys's eyes by getting the giggles onstage in a play called *Mustapha*, by Roger Boyle, 1st Earl of Orrery, 'a most admirable poem, and bravely acted; only both Betterton and [Henry] Harris could not contain from laughing in the midst of a most serious part, from the ridiculous mistake of one of the men upon the stage—which I did not like'.[3]

In spite of this lapse Betterton seems in general to have been a serious-minded character with an exceptionally professional attitude to his art. The fullest and most laudatory accounts of him and of his acting come from the effusive autobiography, published in 1740, of the actor-manager and playmaker Colley Cibber (1671–1757), who worked with him for some years. Betterton was, wrote Cibber, 'an actor as Shakespeare was an author, both without competitors, formed for the mutual assistance and illustration of each other's genius'.[4]

Throughout Betterton's career he prepared his roles with exemplary care, rehearsing his movements and gestures before a mirror and in company with his actress wife. He had a fine voice which he used with great skill—Cibber wrote, 'Could *how* Betterton spoke be as easily known as *what* he spoke, then might you see the Muse of Shakespeare in her triumph, with all her beauties in their best array rising into real life and charming her beholders.'[5] He spoke not only with beauty of tone but with high intelligence as well: 'I never heard a line in tragedy come from Betterton, wherein my judgement, my ear, and my imagination were not fully satisfied.'[6] Physically however he seems not to have been especially well graced, though the account given of him late in life by a comic actor, Anthony Aston, sounds like a malicious caricature rather than an objective description:

Mr. Betterton, although a superlative good actor, laboured under an ill figure, being clumsily made, having a great head, a short thick neck, stooped in the shoulders, and had fat short arms, which he rarely lifted higher than his stomach. His left hand frequently lodged in his breast, between his coat and waistcoat, while with his right he prepared his speech. His actions were few, but just. He had little eyes and a broad face, a little pock-fretten, a corpulent body, and thick legs, with large feet.[7]

Whatever he looked like, Betterton could clearly inhabit a role in a manner that conveyed total conviction. Cibber wrote, 'The most that a Vandyke can arrive at, is to make his portraits of great persons seem to *think;* a Shakespeare goes farther yet, and tells you *what* his pictures thought; a Betterton steps beyond them both, and calls them from the grave to breathe and be themselves again in feature, speech, and motion.'[8] The essayist Richard Steele's praise of Betterton's Othello indicates that he could flesh out the words to convey passionate and complex emotions, acting between as well on the lines:

The wonderful agony which he appeared in when he examined the circumstance of the handkerchief in Othello; the mixture of love that intruded upon his mind, upon the innocent answers Desdemona makes, betrayed in his gesture such a variety and vicissitude of passions as would admonish a man to be afraid of his own heart, and perfectly convince him that it is to stab it, to admit that worst of daggers, jealousy. Whoever reads in his closet this admirable scene will find that he cannot, except he has as warm an imagination as Shakespeare himself, find any but dry, incoherent, and broken sentences; but a reader that has seen Betterton act it observes there could not be a word added, that longer speeches had been unnatural, nay impossible, in Othello's circumstances.[9]

And Betterton was versatile, playing a wide of Shakespearian roles— Sir Toby Belch, Mercutio, Hotspur, Othello, Macbeth, Henry VIII, and Pericles, and varying his style to suit each of them. Cibber wrote:

A farther excellence in Betterton was that he could vary his spirit to the different characters he acted. Those wild impatient starts, that fierce and flashing fire which he threw into Hotspur never came from the unruffled temper of his Brutus—for I have more than once seen a Brutus as warm as Hotspur—when the Betterton Brutus was provoked in his dispute with Cassius his spirit flew only to his eye; his steady look alone supplied that terror.[10]

There can be no question that Betterton's greatest role was Hamlet, and luckily the text prepared by Davenant, though considerably shortened—as it almost invariably has been even to our own day— was by no means as drastically rewritten as most of Shakespeare's other plays at this time. We are lucky to have descriptions of Betterton's performance which give some idea of why it made so great an impact on contemporary playgoers:

I have lately been told by a gentleman who has frequently seen Mr Betterton perform this part of Hamlet, that he observed his countenance, which was naturally ruddy and sanguine, in the scene of the third act, when his father's ghost appears, through the violent and sudden emotions of amazement and horror, turn instantly, on the sight of his father's spirit, as pale as his neckcloth, when every article of his body seemed to be affected with a tremor inexpressible; so that had his father's ghost actually risen before him, he could not have been seized with more real agonies; and this was felt so strongly by the audience, that the blood seemed to shudder in their veins likewise, and they, in some measure, partook of the astonishment and horror with which they saw this excellent actor affected.[11]

It was presumably Betterton's greatness as a Shakespeare actor that led the playwright Nicholas Rowe to invite him late in life to travel to Stratford in the hope of gathering new material for the first-ever biography of Shakespeare which Rowe was writing for inclusion in his edition of the plays, published in 1709.

Betterton, who lived modestly throughout his life, is the first actor to have been buried in Westminster Abbey. His grave, unmarked, is 'over against the third pillar from the south end next to the garden'.[12]

👑

Charles Macklin

Figure 5.1. Charles Macklin as Shylock: an oil painting by Johann Zoffany. © Holburne Museum (Somerset Maugham Collection)

1699–1797. *Principal Shakespeare roles*: Iago, Malvolio, Shylock, Macbeth.

Acting styles fluctuate between two extremes. Some players attempt to create an impression of naturalism, of truth to life, of the reproduction onstage (and, more recently, on film) of an imitation of how people behave in real life. The result at its worst is slovenly speech, ungainly movement, and inadequate projection. At the other extreme are those actors who, acknowledging the artificiality of what they are doing, use exaggerated gestures, unnaturally heightened speech, and over-stylized intonation. Fashions in performance tend to shift in a process of reaction and counter-reaction, though they may coexist simultaneously. Even in Shakespeare's time there appears to have been a clear contrast between the 'majestic' style of the heroically built Edward Alleyn, doubtless encouraged by, and indeed often appropriate to, what Jonson called the 'mighty line' of many of the plays that Christopher Marlowe wrote for him, and the more naturalistic manner advocated by Hamlet in his famous advice to the players: 'Speak the speech, I pray you, trippingly on the tongue . . . and do not saw the air too much with your hand, thus' (3.2.1–5)—a style that was presumably practised by Burbage.

Figure 5.2. A caricature of James Quin, wearing the plumed helmet and carrying the truncheon often associated with tragic heroes, as Coriolanus hearing the pleas of his mother, Volumnia, on behalf of Rome. Private Collection/Bridgeman Images

The high praise awarded after the Restoration to Betterton seems to suggest that he satisfied playgoers of his time by steering a middle path between extremes of stylization and naturalism. But in the early part of the eighteenth century acting styles, at least in tragic roles, ossified into a form of declamatory mannerism which, though it clearly pleased some theatregoers, earned the derision of what Hamlet calls 'the judicious' spectators (3.2.26). It cannot have been helped by the fashion of performing male tragic roles while wearing a kind of flared skirt and on the head a full-bottomed periwig topped by a plumed helmet, and with a truncheon held in the hand for emphasis (analogous to the custom of emphasizing a speech by pointing an arm and finger at the person addressed which is adopted by many—perhaps too many, and too often—English actors at the present time). This practice is illustrated in a well-known caricature of James Quin (1693–1756) in the role of Coriolanus.

Joseph Addison commented on the absurdity of the convention in a *Spectator* essay of 18 April 1711:

The ordinary Method of making an Hero, is to clap a huge Plume of Feathers upon his Head, which rises so very high, that there is often a greater Length from his Chin to the Top of his Head, than to the sole of his Foot. One would believe, that we thought a great Man and a tall Man the same thing. This very much embarrasses the Actor, who is forced to hold his Neck extremely stiff and steady all the while he speaks; and notwithstanding any Anxieties which he pretends for his Mistress, his Country, or his Friends, one may see by his Action, that his greatest Care and Concern is to keep the Plume of Feathers from falling off his Head. For my own part, when I see a Man uttering his Complaints under such a Mountain of Feathers, I am apt to look upon him rather as an unfortunate Lunatick, than a distressed Hero.

The use of a plume of feathers to dignify a tragic hero appears to have been abandoned in the more naturalistic performances of David Garrick but recurs frequently, with variations, in later times. It is, for example, seen again early in the nineteenth century in a portrait of G. F. Cooke as Richard III, and it occurred as recently as in John Barton's 1973 production of *Richard II*, starring Richard Pasco and Ian Richardson (see Chapters 31 and 32).

Quin, a portly man, impressed many of his contemporaries as a great actor, especially in the role of Falstaff, but as the years passed his style came to seem old-fashioned. The principal leader of reaction against it was the self-educated, Irish-born Charles Macklin, colourful, aggressive, hard-drinking, and independent-minded. Born around 1700, he started his professional life as a strolling player undertaking any role that was required of him, writing occasional prologues, epilogues, and songs which he performed himself, and appearing in the harlequinades and afterpieces that regularly supplemented the company's central offerings. When he made his London debut in 1725 he was criticized for not employing the stylized form of delivery then in vogue. He wrote, 'I spoke so familiar, Sir, and so little in the hoity-toity tone of the tragedy of that day, that the manager told me I had better go to grass for another year or two.'[1] But he was strong-minded enough to resist pressure to conform to contemporary fashions and to develop his own style. At a time when, because of a feud with Garrick, he was out of work, he undertook to train a group of amateur actors, advising them to avoid 'all the cant and cadence of tragedy'. A beginner should 'first speak the passage as he would in common life, if he had occasion to pronounce the same words; and then giving them more force, but preserving the same accent, to deliver them on the stage. Where the player was faulty in his stops or accents, he set him right; and with nothing more than this attention to what was natural he produced out of the most ignorant persons players that surprised everybody.'[2] He organized performances of *Othello* at the Haymarket theatre, with himself as Iago, receiving praise for the 'chastity' of his style, avoiding claptrap and melodramatic excess. And he wrote a treatise on the art of acting which unfortunately was lost at sea. The didacticism evident in these endeavours showed itself later in his career when, in 1754, he delivered the first series of lectures on Shakespeare's plays as well as giving demonstrations of the art of public speaking. The project ended in his bankruptcy. He was also a successful playwright. His pseudo-Shakespearian tragedy *Henry VII, or, The Popish Impostor* of 1746 achieved only two performances, but his comedies *Love à la Mode* (1769) and *The Man of the World* not only provided him with roles in which he could excel but became standard repertory pieces.

From 1733 Macklin's career centred on London, where he played a wide range of roles, some relatively insignificant, in several different theatres. In 1735 he became involved in a green-room quarrel which had tragic consequences. Seeing a minor member of the company, Thomas Hallam, wearing a wig that he needed for his own role, he lost his temper; anger mounted to such a pitch that Macklin thrust a stick into Hallam's face, penetrating his left eye. Horrified at what he had done, he threw the stick into the chimney piece. Hallam said to the composer Thomas Arne's son, who was playing a small role, 'Whip up your clothes, you little bitch, and urine in my eye'—as an antiseptic measure—but when the boy could not do so Macklin did the office for him, then went onstage to play his part in the farce. On returning to the green room and finding Hallam in dire straits, he fled in panic. Hallam died and Macklin was tried for murder, but eventually, after speaking skilfully in his own defence, was found guilty only of manslaughter. He was sentenced to be branded on the hand and discharged.[3]

Always immensely hard-working, as a member of the Drury Lane company Macklin played a wide range of roles large and small, including Malvolio in an unsuccessful *Twelfth Night* of 1740. His big break came in the following year when the manager decided to revive *The Merchant of Venice*. Shakespeare's romantic comedies had been largely neglected since the Restoration, and this one had been acted only in a heavily adapted version of 1701 by George Granville, Lord Lansdowne, which enlarged the roles of Antonio and Bassanio, omitted Morocco, Aragon, the Gobbos, Salarino, Salario, and Tubal, and (although the play is retitled *The Jew of Venice*) diminished the role of Shylock. It added a banquet scene in which Shylock raised a toast to money, interpolated additional items, and played fast and loose with Shakespeare's language. During a series of revivals Shylock was played by a succession of comic actors. Macklin prepared for the role with great and characteristic care, studying Josephus' popular *History of the Jews*, written early in the Christian era, which had appeared in a new translation in 1737. He aimed at authenticity of costume, discovering that Italian Jews regularly wore red hats. And according to a piece published in 1754, 'He made daily visits to the centre of business, the 'change and the adjacent coffee-houses, that by a frequent intercourse and conversation with "the unforeskinned race" he might habituate himself to their air and deportment.'[4] (Though as Shylock he had to wield a knife, there is no reason to suppose that he went so far as to submit himself to one.) Macklin retained the hooked nose and red hair traditionally associated with the role, adding a red beard and hat. The text of the play in which he acted, though not unaltered—it included interpolated songs by Thomas Arne and abbreviated both Portia's and Bassanio's roles—was at least closer to the original than Lansdowne's. Macklin approached the first night nervously, holding his energies in reserve until the third act, but then, he told a friend,

I threw out all my fire, and as the contrasted passions of joy for the merchant's losses and grief for the elopement of Jessica open a fine field for the actor's powers, I had the good fortune to please beyond my warmest expectations. The whole house was in an uproar of applause . . . The trial scene wound up the fullness of my reputation . . . here I was well listened to, and here I made such a silent yet forcible impression on my audience that I retired from this great attempt most perfectly satisfied.[5]

The phrase 'I was well listened to' is revealing: audiences of the time could not be relied on to give the actors their full attention.

Macklin's reputation was made. This was one of the great performances of the century and one that he was to go on repeating to unfailing acclaim in London and in theatres up and down the land year after year, decade after decade, until the sad moment in 1789 when, around 90 years old and in failing memory, he stumbled through only a few speeches before yielding the role to his understudy. No doubt the detail of his performances varied over the years, but it is clear that his was a serious, almost tragic interpretation, executed with a passion and ferocity that allegedly rendered King George II sleepless (after, not during, the performance). Francis Gentleman wrote in 1770 that 'in his malevolence there is a forcible and terrifying ferocity; in the third act scene where alternate passions reign he breaks the tones of his utterance and varies his countenance admirably; in the dumb action of the trial Scene he is amazingly descriptive'.[6] But the most particularized account of his interpretation comes from the German philosopher and scientist Georg Christoph Lichtenberg who saw Macklin during a visit to England in 1775, close on thirty years after he first played the role. 'The first words he utters when he comes onto the stage are slowly and impressively spoken. "Three thousand ducats." The double th and the two *sibilants*, especially the second after the *t*, which Macklin lisps as lickerishly as if he were savouring the ducats and all that they would buy.'[7] And to Lichtenberg the interpretation was clearly anti-Semitic. 'The sight of this Jew is more than sufficient to awaken at once in the best-regulated mind all the prejudices of childhood against this people.'[8]

Macklin's sensational and long-continuing fame as Shylock over-shadowed his other Shakespearian performances but his Macbeth, given at Covent Garden when he was already well over 70 years old, was ground-breaking above all because in it he abandoned the custom of performing Shakespeare in dress of the period and adopted what he called 'the old Caledonian habit'; he wore tartan stockings and a 'Balmoral bonnet'—but not a kilt, which would have been inauthentic for the period in which the play was set.[9] And he was praised for showing 'the same attention to the subordinate characters as to the scenes, decorations, music and other incidental parts of the perform-ance'.[10] As we shall see, this innovation foreshadows the staging prac-tices of the Romantic period. And by the time Macklin's long life came to its end, in 1797, that period was already well under way, his successor David Garrick's triumphant career was over, and the Shakespearian stage was dominated by members of the Kemble family, not least John Philip and his sister Sarah Siddons.

Figure 6.1. An early copy of Nathaniel Dance's painting of David Garrick as Richard III. Stratford-upon-Avon Town Council

David Garrick

1717–79. *Principal Shakespeare roles*: Richard III, Romeo, Hamlet, Benedick, Macbeth, Lear.

The year 1741 saw both Charles Macklin's triumph in the role of Shylock and, only a few months later—on 19 October—the sensational debut at a minor, suburban playhouse of an inexperienced 24-year-old actor who was to become one of the most important figures in the history of Shakespearian performance and appreciation. David Garrick, who played Richard III in Colley Cibber's long-popular version of Shakespeare's play, was perhaps the most diversely talented great actor ever to grace the British stage. He was also a highly successful playwright, an innovative theatre manager, an influential student of the history of English drama, an indefatigable letter-writer, and a venerator of Shakespeare whose celebration of the dramatist at Stratford-upon-Avon in 1769 known as the Shakespeare (or sometimes the Garrick) Jubilee is a landmark in the development of Shakespeare's reputation.

Garrick's career is more fully recorded than those of any of his predecessors and many of his successors, partly because he was highly acclaimed almost as soon as he stepped on a stage, and also because he moved among the most distinguished men of letters—Samuel Johnson was his friend from youth—and artists—such as Thomas Gainsborough—of his age. He loved to be painted—there are probably more paintings and engravings of him in his roles than of any other actor of any period. Not until the age of photography and sound recording has an actor's career been so amply documented.

Like many great actors, such as Edmund Kean, Laurence Olivier, and Antony Sher, Garrick was not particularly tall, and he was of

relatively slight build. He had expressive eyes, startling powers of
mimicry, and extraordinarily mobile features enabling a virtuosic
range of facial expression which he delighted to display both on- and
offstage. The French philosopher Denis Diderot, who met him in
Paris, wrote:

> Garrick will put his head between two folding doors, and in the course of five
> or six seconds his expression will change successively from wild delight to
> temperate pleasure, from this to tranquillity, from tranquillity to surprise, from
> surprise to blank astonishment, from that to sorrow, from sorrow to the air of
> one overwhelmed, from that to fright, from fright to horror, from horror to
> despair, and thence he will go up again to the point from which he started.[1]

His acting was characterized by a speed of movement and of utterance which contrasted forcibly with the mode of the early years of the
century epitomized in the style of James Quin. The dramatist Richard
Cumberland, who had worked closely with Garrick, whom he calls
'this heaven-born actor',[2] described in his memoirs of 1806 a performance of Nicholas Rowe's *The Fair Penitent* in which 'Quin presented
himself upon the rising of the curtain in a green velvet coat embroi-
dered down the seams, an enormous full-bottomed periwig, rolled
stockings and high-heeled square-toed shoes' and spoke 'with very
little variation of cadence and in a deep full tone accompanied by a
sawing kind of action which had more of the senate than of the stage in
it'; he 'rolled out his heroics with an air of dignified indifference that
seemed to disdain the plaudits that were bestowed upon him'. Cumberland felt great relief when he 'beheld little Garrick, then young and
light and alive in every muscle and every feature, come bounding on
the stage . . . . it seemed as if a whole century had been stepped over in
the transition of a single scene'.[3] And even Macklin wrote, perhaps a
little enviously, that Garrick 'huddled all passions into strut and
quickness—bustle was his favourite . . . . "Give me a horse!"—"Bind
up my Wounds!"—"have mercy Jesu!"—all bustle!—everything is
turned into bustle!'[4] King George III is said to have put it more bluntly:
'He never could stand still. He was a great fidget.'[5] For all this he could
command extreme pathos in, for example, the scene of reunion
between Lear and Cordelia.

Garrick was supremely professional in an age when this could not be
taken for granted, as is clear from a review of his debut performance as
Richard III which praises its negative virtues:

He is not less happy in his mien and gait, in which he is neither strutting or mincing, neither stiff nor slouching. When three or four are on the stage with him, he is attentive to whatever is spoke, and never drops his character when he has finished a speech by either looking contemptibly on an inferior performer, unnecessary spitting, or suffering his eyes to wander through the whole circle of spectators.[6]

One wonders how much spitting would have been thought acceptable.

Businesslike, relatively untemperamental, sober (unlike some of his rip-roaring successors) though merry, a respectable and responsible citizen, Garrick rapidly became the acknowledged leader of his profession, serving as joint manager of Drury Lane from as early as 1747 and continuing in that position till 1776. When he took over, playgoers were permitted to move around behind the scenes and to watch the action from the wings, sometimes in view of the audience in the pit, to occupy seats on the stage, and even to stroll around on it during the course of a play. This practice was particularly popular among fashionable gentlemen and they objected vehemently when Garrick sought to put an end to it, but finally he succeeded. He insisted on strict discipline among his company of actors. He introduced technical reforms in lighting and scenic devices, some of them resulting from study of the French theatre during his two extended visits to Paris.

Like Betterton, Garrick was especially famous in the role of Hamlet, which he played repeatedly from 1742 till he retired at the age of 59 in 1776. We are lucky to have Georg Lichtenberg's unusually precise account of a performance that he saw during a visit to London in 1775, late in Garrick's career. During the eighteenth and nineteenth centuries actors were often famous for particularly effective moments in their performances which became known as 'points', and would be eagerly anticipated, and sometime vociferously applauded, by their fans. In *Hamlet*, Garrick's start on seeing the ghost was such a 'point', aided, astonishingly, by the use of a mechanical wig which could be manipulated so as to cause a shock of hair to rise on the words 'Look, my lord, it comes!' Lichtenberg's account of this brief episode is the most detailed attempt made up to its time to describe great acting. It also tells us much about Garrick's audience:

Hamlet has folded his arms . . . and pulled his hat down over his eyes; it is a cold night and just twelve o'clock; the theatre is darkened, and the whole audience of some thousands are as quiet, and their faces as motionless, as though they were painted on the walls of the theatre; even from the farthest end of the playhouse one could hear a pin drop. Suddenly, as Hamlet moves towards the back of the stage slightly to the left and turns his back on the audience, Horatio starts, and saying: 'Look, my lord, it comes,' points to the right, where the ghost has already appeared and stands motionless, before anyone is aware of him. At these words Garrick turns sharply and at the same moment staggers back two or three paces with his knees giving way under him; his hat falls to the ground and both his arms, especially the left, are stretched out nearly to their full length, with the hands as high as his head, the right arm more bent and the hand lower, and the fingers apart; his mouth is open: thus he stands rooted to the spot, with legs apart, but no loss of dignity, supported by his friends, who are better acquainted with the apparition and fear lest he should collapse. His whole demeanour is so expressive of terror that it made my flesh creep even before he began to speak. The almost terror-struck silence of the audience, which preceded this appearance and filled one with a sense of insecurity, probably did much to enhance this effect. At last he speaks, not at the beginning, but at the end of a breath, with a trembling voice: 'Angels and ministers of grace defend us!'[7]

After his triumph as Hamlet Garrick might have been expected to tackle Romeo, but he appears to have doubted his suitability for the role—or perhaps to have felt that it was not substantial enough for him. When he finally came to play it he expanded the death scene. He put the play on in 1748 in an adapted and simplified version which includes an elaborate, musical funeral scene for Juliet complete with torches, bells, and choral singing, and which causes her to wake up in the vault before Romeo dies, giving the lovers opportunity for a long last conversation. It reads absurdly now. 'Bless me, how cold it is!' says Juliet. But it went on being acted well into the nineteenth century.

At first Garrick's most talented rival, Spranger Barry (1719–77), played Romeo, but when he moved from Drury Lane to Covent Garden Garrick undertook it himself, inaugurating a battle of the Romeos—both houses put the play on for twelve successive nights until Covent Garden took it off when their Juliet, Susannah Cibber, fell ill, and Garrick celebrated his victory with a final, thirteenth performance. Barry seems to have been more successful in the love scenes; a lady spectator is said to have declared, 'Had I been Juliet . . . to Garrick's Romeo, so ardent and impassioned was he, I should have expected he would have *come up* to me in the balcony; but had I been Juliet to Barry's Romeo, so tender, so eloquent and so seductive was he, I should certainly have *gone down* to him.'[8] But Garrick triumphed in the tomb. Indeed he had a special talent for expiring onstage, excelling, as a critic wrote, 'in the expression of convulsive throes and dying

Mr GARRICK in the Character of HAMLET
Act I. Scene 4.th

Printed for R. Sayer, N.53, Fleet Street, & J. Smith, N.35 Cheapside, 16 Octr 1769. 5

Figure 6.2. An engraving of David Garrick as Hamlet seeing the ghost of his father, Drury Lane Theatre, London, 1756. Reproduced by permission of the Shakespeare Birthplace Trust

agonies'.[9] This ability served him especially well in *Macbeth*, which he played in his own version of the adaptation by Sir William Davenant, helping Shakespeare out by adding a moralistic dying speech:

> Tis done! The scene of life will quickly close.
> Ambition's vain delusive dreams are fled,
> And now I wake to darkness, guilt and horror.

I cannot bear it! Let me shake it off—
It will not be; my soul is clogged with blood—
I cannot rise! I dare not ask for mercy—
It is too late; hell drags me down; I sink,
I sink—my soul is fled for ever! O—O—*(dies)*

Figure 6.3. An engraving of Spranger Barry and Maria Isabella Nossiter
as Romeo and Juliet, Covent Garden, London, 1753. Reproduced by permission
of the Shakespeare Birthplace Trust

In spite of its echoes of the closing speech of Marlowe's *Dr Faustus* this is claptrap, but Garrick exercised on it his transformative power as an actor, provoking the critic Francis Gentleman to ask, 'Who has heard his speech, after receiving his death wound, uttered with the utmost agony of body and mind, but trembles at the idea of future punishment, and almost pities the expiring wretch, though stained with crimes of the deepest dye?'[10] Macbeth was one of Garrick's finest roles till 1768, when he abandoned it on the death of Hannah Pritchard, who matched him as Lady Macbeth. The characteristically bizarre painting by Henry Fuseli is suggestive of the intensity of emotion that the actors brought to their roles in the 'dagger' scene; Johann Zoffany's version of the same scene is less impressionistic but more informative.

Like many of our earlier actors, Garrick had no inhibitions about playing characters whose age differed dramatically from his own. He undertook King Lear with great success as early as 1742, when he was only 25, and continued in the role until his final season as an actor, when, aged close on 60, he also played Benedick and Hamlet. Mostly he used Nahum Tate's adaptation, notorious above all for its happy

Figure 6.4. Henry Fuseli's impressionistic oil painting of David Garrick and Hannah Pritchard in the sleep-walking scene from *Macbeth*. The Art Archive/DeA Picture Library

Figure 6.5. Johann Zoffany's more naturalistic painting of David Garrick and Hannah Pritchard in the sleep-walking scene from *Macbeth*. The Art Archive/ Garrick Club

ending in which Lear, Kent, and Gloucester go into peaceful retirement, and Edgar marries Cordelia. For all the execration that has been poured upon it, this remains one of the most successful plays in the history of the English theatre. Towards the end of his career, however, Garrick restored some passages from the original. His final performance in the role evoked an extraordinary tribute from Sir Henry Bate Dudley, who wrote:

The curse at the close of the first act,—his phrenetic appeal to heaven at the end of the second on Regan's ingratitude, were two such enthusiastic scenes of human exertion, that they caused a kind of momentary petrifaction through the house, which he soon dissolved as universally into tears.—Even the unfeeling Regan and Goneril, forgetful of their characteristic cruelty, played through the whole of their parts with aching bosoms and streaming eyes.—In a word, we never saw before so exquisite a theatrical performance, or one so loudly and universally applauded.[11]

Admittedly, the fact that this was a farewell performance of a greatly loved actor is likely to have played its part in the emotional effect of the occasion.

WHO WAS THE FIRST GREAT
SHAKESPEARE ACTRESS?

When women first appeared on the English stage, in 1660, Shakespeare's reputation was at a relatively low ebb. Many of the plays which provide his best female roles, especially the romantic comedies but also including for instance *Measure for Measure*, *Troilus and Cressida*, *Antony and Cleopatra*, *Cymbeline*, *Coriolanus*, and *The Winter's Tale*, had fallen into disfavour. In the years that followed, other plays, such as *Romeo and Juliet*, *Richard III*, and *Macbeth*, were acted only in radically adapted texts which distorted the female roles. Moreover, evidence is scarce; theatre criticism was slow to develop and accounts of performances tend to be anecdotal and effusively uncritical.

The first female Juliet appears to have been Mary Saunderson, to Henry Harris's Romeo in 1662 when her future husband, Thomas Betterton, played Mercutio. Later she acted admirably as Ophelia and Lady Macbeth but nothing I have read characterizes her as great. Elizabeth Barry (*c*.1658–1713) succeeded her as Betterton's leading lady, excelling in pathetic roles and achieving her greatest successes in the heroic tragedies of her own time. Conversely Anne Bracegirdle (*c*.1671–1748), renowned for her modesty in an age when most actresses were notorious for flamboyant sexuality, was clearly a great comic actress. She was the first Millamant in William Congreve's *The Way of the World* (1700), but her principal Shakespeare roles were given in heavily adapted texts—Charles Gildon's version of *Measure for Measure* and George Granville, Lord Lansdowne's of *The Merchant of Venice*, in which she became the first woman to play any version of Portia.

Another fine comedienne, Anne Oldfield (1683–1730), played almost no Shakespeare. Margaret ('Peg') Woffington (*c*.1714–60) worked with

David Garrick and was for a while his lover; in breeches roles she appealed especially to women in the audience, but her harsh voice resulted in her being dubbed 'the screech-owl of tragedy'.[1] Garrick's principal leading lady, Hannah Pritchard (1711–68), supported him successfully in *Macbeth* even though, by her own admission, she had read only the scenes in which she appeared; this provoked Samuel Johnson to tell Sarah Siddons that 'she no more thought of the play . . . than a shoemaker thinks of the skin out of which the piece of leather of which he is making a pair of shoes is cut'.[2]

And Sarah Siddons (1755–1831) is the first indisputably great Shakespeare actress, a performer of towering reputation whose art inspired eloquent tributes in both prose and verse from some of the finest writers of her time, as well as almost as many paintings and drawings as there are of Garrick. They include a splendid canvas by Gainsborough and Sir Joshua Reynolds's commanding portrait of her as Melpomene, the Greek muse of tragedy. Shadowily visible behind her stand embodiments of the Aristotelian emotions of tragic passion, Pity and Terror.

Figure 7.1. Sarah Siddons as The Tragic Muse: oil painting by Sir Joshua Reynolds, 1784. Huntington Library/SuperStock

Sarah Siddons

1755–1831. *Principal Shakespeare roles*: Lady Macbeth, Constance, Queen Katherine, Isabella, Hermione, Volumnia.

The eldest child of a strolling player and theatre manager, Roger Kemble, and his actress wife Sarah Ward, Siddons had eleven siblings; all who survived infancy went on the stage, where they enjoyed varying degrees of success—Stephen (1758–1822) achieved fame principally for being able to play Falstaff without padding. The biographer James Boaden unkindly said that when he blacked up as Othello he 'parted with his only agreeable distinction'.[1] Charles (1775–1854) was the most versatile member of the family, successful especially in romantic leads. In 1822 he followed his brother John Philip as manager of Covent Garden and put on a production of *King John* with himself as the Bastard, Falconbridge, which inaugurated a spectacular, historically orientated production style that came to dominate the English stage for close on a century. The costumes were designed by James Robinson Planché, a member of the College of Heralds and an expert on historical dress. Most successful of Sarah's siblings was John Philip Kemble (see Chapter 9), who became the principal male actor and theatre manager of the Romantic period. Sarah's niece, Fanny Kemble, who married an American plantation owner and became a campaigner for the abolition of slavery, also achieved great distinction as an actress. Sarah frequently acted with John, and was to play with all three brothers at Covent Garden in *Henry VIII* in 1806 when the artist George Henry Harlow depicted them in a painting of more historical than artistic interest, *The Court for the Trial of Queen Katharine*.

Sarah started to perform for her father's company as an infant phenomenon, taking the singing role of Ariel in an adaptation of *The Tempest* when she was no more than 11 years old. An intelligent and ambitious young woman who, in spite of a peripatetic education, displayed highly developed literary tastes—throughout her life she was liable to recite Milton at the drop of a hat—as well as a talent for sculpture, she laboured to develop her art through years of arduous touring in a wide variety of roles on provincial circuits. A relatively undistinguished fellow actor, Henry Siddons, became her husband in 1773. She seemed to have achieved a major breakthrough in 1775 when Garrick invited her to perform at Drury Lane, but, desperately nervous, ill-costumed, and miscast, received derisory notices. She survived the rest of the season, playing Lady Anne in *Richard III* against Garrick himself, but was not re-engaged. Returning to the provinces, she was soon moving audiences to tears with the intensity of her performances of pathetic roles in Bath and elsewhere. During the next few years she gained invaluable experience in playing, often with great success, over one hundred roles, including Rosalind, Desdemona to her brother John's Othello, Juliet, Imogen, Lady Macbeth, Isabella in *Measure for Measure*, Queen Katherine in *Henry VIII*, Constance in *King John*, and Gertrude. Most of these were to form the basis of her Shakespearian repertoire for the rest of her career. As early as 1775 she became, so far as we know, the first of many women over the centuries to play Hamlet; she would have had to fight a duel with her brother John Philip's Laertes. When she played the Prince again in Dublin in 1802 she was already putting on weight. Nevertheless, overall she seemed to one spectator superior even to John—the greatest Hamlet of the age—and 'the fencing scene in the last act was capital' with the result that 'she astonished the cognoscenti of the audience'. She could have been better costumed: 'Notwithstanding the very fine acting of the character, the effect was considerably injured by the awkwardness of the dress and the feminine gait, which was sometimes ludicrous.' But 'if Mrs S— could correct these, she would be an unrivalled Hamlet.'[2] Her Dublin appearances also provoked a satirical account of her effect upon audiences:

One hundred and nine ladies fainted! forty-six went into fits! and ninety-five had strong hysterics! The world will scarcely credit the truth when they are told that fourteen children, five old women, a one-handed sailor, and six common-council men, were actually drowned in the inundation of tears that flowed from the galleries, lattices, and boxes, to encrease the briny pond in the pit. The water was three feet deep, and the people that were obliged to stand upon the benches, were in that position up to their ankles in tears![3]

Although the nature of Siddons's profession required her to play a wide range of roles, some of them farcical, and even, in her earlier years, to sing and dance, her physical qualities as well as her natural instincts fitted her best to play dignified, aristocratic, queenly women who might however be torn apart by passion and grief. For these reasons she yielded the palm in comedy to others; her Rosalind succeeded rather by hard effort than through the natural affinity with the role of her contemporary Dora Jordan (see Chapter 10). Above all Siddons was the queen of sentimental drama and of tragedy. When she returned to Drury Lane in 1782, at the age of 27, conscious of the need to redeem her London reputation, she chose the deeply pathetic role of the heroine in *Isabella, or the Fatal Marriage*, adapted by Garrick from a play by Thomas Southerne (1660–1746), in which she had wreaked emotional havoc in the breasts of the ladies of Bath—this was, after all, the Age of Sentiment. Her success was instantaneous and sensational, and she was to remain the idol of the English stage till she retired, in 1812.

Over a career lasting more than forty years Sarah Siddons's physical attributes cannot have remained constant, but in the early stages she struck many of those who saw her as strikingly beautiful—even, says Boaden, as 'more beautiful than she is'.[4] This curious statement probably means that her face lit up when her pronounced features—her nose and chin were prominent—were animated. She had a mass of hair—'generally', she wrote, 'braided into a small compass, so as to ascertain the size and shape of my head'[5]—which, said Horace Walpole, 'is either red, or she has no objection to its being thought so' (he suggests that she used 'red powder' to tint it; she was later to deny this).[6] A life mask taken around the time she retired shows unusually full lips. Of a little more than average height, she moved with exceptional grace and dignity. Her black eyes could flash with ferocity, and the tone of her voice was 'melodious, clear, articulate, and thrilling'.[7]

No less important to her success than her physical qualities was the intensity of her imaginative responses to the characters she played along with her extraordinary powers of self-identification. These are illustrated early in her career by her vivid account of how, aged only 20, she prepared for the role of Lady Macbeth.

Being then only twenty years of age, I believed, as many others do believe, that little more was necessary than to get the words into my head; for the necessity of discrimination, and the development of character, at that time of my life, had scarcely entered into my imagination.... I went on with tolerable composure, in the silence of the night, (a night I never can forget,) till I came to the assassination scene, when the horrors of the scene rose to a degree that made it impossible for me to get farther. I snatched up my candle, and hurried out of the room, in a paroxysm of terror. My dress was of silk, and the rustling of it, as I ascended the stairs to go to bed, seemed to my panic-struck fancy like the movement of a spectre pursuing me. At last I reached my chamber, where I found my husband fast asleep. I clapt my candlestick down upon the table, without the power of putting the candle out; and I threw myself on the bed, without daring to stay even to take off my clothes. At peep of day I rose to resume my task; but so little did I know of my part when I appeared in it, at night, that my shame and confusion cured me of procrastinating my business for the remainder of my life.[8]

She goes on to recall how, when she came to play the part in London some six years later, Sheridan (the theatre manager), hearing that she intended to put down the candle in the sleepwalking scene rather than continuing to hold it as she washed her hands, implored her not to defy convention by doing so; but she stood her ground, confident of her 'observation of the accuracy with which somnambulists perform all the acts of walking persons ... and the innovation was received with approbation. Mr Sheridan himself came to me, after the play, and most ingenuously congratulated me on my obstinacy.'[9]

These anecdotes reveal the intensity of Siddons's imaginative response to a text: she had a constantly renewed and vibrant responsiveness to language and to dramatic situations. Her powers of observation were remarkable, and she had a sympathetic depth of human understanding which, in her maturity, she brought to bear on the roles she played. And she had technique, honed by years of disciplined study, in abundance. This enabled her to project her performances even into the vast auditorium—holding more than 3,600 spectators, well over three times the capacity of the current Olivier auditorium of the National Theatre—of the Drury Lane that opened in 1794 after the demolition of the one in which Garrick had played, which resulted in large-scale performances of extraordinary intensity.

Siddons's technique derived from a totally professional attitude to her art. Though—or perhaps because—she was a highly nervous performer, she had, Boaden writes, 'amazing self-possession' which enabled her to overcome self-consciousness. 'When Mrs Siddons quitted her dressing room, I believe she left there the last thought about herself... It was this devotion to what she was about, that left so little *inequality* in her numerous repetitions of the same part.'[10] Similarly Thomas Holcroft wrote, 'Her eyes never wander, her passions are as active while she is silent as when she is speaking.'[11]

The depth of her involvement in a role is strikingly illustrated by John Charles Young's description of her performance in Kemble's version of *Coriolanus*:

She was no longer Sarah Siddons, tied down to the directions of the prompter's book—or trammelled by old traditions—she was Volumnia, the proud mother of a proud son and conquering hero. So that, when it was time for her to come on, instead of dropping each foot at equi-distance in its place, with mechanical exactitude, and in cadence subservient to the orchestra; deaf to the guidance of her woman's ear, but sensitive to the throbbings of her haughty mother's heart, with flashing eye and proudest smile, and head erect, and hands pressed firmly on her bosom, as if to repress by manual force its triumphant swellings, she towered above all around, and rolled, and almost reeled across the stage; her very soul, as it were, dilating, and rioting in its exultation; until her action lost all grace, and, yet, became so true to nature, so picturesque, and so descriptive, that pit and gallery sprang to their feet electrified by the transcendent execution of an original conception.[12]

And even while she was still in her dressing room she was involved in the play's action. Constance in *King John*—then a far more popular play than it later became—was one of her greatest roles. She relates that

Whenever I was called upon to personate the character of Constance, I never, from the beginning of the play to the end of my part in it, once suffered my dressing-room door to be closed, in order that my attention might be constantly fixed on those distressing events which, by this means, I could plainly hear going on upon the stage, the terrible effects of which progress were to be represented by me. Moreover, I never omitted to place myself, with Arthur in my hand, to hear the march, when, upon the reconciliation of England and France, they enter the gates of Angiers... because the sickening sounds of that march would usually cause the bitter tears of rage, disappointment, betrayed confidence, baffled ambition, and, above all, the agonizing feelings of maternal affection to gush into my eyes. In short, the spirit of the whole drama took possession of my mind and frame, by my attention being incessantly riveted to the passing scenes.[13]

Siddons decided to retire from the stage in 1812. Warning signs had started to appear: 'when she knelt to the Duke in *Measure for Measure*, two attendants had to come forward to help her to rise; and, to save appearances, the awkward shift was resorted to of making the same ceremonial attend on the rising up of a younger actress who did not need such support'.[14] Nevertheless, during her farewell season she performed fifty-seven times in fourteen different characters, including the Shakespearian roles of Constance, Queen Katherine, Isabella, Hermione, and Volumnia. Lady Macbeth headed the list with ten performances and brought her career to a triumphant (if not utterly final) close. After the sleepwalking scene at the final performance, writes her official biographer Thomas Campbell, 'the applause of the spectators became ungovernable: they stood on the benches, and demanded that the performance of the piece should not go further than the last scene in which she appeared'. So the curtain fell. Twenty minutes later Siddons, dressed in white, delivered a farewell address, after which 'Mr Kemble led her off the stage, amidst the deepest manifestations of public feeling'.[15]

It was not actually the end. Regretting her ill-judged emergence from retirement four years later, William Hazlitt was to write, 'She was not less than a goddess, or than a prophetess inspired by the gods. Power was seated on her brow, passion emanated from her breast as from a shrine. She was tragedy personified.... To have seen Mrs Siddons was an event in everyone's life.'[16] And even after that she made occasional comebacks and gave readings of Milton and of Shakespeare plays in which she played all the roles. It was a somewhat sad coda to the life of a tragic actress of Wagnerian stature.

Figure 8.1. George Frederick Cooke as Richard III; an anonymous oil painting of about 1805. From the Somerset Maugham Collection, courtesy of Theatre Royal, Bath

George Frederick Cooke

1756–1811. *Principal Shakespeare roles*: Richard III, Falstaff, Iago, Macbeth.

It is a far cry from the self-discipline, the worldly success, and the ultimate affluence of David Garrick to the shambolic career of the turbulent, alcoholic, self-hating, and frequently debt-ridden George Frederick Cooke. But at his best Cooke was a great Shakespeare actor. When sober, he was diligent, cultivated, and gentlemanly. A fellow actor, Charles Mathews, wrote: 'He is one of the most intelligent men and agreeable companions I ever met with, and I think myself extremely fortunate in getting into the same house [i. e. theatre company] with him.'[1] But another colleague, S. W. Ryley, wrote that when Cooke was drunk, 'his interesting suavity of manners changes to brutal invective; the feelings of his nearest and dearest friends are sacrificed; his best benefactor wounded, either in his own person, or that of his tenderest connection, and the ears of delicacy assaulted, by abuse of the grossest nature'.[2] His friend and biographer William Dunlap says that Cooke was, understandably, 'mortified' when he read this.[3]

Born probably in 1756, brought up in Berwick in the north of England, Cooke became stage-struck as an 11-year-old when he saw strolling actors from Edinburgh perform in the local town hall. A couple of years later, along with schoolmates, he put on plays in a disused barn, playing Horatio in *Hamlet*. There's a story that, hoping to see a visiting company in *Macbeth* without paying, he clambered into what turned out to be a thunder-barrel containing two 24-pound cannonballs. He stayed mum as the end of the barrel was sealed with carpeting and it was placed ready to explode on the first appearance of the witches. Then the property man, cursing because

the cannon bullets were so damned heavy, placed the complicated machine in readiness: the witches entered midst flames of rosin; the thunder-bell rang, the barrel received its impetus, and away rolled George Frederick and his ponderous companions. Silence would now have been no virtue, and he roared most manfully, to the surprise of the thunderer, who neglecting to stop the rolling machine, it entered on the stage, and George Frederick bursting off the carpet head of the barrel, appeared before the audience, just as the witches had agreed to meet again 'When the hurly-burly's done.'[4]

On leaving school Cooke was apprenticed to a printer, but he continued to act and, after a series of colourful adventures, joined a professional company in Lincoln at the age of 17. As a touring player he was, and had to be, game for anything, even singing and dancing. For close on thirty years he undertook an extraordinarily wide range of parts in numerous provincial theatres in Ireland as well as in England with increasing success in spite of a series of lapses into alcoholic torpor. At last he emerged on the London theatrical scene as a challenger to the pre-eminence of John Philip Kemble in 1800.

Cooke prepared diligently for his roles and worked himself hard. Even after triumphing at Covent Garden as Richard III on 15 June 1801 he set off the next day for a tour in England and Scotland during which in the space of thirteen weeks 'he gave at least sixty performances with five different companies, and in six different theatres', up and down the country. During this tour he undertook no fewer than twenty-one different roles, including Richard III, Shylock, Macbeth, Hamlet, Iago, Jaques, Othello, Petruccio, and Mercutio. This meant playing five or six nights a week, often with little rehearsal. At the end of it all he had a total breakdown. He was, as usual, lurching unsteadily between triumph and ignominious self-defeat, thrilling audiences with brilliant performances while often alienating them by his drunken behaviour on- and offstage along with cancellations brought about sometimes by genuine ill-health but far more frequently by what came euphemistically to be called his 'old complaint'. There was a terrible occasion at Covent Garden, recorded by the prompter, when he was playing the Ghost to Kemble's Hamlet:

The Ghost was drunk, and found so much difficulty in expressing his 'mission' and in keeping himself above ground that the Pit 'rose at him' indignantly, to which he replied with a motion of defiance whereupon a row ensued which for some time interrupted the progress of the Tragedy.[5]

He made, and spent, a lot of money. In his early fifties, in 1808, having left England to escape his debts, he became the first English actor to triumph on the American stage; but there too he antagonized audiences as well as thrilling them, and he died of drink in Manhattan in 1812.

Partly because much of Cooke's acting took place outside London, and so escaped the attention of the leading newspaper critics, his career is less well documented than those of his major contemporaries, so it's more difficult to discover why, at his best, he made so powerful an impression on his audiences. He was a man of commanding presence, 5 feet 10 inches tall, with prominent nose and chin. Christian Goede, contrasting him with Kemble, writes that the latter's 'countenance is the most noble and refined, but the muscles are not so flexible and subject to command, as Cooke's'.[6] His voice was powerful but could be harsh, especially when affected by drink. Like Macklin and Garrick, both of whom he had seen perform, he impressed audiences by the relative naturalism of his vocal delivery. He is said to have cultivated this, as Macklin had, by studying verse as if it were prose so as to avoid a sing-song delivery. In this he probably gained by contrast with the elevated style of his principal rival, John Philip Kemble. It is a technique that, effective in the roles that suited him best, must have done him a disservice in lyrical roles such as Romeo and parts of Hamlet (which he played with relatively little success—indeed in it Leigh Hunt wrote that 'the most accomplished character on the stage is converted into an unpolished, obstinate, sarcastic madman'[7]). Sarcasm was his forte. The theatre historian James Boaden wrote, 'He was formed for the sarcastic, like Macklin, his features and utterance were only harmonious in *discord* . . . . He was an *Apemantus*'—the cynic philosopher of *Timon of Athens*—'not a Kent.'[8] He could be a great comedian though rather in a satirical than in a genial style; he brought dignity to the Falstaff of *Henry IV Part One*, but in *The Merry Wives of Windsor* 'was shrewd and sarcastic, but wanted easy flowing humour'.[9]

Like all great actors, Cooke could make strikingly effective use of his eyes, 'which are fiery, dark, and at times terribly expressive, with prominent lids and flexible brows.'[10] The American artist Thomas

Sully's portrait of him late in his career as Richard III, his most famous Shakespeare role, shows him as a glowering figure, his height increased by the plumed headdress that had been conventional in the early years of the eighteenth century but which Macklin and Garrick appear to have dispensed with. But later still, Leigh Hunt, reviewing Edmund Kean in 1815 as Richard III, was to suggest that he 'ought not to get under such a large hat and feathers as he seems fond of'.[11]

Cooke's somewhat threatening appearance makes it understandable that Charles Mathews should write, 'His figure and face are much more adapted to the villain than the lover.'[12] His capacity to portray sarcastic villains found expression supremely in Richard III, and also in Iago and Shylock. During his first Covent Garden appearance as Shylock, 'he was greeted with shouts of applause' especially for

The gloomy satisfaction that seemed to accompany the recollection of the bond by which he had Antonio 'on the hip,' and the savage exultation of his laugh, when the full amount of his enemy's loss is stated, were frightfully impressive. The transitions were made in a masterly manner, and the speech in which Shylock urges his own wrongs, and vindicates his tribe, formed a climax of as well-wrought passion as can be conceived.[13]

The great essayist and critic Leigh Hunt wrote that Cooke could act 'as if villainy was pure luxury in him, and with such a soft inward retreating of his voice—a wrapping up of himself, as it were, in velvet—so different from his ordinary rough way, that sometimes one could almost have wished to abuse him'.[14] That evocative phrase 'soft inward retreating of [the] voice' seems applicable to Cooke's speaking of a passage in *Macbeth* as described by Dunlap, who quotes Macbeth's 'Wherefore was that cry?' followed by Seyton's 'The Queen, my lord, is dead.' Then, he says,

With a suppressed agitation [he] gave:
'She should have died—'
And then, after a pause, with a tone lowered almost to a whisper,
'—hereafter' So, again,
'It is a tale told by an idiot, full of sound and fury,
Signifying—'
He sunk his voice, and with a tone of suppressed feeling, and heart-breaking disappointment, repeated the word '—nothing.'[15]

The twentieth-century scholar Dennis Bartholomeusz, quoting this passage, remarks, 'Sir John Gielgud brought out the disillusionment in this line, in much the same fashion, when he played Macbeth more than a hundred years after George Frederick Cooke.'[16]

And Cooke could mine a simple phrase for new depths of meaning. When he played Iago in Philadelphia a spectator wrote of his response to Othello's demand that he kill Cassio, 'Cooke used to start as if he appeared horrified at the deed, appeared to hesitate, and then, with sudden impulse, drew his hand across his face, looked at the Moor, which told plainly, "I do this for love of thee," and then, in a voice almost choked—"My friend is dead!" The effect was irresistible . . . . It was responded to by three immense bursts of applause, succeeded by a dread pause, as if the audience was lost in contemplation of its sudden sublimity.'[17]

Figure 9.1. John Philip Kemble as Coriolanus; copy of an oil painting by Sir Thomas Lawrence. The City of London, Guildhall Art Gallery

John Philip Kemble

1757–1823. *Principal Shakespeare roles*: Hamlet, Macbeth, Prospero, Coriolanus, Lear.

Mrs Siddons's slightly younger brother, John Philip Kemble, resembled David Garrick in being both the leading actor and, for close on thirty years, the dominant theatre manager of his time. But physically and temperamentally the men were very different. Kemble's acting style represented a swing back towards the stylized, declamatory mode that Macklin had fought against and that Garrick had banished. Sir Walter Scott, a friend and admirer, writing after Kemble's death, drew an illuminating contrast:

> Garrick was short though well formed, airy and light in all his movements, possessed of a countenance capable of the most acute or the most stolid, the most tragic or the most ridiculous expression. Kemble, on the contrary, was tall and stately, his person on a scale suited for the stage, and almost too large for a private apartment, with a countenance like the finest models of the antique, and motions and manners corresponding to the splendid cast of his form and features.[1]

These qualities are apparent from Sir Thomas Lawrence's grand and imposing portraits of Kemble in two of his finest and most characteristic roles, Hamlet and Coriolanus. They fitted him also for the romantic, brooding heroes of Gothic romances in which he excelled.

Vocally he was limited. Garrick's voice, according to Scott, was 'full, melodious, commanding, and he might exert it with unsparing profusion'. Kemble's, 'though perfectly distinct and impressive, was early affected by an asthmatic tendency, which rendered it necessary for him to husband his efforts, and reserve them for those bursts of passion to which he gave such sublime effect'.

Problems resulting from asthma were exacerbated by drink and opiates. Partly for these reasons, his range was limited. He failed in roles, notably Romeo, which call for romantic ardour, and though he often played comedy, and even aspired to Falstaff, this, as Scott makes clear with kindly irony, was not his natural metier.

Mirth, when he exhibited it, never exceeded a species of gaiety chastened with gravity; his smile seemed always as if it were the rare inhabitant of that noble countenance. There was unquestionably great sweetness of expression in that smile, but it indicated more of benevolence than of gaiety—the momentary stooping of a mind usually strung to a serious mood to the joy which enlivened the meaner natures around him.[2]

The Coriolanus-like inflexibility of his public persona, amounting at times to an arrogant disrespect for his audiences, frequently aroused disapproval and enmity, most spectacularly in 1809 when in his capacity as manager he raised the price of seats in the theatre that replaced Covent Garden following the disastrous fire that destroyed the earlier building. Three months of rioting ensued, and eventually he had to make a public apology.

Educated at the Roman Catholic seminary in Rheims, and possibly intended for the priesthood, Kemble early developed scholarly and intellectual interests. Throughout his life (in this like Garrick) he was an avid book collector; on his retirement he sold his collection of 4,000 plays and forty volumes of playbills to the Duke of Devonshire. His intellectual interests and ambitions shaped his theatrical career. He wrote plays of his own, and in 1780 made a version of *The Comedy of Errors* called *Oh! It's Impossible* which, perhaps happily, does not survive. In 1786 he published a critical essay, *Macbeth Reconsidered*, dedicating it to his friend, the great scholar Edmond Malone. He studied his roles with meticulous care. He was often accused of pedantry, and was publicly mocked when he insisted on pronouncing the word 'aches' in Prospero's line: 'For this be sure tonight thou shalt have aches' with two syllables, as 'aitches'. 'Night after night', writes Scott, 'he menaced Caliban with *aitches*, and night after night was for so doing assailed by a party in the pit with a ferocity worthy of Caliban himself.'[3]

But for all his learning and his study of early texts and scholarly editions, Kemble was far from being a textual purist. He played

Cibber's adaptation of *Richard III*, Garrick's of *Romeo and Juliet*, and in 1809 put back into *King Lear* much of Tate's verse which Garrick, half a century earlier, had banished in favour of the original. He played *Coriolanus* in a bastardized version of an adaptation by Thomas Sheridan which borrowed from a poetic drama on the same subject by James Thomson. He revised many of Shakespeare's plays to suit his personal interpretation of his roles, studiously developing intellectually overarching conceptions of them, seeking to identify a character's ruling passion, stripping away anything that he regarded as irrelevant to this. *Hamlet* became a study in genteel melancholy. Writing of his Macbeth, Scott identified and praised his 'exquisitely and minutely elaborate delineation of guilty ambition, drawn on from crime to crime, while the avenging furies at once scourge him for former guilt, and urge him to further enormities'.[4] In the banquet scene he caused Banquo's ghost to appear only to himself—an innovation which, focusing attention more firmly on the actor playing Macbeth, has often been followed since his time. More trivially, he invented personal names for many minor roles. In *The Two Gentlemen of Verona*, for example (in which, incongruously, he played Valentine), the anonymous outlaws became Ubaldo, Luigi, Carlos, Stephano, Giacomo, Rodolfo, and Valerio. Whimsical though this may seem, it may have been useful as a way of boosting minor actors' egos and, more practically, of identifying them during rehearsals.

As an impresario Kemble had a strong sense of theatrical values. His scenically spectacular productions, especially at Covent Garden, which he managed from 1808 to 1817, employed many extras for crowd scenes in for instance *Henry VIII* and *Coriolanus*, making him, according to the theatre historian G. C. D. Odell, the 'first great "producer" of the English stage'.[5] His version of *Coriolanus* introduced a ceremony after the hero's victory in which 'no fewer than 240 persons marched, in stately procession, across the stage'; they included 'sword-bearers, and standard-bearers, and cup-bearers, and senators, and silver eagle bearers, with the S. P. Q. R. upon them, and trumpeters, and drummers, and priests, and dancing-girls, etc.,. etc.'.[6] He chose this play for his farewell to the stage, a triumphant and highly emotional occasion. The German translator of Shakespeare, Ludwig Tieck, was there. He deplored the adaptation and described the interpolated ceremony as a 'superfluous pageant' which 'consumed a great deal of time'. Nevertheless Kemble, husbanding his resources as usual, rose to greatness in the final scene. 'Greatest and most exciting of all was the close; without exaggeration it might be pronounced sublime.'[7] And at the end of the performance the thousands present 'produced a supernatural clangour and jubilation, men and women shouting, clapping, smiting the sides of the boxes might and main, with fans and with sticks, while, to add to the tumult, everybody was making what noise he could with his feet'. And after Kemble had spoken his last farewell, 'the storm broke forth again with all its force.'[8]

Kemble's limitations and inflexibilities, his often humourless pedantry, and his waywardness with Shakespeare's texts, might easily seem to disqualify him from the ranks of the greatest Shakespeare actors. Hazlitt had reservations even about his finest role, Coriolanus, in which, he wrote mischievously, his 'supercilious airs and *nonchalance* . . . remind one of the unaccountable abstracted air, the contracted eyebrows and suspended chin of a man who is just going to sneeze'.[9] But whatever his reservations, Hazlitt considered that 'in embodying a high idea of certain characters, which belong rather to sentiment than passion, to energy of will, than to loftiness or to originality of imagination, he was the most excellent actor of his time'.[10]

It is clear from this and other contemporary accounts that at times Kemble transcended his limitations, even perhaps turned them into virtues, by the sheer intensity of the passion with which—in some ways like his most famous sister—he bludgeoned his way into the imaginations of his audiences. Scott thought him 'unapproachable' as Macbeth, singling out a specific subtlety: 'We can never forget the rueful horror of his look, which by strong exertion he endeavours to conceal, when on the morning succeeding the murder he receives Lennox and Macduff in the ante-chamber of Duncan.'[11] He appears to have been at his greatest in climactic scenes. Writing again of his Macbeth, his fellow actor W. C. Macready said,

when the news was brought, 'The queen, my lord, is dead,' he seemed struck to the heart; gradually collecting himself he sighed out, 'She should have died hereafter!' Then as if with the inspiration of despair, he hurried out, distinctly and pathetically, the lines,

> Tomorrow, and tomorrow, and tomorrow,
> Creeps in this petty pace from day to day . . .

. . . rising to a climax of desperation that brought down the enthusiastic cheers of the closely packed theatre.[12]

And his death scene as Coriolanus, as described by Scott, sounds almost as terrifying as Olivier's was to be 150 years later (see Chapter 26): 'There was no precaution, no support; in the midst of the exclamation against Tullus Aufidius, he dropped as dead and as flat on the stage as if the swords had really met within his body. We have repeatedly heard screams from the female part of the audience when he presented this scene, which had the most striking resemblance to actual and instant death we ever witnessed.'[13]

In the later years of Kemble's career the pendulum of naturalism versus stylization began to swing against him. G. F. Cooke's triumph as Richard III as early as 1801 dealt a blow to his supremacy. Even more significant was the rise to fame a decade later of an actor who, as a young boy, is said to have swollen the ranks of the witches in Kemble's production of *Macbeth*: Edmund Kean.

Figure 10.1. Dorothy Jordan (left) as the Comic Muse, oil painting by John Hoppner. © National Portrait Gallery, London

Dora Jordan

Born Dorothea Bland, 1761–1816. *Principal Shakespeare roles*: Viola, Rosalind, Ophelia, Helen in *All's Well That Ends Well*, Mistress Ford, Beatrice, Miranda

Two years after Joshua Reynolds painted Sarah Siddons as the Tragic Muse, John Hoppner's no less grand, ambitiously allegorical canvas entitled *Mrs Jordan as The Comic Muse supported by Euphrosyne, who represses the advances of a Satyr* was shown, as Reynolds's had been, at the Royal Academy. Dora Jordan, holding the mask of comedy, flees from the leering approaches of a horned satyr into the protective embrace of the goddess of mirth, one of the Three Graces of Greek mythology, whose arm is outstretched as if to banish the satyr. Jordan's biographer, Claire Tomalin, asks, 'Did the Satyr represent the male theatre-goer, who regarded the actress as legitimate sexual prey?'[1]

The 25-year-old actress, then in the first flush of her popularity, was certainly an object of sexual desire for many men both on- and offstage, and continued to be so for many years. Born in London of parents who were not legally married, who assumed the name of Bland, and who normally lived in Ireland, she was baptized at the church of St Martin-in-the-Fields on 5 December 1761. Her mother, Grace, along with two sisters, had acted successfully on the Dublin stage, playing both Juliet and Desdemona at the popular and successful Smock Alley Theatre run by Thomas, father of Richard Brinsley Sheridan. Grace's Othello, Tate Wilkinson, became an immensely successful theatre manager in the north of England and was to play a significant role in the family's lives. When a young and pregnant Dora travelled from Ireland to act for him in York, he recommended that she should attempt to avoid scandal by adopting a married name. 'Why,' he allegedly said, 'my dear, you have crossed the water, so I'll call you Jordan.'

Dorothy, known as Dora, had started to work as a milliner's assistant when she was 14, but, a nervous tyro, took her first stage role only about three years later. She was an attractive young woman of moderate height, not apparently a great beauty but vivacious, bubbly in temperament, with a mop of curly brown hair, lively eyes, a good singing voice, and an infectious laugh. Leigh Hunt was to write,

Mrs Jordan always appeared to us unrivalled in a laugh. A stage-laugh generally follows the speech which it should accompany, and is as good a set Ha, ha, ha! as the author has put down in his book; but the laughter of Mrs. Jordan, in all its branches, from the giggle to the full burst, is social and genuine; it clips, as it were, and tickles the dialogue; it breaks in and about her words, like sparkles of bubbling water; and when the whole stream comes out, nothing can be fuller of heart and soul.[2]

According to Wilkinson she 'sported the best leg ever seen on the stage',[3] an asset that was to stand her in great stead when she came to play in male costume, not only as Viola, Rosalind, and Imogen but in many other breeches roles, as they were called. Her sexual appeal both on- and offstage brought her many admirers and numerous professionally inconvenient pregnancies, not least by the Duke of Clarence (later King William IV), with whom she was to live for some twenty years and to whom she bore at least ten children.

Dora was a naturally talented woman whose success as an actress was not simply the result of her physical charms. When she played her first Shakespeare role, Phoebe in *As You Like It*, in Dublin, a member of the Sheridan family predicted that she would become 'the first comic actress in England... For her chastity of acting, naïveté, and *being* the character she represents, young as she is, she surpasses what could have been expected.'[4] Her apparent spontaneity resulted from hard work. The great Victorian actor W. C. Macready, who took acting lessons from her as a young man, praised her 'discrimination, an identity with the character, an artistic arrangement of the scene, that made all appear spontaneous and accidental, though elaborated with the greatest care'.[5]

Dora made her London debut in *The Country Girl*, Garrick's cleaned-up adaptation of Wycherley's bawdy restoration comedy *The Country Wife* in 1785, at Drury Lane, managed by Richard Sheridan, after which his sister-in-law, Mary Tickell, wrote that 'she has more genius in her little finger than Miss Brunton'—a young and successful actress who was to win great fame in America—'in her whole body'. This witness's praise of her vocal qualities and skill is especially revealing. 'Her voice is harmony itself... and it has certain little breaks and undescribable tones which in simple archness have a wonderful effect, and I think (without exception even of Mrs Siddons) she has the most *distinct* delivery of any actor or actress I ever heard.'[6] To a modern reader the 'little breaks' in the voice irresistibly look forward to the speaking of Judi Dench. And one of the few accounts of Dora's acting that attempt to convey an impression of specific moments of a performance is Charles Lamb's praise of her verse speaking as Viola, a role in which Dench excelled:

There is no giving an account how she delivered the disguised story of her love for Orsino. It was no set speech that she had foreseen, so as to weave it into an harmonious period, line necessarily following line, to make up the music... but, when she had declared her sister's history to be a 'blank', and that she 'never told her love', there was a pause, as if the story had ended—and then the image of the 'worm in the bud' came up as a new suggestion—and the heightened image of 'Patience' still followed after that, as by some growing (and not mechanical) process, thought springing up after thought, I would almost say, as they were watered by her tears. So in those fine lines—

> Write loyal canto[n]s of contemned love—
> Hollow your name to the reverberate hills—

there was no preparation made in the foregoing image for that which was to follow. She used no rhetoric in her passion; or it was nature's own rhetoric, most legitimate then, when it seemed altogether without rule or law.[7]

Though Mrs Jordan was above all a comic actress, she played non-Shakespearian tragic roles, and Leigh Hunt writes of 'her peculiar excellence in the artless miseries of Ophelia', especially in her mad scenes: 'her little bewildered songs in particular, like all her songs, indeed, pierce to our feelings with a most original simplicity'.[8] In later life she became portly but continued to enchant her admirers even when still playing Shakespeare's younger heroines.

She never married and her debt-ridden royal lover abandoned her after twenty years of cohabitation. A loyal and tender-hearted parent, Dora incurred many debts, went to live in France, and died there in poverty. Fifteen years later the penitent King commissioned a statue of her with two of her children from the eminent sculptor George Chantrey. Among her descendants are many men and women who have attained great distinction in public life to the present day— authors, soldiers, and eminent politicians including a prime minister, David Cameron.

Edmund Kean

1787?–1833. *Principal Shakespeare roles*: Shylock, Richard III, Hamlet, Othello, Iago, Macbeth, Timon, Lear.

Figure 11.1. Edmund Kean as Sir Giles Overreach in *A New Way to Pay Old Debts*, by Philip Massinger: oil painting by George Clint. The Art Archive/Victoria and Albert Museum, London/Sally Chappell

The poet Samuel Taylor Coleridge said of Edmund Kean, 'To see him act, is like reading Shakspere by flashes of lightning.'[1] It is perhaps the most famous remark ever made about an actor. And it is strikingly consonant with George Clint's brilliant portrait of Kean as Sir Giles Overreach in Philip Massinger's play *A New Way to Pay Old Debts* which provided a warhorse role for generations of star actors up to the time of Donald Wolfit. The staring dark eyes, the raised brows, the half-open mouth in a jutting jaw, the neck outstretched from a loose-fitting collar, the long black locks unkempt in disarray, and the outstretched arm create an impression of violent impetuosity such as might have inspired Coleridge's remark.

In fact, however, though it is often taken to imply that Kean provided a stunning sequence of illuminations of Shakespeare's text, it is not an unequivocal compliment. It follows the statement that 'His rapid descents from the hyper-tragic to the infra-colloquial, though sometimes productive of great effect, are often unreasonable.' Fanny

Kemble, Mrs Siddons's actress niece, wrote similarly of Kean's 'entire mastery over his audience in all striking, sudden, impassioned passages, in which he has contented himself, leaving unheeded what he could not compass—the unity of conception, the refinement of detail, and evenness of execution'.[2]

These characteristics place Kean at an opposite extreme from John Philip Kemble's search for a single through-line in the roles that he played, for an overriding passion defining the character, and they help to explain why William Hazlitt was able to write that Kean 'has destroyed the Kemble religion . . . in which we were brought up'.[3] In opposition to Kemble's stately, statuesque dignity, Kean acted with the ferocity of an enraged street-urchin, taking his roles by the scruff of their necks and shaking them till they yielded up all that he could wring out of them.

Kean was short, stocky, and strongly built. Though the report of the post-mortem examination of his body, recording that it was 'five feet six inches and three quarters in length' is generally drily scientific in tone, it nevertheless describes the corpse as 'well formed, and the external form of the thorax and abdomen so beautifully developed as to serve as one of the finest models that could possibly be presented to the eye of the sculptor or painter'.[4] Athletic in youth, impetuous, driven by blazing ambition which was fuelled by resentment against a society that had imposed terrible hardships on him and his family in early life, Kean found in a few Shakespearian roles—primarily Shylock, Richard III, and Othello; to a lesser extent Hamlet, Macbeth, Timon, and Lear—an outlet for the passions that gnawed his inwards and that eventually destroyed him.

Theatre was in his blood. He was born at an uncertain date, probably in 1787, the illegitimate son of an actress, Nancy Carey, who worked also as a prostitute. His father was one of three Kean brothers: Edmund, an orator and mimic; Moses, also a mimic and a moderately successful comic actor; and Aaron, of whom little is known. But as he grew up Kean liked to put it about that he was the bastard of Charles Howard, 11th Duke of Norfolk, who may have had an affair with the woman who became Moses's mistress, Charlotte Tidswell. Known as Aunt Tid, she was mainly responsible for the child's upbringing.

Early in life, impelled by the family's poverty, the boy performed as an entertainer in streets, taverns, and drawing rooms, developing skills as a singer, dancer, juggler, tumbler, acrobat, boxer, and fencer that would serve him well in later years. As a lad he may have taken tiny roles in some of Kemble's productions at Drury Lane, and he certainly played the boy Robin in *The Merry Wives of Windsor* there in 1796. He acted in fairground theatres, and by the time he was a late teenager was playing a wide range of roles in provincial repertory theatres, where his acrobatic skills caused him, somewhat to his irritation in view of his aspirations as a tragedian, to be especially in demand as Harlequin in pantomimes. In one of these it was advertised that he would 'leap through a balloon of real fire'.[5]

At the age of 21 he married his Columbine, Mary Chambers, formerly a governess and eight years his senior. They gave their two sons the forenames of the Duke of Norfolk, Howard and Charles. Kean worked hard, if sporadically, to fill in the gaps of his education, picking up an assortment of Latin tags with which he would later besprinkle his letters. For all their social pretensions the family experienced abject poverty. Howard, a beautiful and talented boy, had already performed onstage when, to the deep distress of his parents, he died of whooping cough at the age of 4. Charles, however, overcame his childhood privations. Edmund later sent him to Eton, and though he lacked his father's genius he was to become the leading actor-manager of the mid-nineteenth century.

Already Kean was developing the habits of binge drinking, sometimes for days on end, and womanizing that were to plague him—and his family—for the rest of his life, and to bring it to a premature close. But his ambition to become a great tragedian was deadly serious, and early in his career, probably in 1812, the manager of the Exeter theatrical circuit gave him the opportunity to play most of the great tragic roles—Macbeth, Hamlet, Othello, Richard III—that were to form the basis of his repertoire for the rest of his career. He worked incredibly hard. At a benefit performance for himself in August he played within a single evening Shylock, danced 'a new pas de deux', and played Kojah, 'a noble savage' in a pantomime which he had directed and in which he demonstrated a variety of forms of combat 'with bamboos, Battle axe, shield, and sword'.[6] He drank hard, too; his wife, writing to a friend about the family's poverty and sickness, said that he was 'entirely ruining his health with drink'.[7] But whatever the irregularities of his offstage behaviour, he studied his effects with passionate dedication, developing a technical expertise which became second nature to him and enabled him to go on repeating his signature roles in a great variety of circumstances even when he was no longer able to learn new ones.

Kean's big break came in 1814 at the age of about 26 when, after years of struggle both with his rivals and with his inner daemons, and after plaguing the managers of the London theatres with demands for engagements, he played Shylock in *The Merchant of Venice* at Drury Lane. In doing so, after a single rehearsal on the day of performance, he both established himself as the leading actor of the age and saved the theatre's ailing fortunes. His success was sensational and instantaneous. Rushing back home to his wife, he said, 'Mary, you shall ride in your carriage and Charley shall go to Eton.'[8] They did. William Hazlitt, one of only two critics present in a far from crowded house, wrote on the following day: 'For voice, eye, action, and expression, no actor has come out for many years at all equal to him. The applause from the first scene to the last, was general, loud, and uninterrupted.'[9] And Hazlitt's analysis of Kean's distinctive qualities identifies the characteristics that aroused the audience's enthusiasm:

in giving effect to the conflict of passions arising out of the contrasts of situation, in varied vehemence of declamation, in keenness of sarcasm, in the rapidity of his transitions from one tone and feeling to another, in propriety and novelty of action, presenting a succession of striking pictures, and giving perpetually fresh shocks of delight and surprise, it would be difficult to single out a competitor.[10]

The anonymous critic of *The Examiner*, too, enthused:

There was an animating soul distinguishable in all he said and did, which at once gave a high interest to his performance, and excited those emotions which are always felt at the presence of genius—that is, at the union of great powers with a fine sensibility. It was this that gave fire to his eye, energy to his tones, and such a variety and expressiveness to all his gestures, that one might almost say 'his body thought'.[11]

Less than three weeks later Kean took on the greater challenge of Richard III—still performed in Colley Cibber's radical adaptation of 1699—the role in which great forebears including Garrick, Cooke, and Kemble had triumphed. Not all critics were immediately won over by the originality of his interpretation; some found him at times too undignified and harsh in speech. But others were bowled over, especially by Kean's performance of the final scene. The critic of *The Examiner* enthused, 'We have felt our eyes gush on reading a passage of exquisite poetry, we have been ready to leap at sight of a noble picture, but we never felt stronger emotions, more overpowering sensations, than were kindled by the novel sublimity of his catastrophe.'[12] Hazlitt wrote that Kean was 'more refined than Cooke; more bold, varied, and original than Kemble, in the same character'. And his account of the play's climactic scenes has become one of the classics of theatre criticism:

His manner of bidding his friends good-night, and his pausing with the point of his sword drawn slowly backward and forward on the ground, before he retires to his tent, received shouts of applause. He gave to all the busy scenes of the play the greatest animation and effect. He filled every part of the stage. The concluding scene, in which he is killed by Richmond, was the most brilliant. He fought like one drunk with wounds: and the attitude in which he stands with his hands stretched out, after his sword is taken from him, had a preternatural and terrific grandeur, as if his will could not be disarmed, and the very phantoms of his despair had a withering power.[13]

Kean followed his Richard III with a successful Hamlet, on 12 March, impressing Hazlitt—who expressed reservations about some aspects of the interpretation—especially with an original, if seemingly sentimental, reading of the end of the nunnery scene.

But whatever nice faults might be found in this scene, they were amply redeemed by the manner of his coming back after he has gone to the extremity of the stage, from a pang of parting tenderness to press his lips to Ophelia's hand. It had an electrical effect on the house. It was the finest commentary that was ever made on Shakespeare.[14]

And a couple of months later Kean was to undertake the virtuoso feat of adding Othello and Iago in successive performances to his Drury Lane repertoire. Initially—perhaps because he was young to be playing the weightier role of Othello—he appears to have made an even greater impression as Iago, for Hazlitt 'the most faultless of his performances' because 'the least overdone'.[15] But for many theatregoers Othello, especially in the duel with Iago in the third scene of Act 3 and onwards, was to become his most profoundly moving and satisfying role. For all the complaints that were made about his vocal limitations, he is praised especially for the musicality of his speaking. Even in his later years, when his voice was ravaged by drink, a fellow actor, George Vandenhoff, wrote that 'His delivery of Othello's "Farewell" ran on the same tones and semitones, had the same rests and breaks, the same *forte* and *piano*, the same *crescendo* and *diminuendo*, night after night, as if he spoke it from a musical score. And what beautiful, what thrilling music it was! The music of a broken heart—the cry of a despairing soul!'[16] At the end of Kean's first London season Drury Lane's grateful managers voted him five shares in the theatre and acknowledged that he had saved it from bankruptcy.

After playing for some months in Dublin and elsewhere, Kean returned to Drury Lane for his second season there, adding to his London repertoire Macbeth, in the spectacular semi-operatic version based on William Davenant's Restoration adaptation, soon to be followed by Romeo—a part for which he was temperamentally and physically ill-suited. In March 1815 there followed a rare revival of *Richard II*. The dynamic Kean was miscast as the lyrical King. In Hazlitt's view Kean made Richard 'a character of *passion*, that is, of feeling combined with energy; whereas it is a character of *pathos*, that is to say, of feeling combined with weakness'.[17] The play was given in an odd version by Richard Wroughton in which the Queen mourns over her husband's body in lines adapted from those of the dying Lear, with 'Pray you, undo my button' changed to 'Pray you, undo my lace', and supplemented by a snatch of *Titus Andronicus*. Kean must have been bitterly conscious of the irony that words not present in the version of *King Lear* with a happy ending by Nahum Tate which had been acted for the past 150 years were now being spoken in a different play almost literally over his dead body.

Enterprisingly too he played an abbreviated *Timon of Athens* in 1816. The little-known play received only seven performances but occasioned a review from Leigh Hunt which rises to eloquence in its description of the encounter between Timon and Alcibiades.

First you heard a sprightly quick march playing in the distance; Kean started, listened, and leaned in a fixed and angry manner on his spade, with frowning eyes . . . he seemed as if resolved not to be deceived. The audience were silent; the march threw forth its gallant note nearer and nearer; the Athenian standards appear, then the soldiers come treading on the scene with that air of confident progress which is produced by the accompaniment of music; and at last, while the squalid misanthrope still maintains his posture and keeps his back to the strangers, in steps the young and splendid Alcibiades, in the flush of victorious expectation. It is the encounter of hope with despair.[18]

Kean played Lear for the first time in 1820; the play had been shelved during the last years of the supposedly mad King George III. The text was mostly Tate's sentimentalized version, but in a few performances Kean was at last allowed the original death scene. As often in versions of the tragedies throughout the nineteenth century the curtain fell, to slow music, immediately after the hero's last words. The flame of his genius rapidly consumed him. He led a flamboyant lifestyle, keeping a pet lion and a yacht, a stallion on which he would ride drunkenly up and down the steps of Drury Lane, and employing a secretary whose duties included getting him safely back home after all-night drinking sessions. He spent too much, gave away too much, drank too much, and womanized too much. Scandal after scandal dogged his career and ravaged his domestic life. In 1825 the Drury Lane prompter James Winston, whose journals provide eye-opening accounts of what went on behind the scenes, wrote that after going missing all one night Kean was found 'in his room at the theatre fast asleep wrapt up in a large white greatcoat. He then sent for a potence [presumably a cordial drink], some ginger [reputedly an aphrodisiac], etc., and said, "Send me Lewis or the other woman. I must have a fuck, and then I shall do." He had it. They let him sleep till about six, when they awoke him, dressed him, and he acted but was not very sober.'[19] The role was Hamlet.

In Kean's last years, though he could still play the roles that he had learned as a young man, both his mind and his body began to let him down. He acted in Paris with little success in 1828, and had a terrible fiasco at Drury Lane in 1830 when his memory failed him. In 1832, aged 45, while playing Othello at Covent Garden, he collapsed into the arms of his son Charles, who was playing Iago, saying, 'I am dying—speak to them for me.' He died two months later.

For all his faults and his excesses, in his brief prime Kean must have been—with the possible exception of the more versatile Laurence Olivier—the most electrifying actor of the English stage, transcending his limitations by the imaginative intensity of his acting.

William Charles Macready

Figure 12.1. W. C. Macready as Macbeth: oil painting by George Clint, 1821. © Victoria and Albert Museum, London

1793–1873. *Principal Shakespeare roles*: Romeo, Hamlet, Richard III, Shylock, Benedick, Lear, Macbeth, Coriolanus, Leontes.

The contrast between the racy libertinism of the Regency and the staid respectability associated with the Victorian period is epitomized in the differences between the personalities and the careers of Macready and Edmund Kean, whom Macready admired as an actor but despised as a man. Macready's father was a provincial theatre manager who, not wishing his son to become an actor, sent him to Rugby School for a classical education that would fit him for the Bar or the Church. His tutor, aware of the father's feelings, nevertheless reported to him on the boy's 'wonderful talent for acting and speaking' and referred to the combination within him of 'fine figure, expressions, countenance, elegance, and propriety of action, modulation of voice, and most complete power of representation'.[1] These qualities would seem most naturally to qualify the boy to become an actor, but he himself wanted to make a career in the law. When he was 16, however, his father's financial difficulties, which were to lead to imprisonment for debt and to bankruptcy, became so acute that, with the puritanical sense of duty that was to characterize his entire career, he suppressed his personal desires and started both to train himself as an actor and to take over some of his father's managerial duties.

Descriptions of Macready's looks and of his vocal powers vary wildly. Leigh Hunt described him as 'one of the plainest and most awkwardly made men that ever trod the stage'. But his statement that Macready's voice 'is even coarser than his person' seems to be denied by many reports of the actor's eloquent speaking, including some by Hunt himself.[2] After seeing his Richard III in 1819 Hunt had the magnanimity to write, 'We expected to find declamation, and we found thoughts giving a soul to words.'[3] Of his Coriolanus in the same year Hunt wrote, 'his voice is the finest and most heroical on the stage'.[4] But Macready had a mannerism of interjecting redundant syllables between words, and (like Kean) was 'apt', as Hazlitt wrote of his Coriolanus, 'to be too sudden and theatrical in his contrasts, from a loud utterance to a low one'.[5]

Macready's numerous acting triumphs seem to have resulted rather from high intelligence and dogged hard work than from natural gifts. His self-training was arduous to the point of masochism. Late in life, remarking 'how sparingly, and therefore how effectively, Mrs Siddons'—whom he revered and with whom he had acted as a young man—'had recourse to gesticulation', he described how, in order to overcome the temptation to wave his arms around and to shout, he

would lie down on the floor, or stand straight against a wall, or get my arms within a bandage, and, so pinioned, or confined, repeat the most violent passages of Othello, Lear, Hamlet, Macbeth, or whatever would require most energy and emotion. I would speak the most passionate bursts of rage under the supposed constraints of *whispering them* in the ear of him or her to whom they were addressed, thus keeping both voice and gesture in subjection to the real impulse of feeling.

He would use looking glasses, too, to help him to 'keep the features, perhaps I should say the muscles of the face, undisturbed, whilst intense passion would speak from the eye alone'.[6] Something of this may be seen in George Clint's portrait of him in what was probably his finest role, Macbeth.

At the age of 17, initially almost paralysed with nerves, he made his debut as Romeo with his father's company in Birmingham. Encouraged by the rounds of applause with which contemporary audiences were accustomed to signal approval of specific points of the action, he gradually 'entered into the spirit of the character' and 'felt the passion'; he '"trod on air", became another being, or a happier self'.[7]

From this time forward his professional career was dedicated entirely to the stage as both actor and manager.

He played in Birmingham, Bath, and other provincial towns for six years before appearing in London at Covent Garden in 1816. His first Shakespearian triumph came three years later, as Richard III (playing Cibber's text, which he despised). Reviewers praised his originality, his endurance in so long and arduous a role, his vocal powers, and his intelligence. Leigh Hunt, while admitting that his 'natural style of acting' was indebted to the example of Kean, illuminatingly compared the actors' interpretations, concluding that 'Mr Macready's Richard is a very great addition indeed to his reputation, and no small one to the stock of theatrical pleasure'.[8] And the audience applauded rapturously.

Soon afterwards, risking comparison with his other older contemporary, John Philip Kemble, Macready took on Coriolanus, and triumphed again. The reviewer for the *Morning Herald* praised his 'magic power of imposing an illusive image of physical grandeur upon the very sense of the beholder, merely by some slight change of attitude or action'. Again the audience responded with rapture: 'From the death of Coriolanus to the fall of the curtain the house resounded with applause, and in the pit the waving of hats was universal.'[9] Leigh Hunt, in a finely discriminating notice, praised Macready while finding the rest of the cast 'beneath criticism'. The Volumnia, he wrote, 'belongs to melodrama. A Roman matron did not think it essential to her dignity to step about with her head thrown half a yard back, as if she had a contempt for her own chin.'[10] In the following year Macready first undertook what was probably his greatest role, Macbeth; an illustration shows him, like many of his predecessors, still wearing the plumed cap associated with tragedy. Again he triumphed, partly as a result of his rethinking of traditional business. 'In the banquet scene . . . he made an original and admirable effect. Instead of intimidating the Ghost into a retreat, he fell back, sank into a chair, covered his face with his hands, then looked again, perceived the Ghost had disappeared, and upon being relieved from the fearful vision recovered once more the spring of his soul and body.'[11] A fellow actor, John Coleman, who towards the end of his long life published a racy and highly entertaining memoir, *Fifty Years of an Actor's Life*, wrote, 'For subtlety, intellectuality, and vigour his Macbeth has never been approached in our time, and he was the only possible Lear I have ever seen.'[12] (By this time Sir Henry Irving had played both roles.)

Over his long career Macready played many other Shakespeare roles, some rarely, others frequently. The range is impressive. It includes Richard II (a rare revival), Henry IV, Antony (in *Antony and Cleopatra*), Othello, Iago, Prospero, Cassius, Shylock, the Duke (in *Measure for Measure*), Benedick, Ford, Jaques, Brutus, King John, Wolsey, Iachimo, and Leontes. Inevitably his interpretations, and the degree of success with which he carried them out, fluctuated. Comedy was not his natural element, yet the dramatist and critic John Westland Marston wrote that as Benedick in *Much Ado About Nothing* Macready, in spite of serious anxiety about whether he should play the role, 'gained a triumph which . . . might fairly rank with any that he achieved in tragedy'. He did this partly through mastery of mime: 'In the celebrated soliloquy in the second act, after he has overheard in the arbour that Beatrice loves him, the complex expression of his face as he advanced drew roars from the house before he uttered a word. One might read there the sense of amazement, of gratification, and of perplexity as to the way of reconciling his newly-revealed passion for Beatrice with his late raillery at her and all women.'[13] In 1857, after forty-three tormented years as an actor, Macready, aged 58, was at last able to retire from his despised profession and to retreat into the life of a country gentleman. The occasion was marked by a grand ceremonial dinner organized by Dickens and with innumerable toasts along with an unexpected sonnet from the Poet Laureate, Alfred Lord Tennyson, which also conveyed Shakespeare's assumed approbation of the actor's efforts:

Farewell Macready; moral, grave, sublime;
Our Shakespeare's bland and universal eye
Dwells pleased, through twice two hundred years, on thee.[14]

Macready documented both his public and his private life in voluminous diaries, and although after he died his son destroyed most of the manuscripts for fear they were too revealing, copious selections, as well as Macready's own *Reminiscences*, had already appeared in print. His writings reveal a tormented, conflicted, intensely self-critical soul. Deeply religious and anxious to conform to the highest standards of morality, he frequently castigates himself for lapses of behaviour. On his fortieth birthday, he wrote 'what has my life been? A betrayal of a great trust, an abuse of great abilities!'[15] Trying to impose on others the high standards that he set himself, he could be tyrannical with fellow actors and even with members of his deeply loved family.

Macready's volatile and passionate temperament often aroused enmity. Coleman wrote that in the theatre 'he was dogmatic, opinionated, impatient of contradiction, domineering, and autocratic, irascible, atrabilitarious [*sic – a variant of a Spanish word meaning 'cantankerous*], and overbearing'.[16] These defects had calamitous consequences in the Astor Place Riots of 1849 in New York when the ferocious rivalry between Macready and his American fellow tragedian and one-time friend Edwin Forrest resulted in demonstrations both inside and outside the Astor Opera House which left around twenty-five people dead and more than 120 injured.

Among the many paradoxes of Macready's tumultuous career was his erratic treatment of Shakespeare's texts. He took pride in abandoning Tate's adaptation of *King Lear* in a splendid Covent Garden production of 1838 in which a woman, Priscilla Horton, played the newly restored role of the Fool. The text was however considerably shortened and rearranged. In a detailed review sometimes ascribed to Dickens, John Forster wrote that Macready's Lear, 'remarkable before for a masterly completeness of conception, is heightened by this introduction of the Fool to a surprising degree'. 'Mr Macready's representation of the father at the end,' he wrote, 'broken down to his last despairing struggle, his heart swelling gradually upwards till it bursts in its closing sigh, completed the only perfect picture that we have had of Lear since the age of Betterton'[17]—a reference to the fact that the original play had not been acted since Betterton's time. He made valiant attempts to restore passages of the original *Richard III* to Colley Cibber's adaptation. Yet when he produced *The Tempest* in a visually splendid production also of 1838, although he removed the additions made by Dryden and Davenant in the mid-seventeenth century, he turned the opening storm scene into a wordless spectacle. Less culpably, given the climate of the times, his omissions from *Macbeth* included the Porter scene, with its bawdy innuendoes. During periods of management of both Drury Lane and Covent Garden he did much to raise standards of rehearsal and performance, disciplining his actors rigorously and insisting on high production values.

The most eloquent description of Macready's acting—and indeed one of the most eloquent, not to say effusive, of any Shakespeare performance—comes in Helen Faucit's book *On Some of Shakespeare's Female Characters* (1885). As a young woman Faucit (who later married Sir Theodore Martin, Queen Victoria's biographer) was in love with Macready, and there were even rumours that she was pregnant by him. In 1837, aged 20, she had played a fine Hermione to his Leontes. Many years later she vividly recalled his acting in the scene where what Leontes believes to be Hermione's statue comes to life:

Oh, can I ever forget Mr Macready at this point! At first he stood speechless, as if turned to stone; his face with an awe-struck look upon it. Could this, the very counterpart of his queen, be a wondrous piece of mechanism? Could art so mock the life? He had seen her laid out as dead, the funeral obsequies performed over her, with her dear son beside her. Thus absorbed in wonder, he remained until Paulina said, 'Nay, present your hand.' Tremblingly he advanced, and touched gently the hand held out to him. Then, what a cry came with, 'O, she's warm!' It is impossible to describe Mr Macready here. He was Leontes' very self! His passionate joy at finding Hermione really alive seemed beyond control. Now he was prostrate at her feet, then enfolding her in his arms. I had a slight veil or covering over my head and neck, supposed to make the statue look older. This fell off in an instant. The hair, which came unbound, and fell on my shoulders, was reverently kissed and caressed. The whole change was so sudden, so overwhelming, that I suppose I cried out hysterically, for he whispered to me, 'Don't be frightened, my child! don't be frightened! Control yourself!' All this went on during a tumult of applause that sounded like a storm of hail.[18]

As we shall see in Chapter 13, Macready and Faucit had a real-life relationship that ended in tears.

Figure 13.1. Helen Faucit: undated studio photograph. © National Portrait Gallery, London

Helen Faucit

1814–98. *Principal Shakespeare roles*: Rosalind, Juliet, Portia, Beatrice, Desdemona, Hermione, Lady Macbeth, Imogen.

In Helen Faucit's book which includes her eloquent account of acting with Macready in *The Winter's Tale* (see Chapter 12) she declares her incredulity that Shakespeare could ever have been satisfied with the efforts of 'boys and beardless youths' to perform the women's roles in his plays.

Think of a boy as Juliet! As "heavenly Rosalind"! as "divine Imogen"!... How could any youth, however gifted and specially trained, even faintly suggest these fair and noble women to an audience? Woman's words, woman's thoughts, coming from a man's lips, a man's heart—it is monstrous to think of! One quite pities Shakespeare, who had to put up with seeing his brightest creations thus marred, misrepresented, spoiled.[1]

Helen Faucit, born Helena Faucit Saville in 1814 (not, as her husband recorded and is often repeated, 1817), was above all a womanly woman. Handsome rather than beautiful in her younger days, she had fair skin and curly locks of dark hair, alluring eyes, a prominent nose, and a cleft chin. Her features were mobile and highly expressive. The well-known and beautiful painting of her by Rudolf Lehmann as Juliet which her husband left to what was then the Shakespeare Memorial Theatre idealizes her appearance; more convincing as a likeness is the dignified, self-consciously posed photograph reproduced as Figure 14.1 and taken in 1864, by which time she was in her fiftieth year and had given up regular acting. In her early years, the young Queen Victoria—who later became a warm admirer and close friend, and to whom Helen Faucit dedicated her book on Shakespeare—described her as 'plain and thin' and complained that she 'rants and screams too much'.[2] But when she was in her thirties an admirer described 'the elegance which invariably distinguishes all her movements' and praised 'the proportions of her figure' and 'the deep intonations and flexible richness of voice' which 'penetrate the heart'.[3] No less smitten was John Coleman: 'Her voice, with its infinite varieties of tremulous minors and full flushed resonant crescendoes, was "an alarum to love".'[4] Thomas De Quincey too, in an essay on her performance as Sophocles's Antigone in Edinburgh in 1845, wrote rhapsodically of her 'noble figure', her 'lovely arms', and her 'fine and impassioned voice, deep for a female'. 'Is it', he asked, 'a goddess that moves before us? Perfect she is in form; perfect in attitude . . . We critics, dispersed through the house, in the very teeth of duty and conscience, all at one moment unanimously fell in love with Miss Faucit.'[5]

She was born into a theatrical family, and theatre was in her blood. Sickly and lonely in childhood, she developed an early passion for literature, and especially for Shakespeare. She received early training for the stage from her actor step-uncle, Percy Farren. Her family had links with Edmund Kean, whom she saw perform in his later years at Richmond. She gives a touching account of a 'chance' meeting with him during a walk, looking 'as if come from the grave', when she was 16. And in 1833, a few months after he died, she made a successful debut as Juliet in the Richmond theatre. She was 19 years old. Characteristically of the time the programme also included a pantomimic afterpiece featuring a 'full-length automaton figure' of the great violinist Paganini, then at the height of his fame, which by some feat of trickery fell to pieces after performing 'several favourite airs'. Helen became so carried away with her role that during the 'potion scene' she accidentally crushed the glass phial in her hand and fainted. She recovered and completed the performance to 'cordial applause'. On the following day the glass phial was replaced by a wooden one. Later in the season, when she played Julia in a now-forgotten play by Sheridan Knowles, *The Hunchback*, a critic praised 'her "rare merit" of responding to other actors' words as if hearing them for the first time— her face took their "impress" and her answer "seemed the spontaneous effusion of her own mind." '[6]

For all Helen's initial success it was clear that she needed further study, and her London debut was delayed until 1835 when she scored a triumph at Covent Garden, again playing Knowles's Julia. During the following season—still aged no more than 22—she played nine Shakespeare roles, including some—Beatrice, Hermione, Portia, Kate (in Garrick's *Catherine and Petruchio*, an abbreviation and adaptation of *The Taming of the Shrew*), Desdemona, and Juliet—which, like Julia in *The Hunchback*, she was to repeat many times in her career. She undertook Rosalind, which was to become her best and most popular Shakespeare role, for the first time in 1839. 'Fair and noble women' such as she names in the passage I quoted from her book were her speciality, and one in which she was aided by the Victorian practice of purging Shakespeare's texts of sexual references and innuendo. She did not play racier roles such as Isabella, Mistress Quickly, Mistress Ford, Gertrude, Cleopatra, or Juliet's Nurse (as she might well have done in later life); and she did her best to play down Lady Macbeth's darker side.

Macready, the eminently respectable (and happily married) manager of Covent Garden during her early days in the theatre, became an affectionate but stern mentor. She fell desperately in love with him, and there were even false rumours that he had got her pregnant, but, recognizing the hopelessness of her passion, she threw herself into her acting career with commensurate intensity. Macready and she acted together frequently from 1836 until 1845 when, during a season in Paris, she was so wildly applauded that he became jealous of her success and ended their partnership.

Another early (and softer-hearted) mentor was the elderly (and by this time seriously deaf) Charles Kemble. During his final season as an actor, in 1836, she was to write, he taught her to avoid melodramatic expression of emotion, 'but if pain or death had to be represented, or any sudden or violent shock', to show them 'in their mental rather than in their physical signs. The picture presented . . . must suggest the heroic, the divine in human nature, and not the mere everyday struggles or tortures of this life. . . . Under every circumstance the ideal, the noble, the beautiful, should be given side by side with the real.'[7]

After her break with Macready she acted mainly outside London, in major centres of theatrical activity including Dublin, Manchester, Glasgow, and Edinburgh. Conditions were not always ideal. As a visiting star she played Lady Macbeth with an under-rehearsed and inadequate supporting company in Cork in 1844. Long afterwards a member of her audience wrote:

> I can never forget the horrified expression on the faces of the audience when the great actress was going through the sleep-walking scene—a perceptible shiver seemed to pass through everyone, though the acting was totally devoid of the exaggeration I have witnessed in other performances of the part. [But she had] wretched support. . . . in the scene where Macbeth asks 'How does your patient, doctor?', the poor physician who should have entered at the left came in at the right, whereupon the following occurred:—

MACBETH   (angrily)—Come round here, sir!

DOCTOR—   I beg your pardon, sir. (Goes round)

MACBETH—   It is impossible that I can act any longer. (Bows and retires.)

DOCTOR   (sweeps round the stage and bowing to the audience)—I apologize, (Exit.)[8]

In 1851 Helen Faucit married the biographer, man of letters, and eventually courtier Theodore Martin, who was to be knighted in 1880 as a reward for writing the life of Prince Albert and who later wrote biographies of both Queen Victoria and, after Helen died, of her. Now thoroughly absorbed into high society, Helen wound down her theatrical career while still making occasional appearances and giving dramatic readings. She acted with Henry Irving at the Lyceum as late as 1876, in a play adapted by her husband, and played an elderly Beatrice for the opening of the Shakespeare Memorial Theatre in 1879. Two years later the first of her *Letters on Some of Shakespeare's Heroines* appeared in *Blackwood's Magazine*; they formed the basis of her book published in 1885. After she died at the age of 84 her adoring widower made several attempts to memorialize her including the presentation of Lehmann's portrait of her as Juliet to the Shakespeare Memorial Theatre and a pulpit in her memory in Holy Trinity Church, Stratford-upon-Avon.

An early starter, and a thoughtful, self-critical, and (for all her social success) a highly professional actress, Helen Faucit developed and matured her interpretation of her most successful roles over the years. As her book shows, she saw the characters she played as real, living beings, for whom she imagined lives beyond the action of the plays in which they appear. This links her with the developing interest in character criticism often regarded as typical of the period. And she was anxious to defend her characters from possible accusations of impropriety. Writing of Ophelia, she expresses her belief in Shakespeare's 'trust in the power possessed, at least by sympathetic natures'—such, obviously, as her own—'of filling up his outlines, and giving full and vivid life to the creatures of his brain'.[9] With an element of self-identification, she imagined Ophelia as 'a sweet child, with no playmates of her kind, wandering by the streams, plucking flowers, making wreaths and coronals, learning the names of all the wild flowers in glade and dingle, having many favourites, listening with eager ears when amused or lulled to sleep at night by the country songs, whose words (in true country fashion, not too refined) come back again vividly to her memory, with the fitting melodies, as such things strangely but surely do, only when her wits had flown'. And she thought it important to do so 'because it puts to flight all the coarse suggestions which unimaginative critics have often made, to explain how Ophelia came to utter snatches of such ballads as never ought to issue from a young and cultured woman's lips'.[10]

In her performances she sought psychological truth while at the same time idealizing the women she represented, seeking to see the action and the other characters in the plays from their heroines' viewpoint. She tried to create an impression of spontaneity, of the life and emotional impetus behind every speech, action, and reaction, even in her characters' silent response to what was going on around them. Her success in doing so when she played Rosalind is vouched for in a lengthy review of her book written by a distinguished Irish archaeologist, Margaret Stokes, in a style as gushing as Faucit's own but which nevertheless substantiates its praise with many well-observed descriptions of individual points of action:

When may we hope again to see the airy grace, the youthful elasticity, the high breeding which made that impersonation so irresistibly attractive? Or who will recall the inexpressible charm of her look and manner, when Rosalind resumed her woman's dress, and all the woman's sweetness and refinement and subdued playfulness, as she spoke the epilogue, and left upon the heart a feeling like that of a strain of the sweetest music?

And she adds a tribute that chimes in precisely with the actress's own aims: 'Whatever the character, you realised the noble woman behind.'[11]

To a modern spectator Helen Faucit's interpretations might
well have seemed sentimental and forced. Yet there is no question
that for many of her contemporaries, including the intellectually distinguished George Henry Lewes, she was 'the finest tragic actress on
our stage'.[12]

WHO WAS THE FIRST GREAT AMERICAN SHAKESPEARE ACTOR?

Amateurs are known to have acted plays by Shakespeare in America from 1730, but the earliest professional performances seem to be those given by a company of English actors. Led by Lewis Hallam, they travelled from London to Williamsburg, Virginia to play *The Merchant of Venice* in 1752. Other companies of no great distinction followed, but it was not until the early years of the nineteenth century that leading English actors started to make the often arduous sea journey to appear in the playhouses of New York, Philadelphia, Boston, and other major cities. G. F. Cooke, Edmund Kean, and Junius Brutus Booth (1796–1852) were the most prominent ones to win acclaim, and to enhance Shakespeare's American reputation, by doing so.

When I started to write this book I thought the first-born native American to have a place in it would be Edwin Forrest (1806–72). He was certainly greatly admired by many theatregoers of his time, in England as well as in America. Endowed with a magnificent physique, which he loved to display, and a sonorous voice, he made his professional debut, still no more than 16 years old, in the role of Young Norval in the once popular tragedy of *Douglas* by John Home, receiving a 'torrent of approbation'.[1] Soon afterwards he embarked on an adventurous career as a strolling player, often blacking up in comic negro roles, and even appearing for a while in a circus. When still only 19 years old, in 1825, he had the formative experience of acting with Kean in New York, playing Iago and Richmond to the great man's Othello and Richard III, and not long afterwards he himself undertook Othello, with sensational popular success. He became a star, playing not only in America but also in England, where he became first a friend, then a bitter enemy of Macready. His principal Shakespeare roles besides Othello were Hamlet, Macbeth, King Lear, Richard III, and Coriolanus, in the last of which he could display his physique with special success. He built up a great following in his own country, encouraged native playwriting, and made a fortune. He established a home for retired actors. Theatres built in New York and Philadelphia in the 1920s were named after him.

All this might seem to qualify Forrest as a great Shakespeare actor, but as I read more about him I began to feel that he was primarily a barnstormer, a hunk of a man with a stentorian voice who lacked subtlety, interpretative genius, and all those qualities that make an actor great rather than simply successful and popular. Nothing I have read about him convinces me that he contributed significantly to the interpretative understanding of the roles he played. The problem about his status was formulated by the American theatre historian Charles Shattuck. 'Was he a great actor, or was he only a sort of theatrical frontiersman, a huge, fierce male animal endowed with extraordinary strength of body and voice?'[2] He was, complained the English critic John Forster, in reviews amply supported by accounts of detailed points of the action, above all a literalist, displaying as Othello an 'utter want of imagination',[3] employing as Macbeth a 'succession of. . . vulgar tricks',[4] and closing his performance as Richard III with 'one of the most wretched and melodramatic tricks of the profession . . . While Richard fought with Richmond he had provided himself with long and heavy strips of black hair, which were fixed in such a way that they came tumbling over his forehead, eyes, and face, with every barbarous turn and gesture. The princely Plantagenet . . . was thus accomplished by Mr Forrest in all the points of a savage newly caught from out of the American backwoods.'[5] Forster may be accused of partisanship on behalf of his friend Macready, even of an anti-American bias, but in face of such devastatingly precise criticism I find it impossible to acknowledge Forrest as the first great American Shakespeare actor.

Paradoxically, then, that honour must go to a man born one year later than Forrest whose acting career lay almost entirely outside his native country: Ira Aldridge.

Ira Aldridge

Figure 14.1. 'Head of a Negro in the Character of Othello': oil painting, 1825, by James Northcote believed to represent Ira Aldridge. Manchester Art Gallery, UK/Bridgeman Images

1807–67. *Principal Shakespeare roles*: Othello, Lear, Macbeth, Shylock, Richard III.

Ira Aldridge, known as the African Roscius, was the both the first black actor to achieve great distinction as an interpreter of Shakespeare and the first American to do so. Many legends, some of them self-perpetuated, accrued about his early life. Some said that he was born in Senegal as the son of a prince, others that his father was a slave. Biographers have struggled to sort out fact from fiction. He seems in fact to have been the son of a New York straw-seller who was also a lay preacher. In spite of his humble origins he received a good education at the African Free School in Manhattan. After appearing in amateur and semi-professional theatrical productions as a youth with the short-lived African Theatre Company (with whom he may have played Romeo) he aspired to become a professional actor but when he was around 17 years old, realizing that racial prejudice militated against his acceptance in America, where slavery was still legal in some states, he emigrated to England, where it had been abolished in the year of his birth—though it was to persist in the British colonies until 1838.

A fine oil painting by James Northcote (1746–1831) entitled *Head of a Negro in the Character of Othello* was completed in 1825, the year in which Aldridge first acted in London, at the Royalty Theatre in the East End, playing black characters in a series of melodramas. In the same year, still aged only about 17, he played Othello (the first black actor known to have done so), at the Coburg Theatre (later the Old Vic). Northcote's painting is usually, and plausibly, identified as a portrait of Aldridge. If this is correct he was clearly a handsome young man, exceptionally well developed for his years, and with regular features. A newspaper account of his Othello in 1833 describes his complexion as 'rather a fine dark olive than a deep black, so that its transparency is evident, and on the surface is none of that disagreeable gloss given by the pomatum pot [an ointment which could be used for blackening the skin], and which shines so conspicuously by the aid of the footlights. His features are those of a Negro somewhat refined—the full lip, the flat nose, and the eye tinged with the liquid that discolours the skin; but altogether they are capable of forcible expression.'[1] Portraits and photographs of him in later years show a stocky, eventually somewhat tubby figure.

In England as in America racial prejudice was rife. Charles Lamb, in his essay 'On the tragedies of Shakespeare, considered with reference to their fitness for stage representation' published in 1811, had written, 'I appeal to everyone that has seen "Othello" played, whether he did not find something extremely revolting in the courtship, and wedded caresses of Othello and Desdemona';[2] and Coleridge, lecturing in 1821, had said of Desdemona, 'as we are constituted, and most surely as an English audience was disposed at the beginning of the seventeenth century, it would be something monstrous to conceive this beautiful Venetian girl falling in love with a veritable negro'.[3] Similar attitudes poisoned much newspaper comment on Aldridge's appearances. In 1832 an article in *Figaro in London* spoke of 'a stupid-looking, thick-lipped, ill-formed African calling himself the African Roscius',[4] and when he played Othello at Covent Garden in the following year the same journal referred to him as a 'miserable nigger', a 'wretched upstart' who was 'about to defile the stage'. It threatened, unless he withdrew his name from the playbills, to 'force him to find in the capacity of footman or street-sweeper, that level for which his colour appears to have rendered him peculiarly qualified.'[5] And *The Athenaeum* protested 'in the name of propriety and decency' against 'an interesting actress, and lady-like girl, like Miss Ellen Tree, being subjected ... to the indignity of being pawed about' by the black actor.[6] It must have taken great courage as well as professional dedication on Aldridge's part to go on in face of such opposition. For all this, and although the audience was small, even *The Times* had to concede that Aldridge's performance 'was extremely well received',[7] and the dramatist Sheridan Knowles is said to have 'rushed into his arms, exclaiming, "For the honour of human nature let me embrace you."'[8]

Finding only occasional work in London, and that mainly in minor theatres, Aldridge made a successful career in the provinces, adding white as well as black men, including King Lear, Macbeth, Shylock, and Richard III, to his repertoire, often using white make-up. He tried out many of his roles in Hull, the birthplace of William Wilberforce, the great opponent of slavery. And he played Othello in a now-demolished theatre close to the site of Shakespeare's New Place in Stratford-upon-Avon. No textual purist, he frequently played single scenes and programmes of excerpts from a number of plays, a shortened version of *The Merchant of Venice* that ended with Shylock's defeat, and a text derived from Nahum Tate's adaptation of *King Lear*. He often demonstrated versatility and complicated his audiences' reactions to blackness by playing a comic, drunken black slave in *The Padlock*, by Isaac Bickerstaffe, with music by Charles Dibdin, as an afterpiece to *Othello*, and by singing a comic song, 'Opossum up a gum tree'.[9]

Around 1847, seeking another black Shakespearian role, he played Aaron in a version of the rarely performed *Titus Andronicus* concocted partly by himself. The text has not survived, but reports show that it was so grotesquely altered that the villainous Moor became the play's virtuous hero. In 1852 he undertook the first of many tours in western and eastern Europe where, in spite of acting in English with foreign-speaking casts, he received many state honours and gifts. From time to time he returned to London, playing Othello at the Lyceum in 1852 when *The Athenaeum* wrote much more favourably—though still patronizingly—of the 'sable artist', but although he longed to return to America he never had the confidence to do so. He was especially admired in Russia, playing Lear for the first time in St Petersburg in 1858, but also travelling extensively in remote provinces.

Inevitably over a long career with performances given in an exceptionally wide range of conditions, Aldridge's interpretations of his roles, and the degree of success with which he executed them, varied more than those of most actors. And since he rarely performed in London, they escaped the notice of some of the most experienced theatre critics. There are however detailed accounts of some of his performances written by Continental critics, many of which emphasize the unactor-ish emotional directness of his acting.[10]

Since he acted Aaron in so drastically altered a version of *Titus Andronicus* his performance in that role is scarcely relevant to his qualities as a Shakespeare actor, but a review written after he played it at the Britannia Theatre in London in 1857 at least conveys an impression of the qualities that impressed his audiences. He was 'gentle and impassioned by turns; now, burning with jealousy, as he suspects the honour of the Queen; anon, fierce with rage, as he reflects upon the wrongs which have been done him...and then all tenderness and emotion in the gentler passages with his infant. All these phases of the character Mr. Aldridge delineated with judgment and great force of expression.' And again his emo-tional directness is praised: 'He rants less than almost any tragedian we know...he is thoroughly easy, natural and sensible, albeit he has abundance of physique at his command.'[11] His Russian biographer gives an account of his portrayal of Shylock's final scene which illustrates his skill in inventing emotionally revealing action:

when he hears that one of the punishments will be his adoption of Christianity, he first begins to shudder and lets out a horrified moan. After that, when one of the men seizes him by his robes...Aldridge makes a wonderful mute scene out of it...He violently jerks his clothes out of...the unclean hands of the Christian, then he takes out a handkerchief and very meticulously wipes the place on his garment which was soiled by the unclean touch. After that he looks with repulsion and disgust at his handkerchief which is itself now besmirched, and finally, after having thrown it with indignation at the Chris-tian, he breaks down bitterly, cries and leaves.

And the writer comments that Aldridge 'was drawing on the experi-ence of his own life for the picture of the tragedy of a Jew who is downtrodden and powerless to take revenge'.[12]

Russian accounts of Aldridge as Lear show that in spite of playing a corrupt version of the text he achieved devastating emotional impact at many points of the action.

Above all was his last scene when, with wide open eyes, with tortured face he runs onto the scene carrying the dead Cordelia in his arms. It seemed as if he was about to throw her on the ground and tear to pieces everyone around him, but then his eyes fell on her face and the face of the old man softens, he seats himself on the earth, hugs his daughter to his bosom, smoothes her hair, caresses her, and his whole being becomes transformed into love and sorrow.[13]

And he 'presented the death of the king simply and amazingly; quietly and with just the shadow of a smile on his lips he whispers these last words, convulsively crosses his fingers, then lightly falls into the arms of those around him and his eyes close; no writhing, no shuddering, nothing'.[14]

Othello was of course Aldridge's signature role, and one which he continued to develop over the course of his long career. Aided (like Paul Robeson after him) by a powerful physique and noble voice, he played the role with deep self-identification and at times terrifying passion. The best account that I have come across is by a French reviewer who saw him in St Petersburg, who wrote that the actor 'captivated the entire audience by his harmonious and sonorous voice, by his simple, natural, and dignified declamation'. The critic was especially impressed by 'the scene in the third act when the sentiment of jealousy is excited in the savage Moor'—episodes in which Kean too had been especially admired:

You see his eyes flash, you feel the tears in his voice when he questions Iago, followed by stifled sobs that almost choke him, and when he is at last convinced that his misfortune is beyond doubt, a cry of anger or rather the roaring of a wild beast escapes him, coming from the very bottom of his heart. . . . Real tears roll down his cheek, he foams at the mouth, his eyes flash fire; never have I seen an artist so completely identify himself with the person he represents.[15]

Aldridge became a British citizen in 1863 but died while on tour and was buried in Łódź, Poland, four years later. His daughter Luranah became an opera singer and, encouraged by Cosima Wagner, was cast as one of Valkyries at Bayreuth in 1896, but illness prevented her from appearing. An indisputably great actor, Ira Aldridge was also an indefatigable ambassador for his race.

Charlotte Cushman

Figure 15.1. Charlotte Cushman: daguerreotype, c. 1855. © Everett Collection Historical/Alamy

1816–76. *Principal Shakespeare roles*: Romeo, Desdemona, Emilia, Portia, Rosalind, Gertrude, Lady Macbeth, Queen Katherine

Charlotte Cushman, the first great female American Shakespeare actor, was almost as physically impressive as her male compatriot and contemporary Edwin Forrest. Powerfully built, she had a superb figure but a face which she herself referred to as 'my unfortunate mug'. Still, it served her well. One of her biographers, Clara Erskine Clement, an art historian and world traveller who was a close friend, says that 'no likeness could ever represent her satisfactorily, since it was the flexibility of her features, and the picturing of every passing emotion upon them, that made the face by which her friends and the public knew her'.[1] A delightful 1843 portrait by Thomas Sully, with whose daughter she was in love, idealizes it. The daguerreotype reproduced as Figure 15.1, made around 1855, when she was about 40 years old, provides a more realistic image.

Charlotte was a woman of high intelligence, physical courage, and great independence of mind and spirit. A defier of convention, over the years she had a sequence of passionate affairs, usually with highly talented women, more than one of which led to a form of marriage. Possessed of a fine contralto voice, she aspired at first to be an opera singer, but a teacher misdirected her into higher, soprano roles, and aged under 20 she made her debut as the Countess in Mozart's opera *The Marriage of Figaro*. This had a disastrous effect on her singing voice. After retraining for several months she was guided into acting, making her debut ambitiously and successfully as Lady Macbeth in New Orleans on Shakespeare's (official) birthday, in 1836, when she was still under 20 years old. During the next few years she played a wide variety of roles, including Emilia, Goneril, Romeo, Oberon, and Gertrude at the Park Theatre, New York, and elsewhere. She was at her best in roles that enabled her to tear a passion to tatters, sensationally successful as Nancy in an adaptation of Dickens's *Oliver Twist* and as Meg Merrilies in a play based on Sir Walter Scott's novel *Guy Mannering*. And though she could play Shakespeare's comic heroines, she was more naturally cast in tragedy and melodrama. A spectator wrote of her Emilia: 'I saw a large-sized, fair-complexioned young woman, not of handsome but of impressive presence. The effect of her denunciation of the *Moor* after the murder of *Desdemona*, was electric.'[2] A watershed in her life came when, aged 27, she first acted with Macready during his second American tour. He was unnecessarily cautious not to meet her in private: in his diary for 23 November he wrote, 'She kissed my hand, but I was only kind.' Though he found her rather a pain personally (the obverse may also have been true), he was greatly impressed by her developing talents and recommended her to visit England, where she arrived in late 1844. After initial setbacks and a visit to Paris where she sought work, she made her London debut at the Princess's Theatre, run by Charles Kean, in 1845 where she played Lady Macbeth to Forrest's Macbeth. He failed; she triumphed. It became her most famous Shakespeare role, and one that she played frequently in both England and America. Some accounts of her performances of it are purely adulatory, but her biographer Clara Erskine Clement gives an interestingly frank impression of it along with a general description of her acting style:

at first, before she lost herself in her assumed character, and indeed always in the minor scenes, she was what is termed 'stagy.' She employed the angular motion, the start, the labored breathing, and the stilted declamation which are happily almost obsolete now. This manner was especially noticeable in

'Macbeth', and in the first scene with *Macbeth* Miss Cushman gave full illustration of these peculiarities, but as the play progressed, and she became in truth *Lady Macbeth*, all this staginess disappeared, and she seemed to have forgotten herself; she was acting no longer. She coaxed and chided by turns; was now the queen, again the loving wife, and then the suffering, conscience-stricken woman, with all the naturalness possible.[3]

According to a fellow actor, Lawrence Barrett, Charlotte had a theory that

all through the more important scenes of the play, both *Macbeth* and *Lady Macbeth* were under the influence of wine. She supported her opinion from the text, and believed that Shakespeare supposed it to be apparent that they were drunk. This suits well with the manner which Miss Cushman had at some points in the play, a reckless, swinging way of doing everything and an apparent carelessness of what happened.[4]

At the Princess's she went on to play Beatrice, Portia, and—with special success—the breeches role of Rosalind. Offstage she met and entertained many of the leading intellectual men and women of the day. After a successful provincial tour she moved to the Haymarket to play Romeo to her sister's Juliet for some eighty or more performances in a single season. She insisted against opposition in abandoning Garrick's alterations and reverting to an only slightly shortened version of the original text (a lead which was followed in the following year by Samuel Phelps at Sadler's Wells). Her Romeo astonished the dramatist James Sheridan Knowles—no mean judge—who compared the impact of her acting in Romeo's scene with the Friar favourably with Kean's in the third act of *Othello*. 'I was not prepared for such a triumph of pure genius . . . It was a scene of topmost passion; not simulated passion,—no such thing; real, palpably real. The genuine heart-storm was on,—on in wildest fitfulness of fury; and I listened and gazed and held my breath, while my blood ran hot and cold.'[5] John Coleman was impressed by her overt sexuality in the role: 'Her amorous endearments were of so erotic a character that no man would have dared to indulge in them *coram publico* [in a public place].'[6]

Rather similarly he says of her Rosalind that 'Her comedy was rich and racy. Certain Shakespearian lines, which in this superfine age we have suppressed as indecorous, came lifting off her lips with a sense of enjoyment in which she appeared to revel, and, for the matter of that, so did the modern Athenians [i.e. the audience in Edinburgh, where she was performing].'[7] This performance came as a surprise to those who thought of her primarily as a tragedienne. Her adoring long-time lover and biographer Emma Stebbins, an eminent sculptress, quotes an unnamed reviewer as writing, 'the charm of charms in this impersonation is the hearty sweetness of her laugh; it is contagious from its very sweetness; she seems to laugh from her very soul as she bandies about her jests and makes the love-lorn Orlando the butt of her pretty malicious pleasantries. And even as she feels it, so does her audience.'[8]

Clement, whom I quoted on Cushman's Emilia, saw her frequently in her later career and remarks that even when she played with Macready, from whom she learned much, she could 'throw such energy, physical and mental, into her performance as to weaken, for the time, the impression of Mr. Macready's magnificent acting'.[9] She acted again with Macready in 1847, playing Queen Katherine, in *Henry VIII*, to his Cardinal Wolsey at a benefit performance for him attended by Queen Victoria on the eve of his second American tour at Drury Lane in July 1848. The critic of *The Times* wrote ecstatically that 'the broken up attitude of that ghastly figure in the chair, the benignant smile that seems ever ready to vanish away in death, the flush of banished pride at the unmannerly entrance of the messenger ... the look of approaching beatitude in sleep, when she is cheered by a celestial vision, are so many nuances all truthful to the last degree'.[10] In both its power and its pathos Queen Katherine was a great role for her.

Now established as a star in England, she played frequently and with great success with her sister and in English provincial cities as well as in London and Dublin before returning to America in 1849. After this she worked frequently in both England and America while also spending much time in a female artistic community in Rome. Dogged by serious illness in her later years, she announced her retirement in 1874, but acting, and the subsequent applause, had a therapeutic effect on her, and even after undergoing horrific operations for cancer she continued both to act onstage and to give public readings to adulatory acclaim until she could do so no more.

Lady Macbeth was the last as well as the first role that she played.

Edwin Booth

Figure 16.1. Edwin Booth as Hamlet, Princess's Theatre, London, 1880. Reproduced by permission of the Shakespeare Birthplace Trust

1833–1893. *Principal Shakespeare roles*: Romeo, Shylock, Hamlet, Iago, Othello, Richard III, Benedick.

Often in the history of Shakespearian stage performance great actors have emerged from a family with a theatrical background. This is true, as we have seen, of Sarah Siddons and John Philip Kemble, of Dora Jordan, William Charles Macready, Helen Faucit, and Edmund Kean. The greatest American male actor of the nineteenth century, Edwin Booth—named after Edwin Forrest—also had theatre in his blood. His father, Junius Brutus Booth, who at one time rivalled Edmund Kean at Drury Lane but lapsed into alcoholism and eccentricity bordering on madness, had travelled from England to make the better part of his career in America. And two of Edwin's brothers, John Wilkes Booth and Junius Brutus Booth, Junior, also followed in their father's footsteps.

Like other actors before him, including Cooke, Kean, and Forrest, Edwin came up the hard way. As a boy he often travelled with his father as a kind of minder, trying to keep him sober and to get him to the theatre in time. He made his official stage debut at the age of 15 to his father's Richard III in the tiny role of Tressel, a mute role in Shakespeare's play who speaks only in Colley Cibber's version, but he was soon promoted, even standing in for his father as Richard a couple of years later. The acting members of the family toured in California, playing to miners engaged in the Gold Rush, and Junius senior died of typhoid on board a river steamer when Edwin was 19. It was at this age, in 1853, that Edwin first played Hamlet, which was to become his most famous role. He was soon taking other leading Shakespeare roles including Benedick, Romeo, and Shylock, while also acting in many more ephemeral plays as he developed his skills.

Of average height and comparatively slight in build, Booth—often described as 'lithe'—was not cut out for the kind of heroic roles in which Forrest, whom he soon came to rival and to surpass, excelled. He had sensitive features, flowing black locks, expressive eyes, and lyrical vocal delivery. Even so he hated playing lovers—even Romeo. Booth is the first of the actors in this book of whom a sound recording exists—made under difficult studio conditions, not from a stage performance. The crackly transfer of a wax cylinder on which, in his fifty-seventh year, he speaks lines from Othello's speech to the Senate reveals a musical voice of baritonal quality and gives a sense, however imperfectly, of the beauty and intelligence of his delivery. He respects the iambic metre but keeps the verse flowing with skilful use of enjambment. There is little sign of an American accent and—like Irving at around this time—he usually, but not invariably, pronounces 'my' as 'mi'—'rude am i in mi speech'—'mi boyish days'.

Except for Ira Aldridge, Booth is also the first of the actors discussed here of whom we have photographs in stage costume. Again these early photographs were made not onstage, let alone in actual perform-ance, but in studio conditions which resulted often in artificial poses as the actors strove to remain still for long enough for their images to be recorded on the photographic plate, but at least they give an impression of their facial appearance, their characteristic poses, and their costumes. The image of Booth as Hamlet, cross-gartered like Malvolio, repro-duced in Figure 16.1, records a genuine piece of stage furniture. There also exists a historic photograph of him with his two brothers as Mark Antony (Edwin), Cassius (John Wilkes), and Brutus (Junius Brutus Jr.,) in *Julius Caesar*, the only play in which they acted together.

This was only a few months before John Wilkes took on the real-life role of an assassin, shooting and fatally wounding Abraham Lincoln as he watched a play. By a strange chance, only a few months previously Edwin himself had saved Lincoln's son from almost certain death when the young man fell from a train.

Booth led a riotous life in his youth, to the detriment of his art. 'Before I was eighteen I was a drunkard, at twenty a libertine', he wrote to a friend.[1] But he virtually gave up drinking after the death of his first wife, in 1863, and matured into a deeply thoughtful actor and theatre manager who earned respect and admiration in England and Germany as well as in America, where he became the acknowledged leader of his profession. He played Hamlet repeatedly throughout his career, developing and maturing his interpretation even after his unprecedented run of 100 performances in 1865. His brother's assassination of Lincoln and the subsequent hatred of the family name caused a hiatus in his career, but his return to the stage some nine months later, again as Hamlet, was greeted with rapturous acclamation.

Though serious in his approach to his craft and to Shakespeare Booth was not a scholar, being content by and large to accept the standard theatre texts of his time, with their omissions, transpositions, and prudish expurgations. He did however contribute detailed performance notes to H. H. Furness's Variorum editions of *The Merchant of Venice* and *Othello*. His acting editions of sixteen plays were published in collaboration with the theatre historian William Winter, a devoted admirer.

As a theatre manager, financier, and producer Booth furthered the movement towards pictorialism and historical reconstruction which had been fostered in England during the 1850s especially in the Princess's Theatre productions of Charles Kean, with whom he was to act. In 1864 Booth emulated Kean in productions at the Winter Garden Theatre in New York which he opened with a production of *Hamlet* aiming to reproduce the tenth-century court of Elsinore in elaborate detail. Its success with the public was so great that it ran for a record 100 consecutive performances, coming to an end only three weeks before his brother shot Lincoln. This theatre burnt down in 1867. Nothing daunted, Booth embarked on the financing and building of Booth's Theatre which offered previously unrivalled facilities for scenically spectacular productions, with innovative lighting and a new system of scene shifting with hydraulic lifts which permitted fully furnished sets to be rapidly raised and lowered from under and above the stage.

He opened the theatre in 1869 with a spectacular *Romeo and Juliet* produced, the playbill proclaimed, 'in strict accordance with historical propriety in every respect, following closely the text of Shakespeare'.[2] In fact the text was heavily bowdlerized, shortened, and rearranged. The production failed to please the critics but scored a popular success. It was followed by an *Othello* in which Booth initially played the Moor but soon took over as Iago with far greater success. Something similar was to happen in England in 1880 when Henry Irving generously proposed that they should alternate the roles at the Lyceum. Though Booth's Othello was admired, the role of Iago brought him greater acclaim. Here, as in Richard III, Hamlet, and to a lesser extent Benedick, he could deploy his special talent for portraying intelligence and irony. His Iago was multifaceted. 'To Othello', a critic wrote,

he is the truthful, respectful adherent and friend whose duty makes a painful disclosure obligatory upon him. To Desdemona he is the courteous servant, whom her beauty and her distress command. To Cassio he is the open and generous fellow-soldier, ready to take his part in disgrace. To Roderigo he is a dashing buck, whose villainy and whose pretensions the poor fool equally admires. To Emilia alone is he the inscrutable, black-browed schemer, whom she distrusts, but does not understand.[3]

In other words, the actor was acting the quintessential actor by pretending not to be acting. Booth himself wrote, 'Don't *act* the villain, don't *look* it or *speak* it (by scowling and growling, I mean), but *think* it all the time. Be genial, sometimes jovial, always gentlemanly. Quick in motion as in thought; lithe and sinuous as a snake.'[4] But as the play approached its climax Booth expressed the full depths of Iago's villainy, raising his hand after killing Roderigo as if he intended to kill Cassio too, grinding his teeth as he said 'From this time forth I never will speak word', and finally, as the curtain came down on Othello's suicide, starting forward as if to gloat over his death.

Perhaps the most spectacular of Booth's productions in his own theatre was a strongly cast *Julius Caesar* (1871–2), which offered anachronistic but visually splendid reproductions of Augustan (instead of Republican) Rome peopled in the crowd scenes by vast numbers of well-drilled supernumeraries. Booth himself played a thoughtful Brutus for most of the long run, but during the last two weeks demonstrated his versatility by taking over first Cassius then Mark Antony.

Altogether Booth put on eight Shakespeare productions at his own theatre, including Cibber's *Richard III* (returning in 1876 to a version based on the original), and *Macbeth* (a role for which he was not well suited). Eventually the financial strain defeated him and he was declared bankrupt in 1874. But he manfully rebuilt his career, as he had done after his brother's assassination of Lincoln, depending now more centrally on his personal acting skills than on spectacular production methods. Visits to England in 1880 and 1882 were followed by a successful tour of Germany and Austria in which, like Aldridge before him, he acted in English while the rest of the cast spoke German. Recovering his fortunes he founded the Players' Club in New York in 1888 as a meeting place for actors and other intellectuals. Like Irving in England, he was helping to raise the social status of his profession. He ended his acting career with a final performance of Hamlet in 1891.

This role, which he played hundreds of times over a period of close on forty years, formed the cornerstone of his career. His interpretation developed and matured along with both his technique and his experience of life, though also of course in his later years his portrayal of a young prince decreased in plausibility. Though Booth was acting before the age of extensive mechanical reproduction, the impact he made on some of those who saw him play Hamlet resulted in exceptionally detailed accounts of performances given at different phases of his career, which can be supplemented by numerous reviews, personal accounts, promptbooks, and other documents, all of which enabled the great theatre historian Charles Shattuck to provide, in *The Hamlet of Edwin Booth* (1969), what may well be the fullest record of any theatrical performance before the invention of film.

Booth's first Hamlet, given in 1853, his twentieth year, in San Francisco, was reviewed enthusiastically by a young Harvard graduate, Ferdinand Cartwright Ewer, who became a distinguished theologian. Ewer was impressed above all by what he called Booth's 'flexibility'. Hamlet, he wrote later, should be 'Melancholy without gloom, contemplative yet without misanthropy, philosophical yet enjoying playfulness in social converse, a man by himself yet with ardent feelings of friendship, a thorough knower of human nature'. He 'stands the type of all that is firm, dignified, gentlemanly and to be respected in a man'.[5] The young Booth was deeply impressed by Ewer's criticism and strove to put his view of the character into practice later. In Boston in 1862 a reviewer wrote that 'His conception of the character seems riper—

more natural—the result of deeper study. There is no claptrap—no false excitement—for the purpose of producing an effect upon the audience; but every word and gesture will bear the closest criticism and most searching analysis.'[6] Above all Booth was praised for an integrity of conception which gave an appearance of naturalness, of a consistent, developing character rather than a bundle of actor's points. By the time of the 'hundred nights Hamlet', in 1864, he was acknowledged as the leading American actor of the time. The visual beauty of his production was praised, and Booth, according to the critic of *Harper's Magazine*, portrayed 'Hamlet as he lived in Shakespeare's world'. It is 'not in any particular scene, or passage, or look, or movement that conveys the impression; it is the consistency of every part with every other, the pervasive sense of a true gentleman sadly strained and jarred'.[7]

It is however the Hamlet given at the Winter Garden in New York in 1870 that is most fully recorded. A 20-year-old theatregoer named Charles W. Clarke who studied the play intensely and learned the entire text by heart, saw Booth play the role eight times and wrote an amazingly full account of it in which he tried, as Charles Shattuck writes, 'to capture every one of Booth's movements, gestures, looks, and vocal effects which could be expressed in writing'.[8] It is an astonishing tribute to an actor who inspired deep admiration and loyalty.

In later years Booth's Hamlet became an American institution, revered even as his hair greyed, his energies ebbed, his voice faded, and rivals appeared on the horizon. His farewell performance, attended by an audience numbering over three thousand, most of whom could hear little of what he said, was a sad anticlimax to a great career.

Henry Irving

Figure 17.1. Henry Irving off duty: unfinished oil painting, 1880, by Jules Bastien Lepage. © National Portrait Gallery, London

1838–1905. *Principal Shakespeare roles*: Benedick, Shylock, Hamlet, Lear, Othello, Iago, Macbeth, Iachimo, Coriolanus, Lear.

Unlike Edwin Booth (with whom he acted in his early years) Henry Irving, born John Henry Brodribb in 1838, became an actor against his parents' wishes and in spite of natural disadvantages—he had to conquer a stammer—and achieved success only after a long and arduous apprenticeship. He left school at the age of 13 and worked for a while in London as a clerk, but was inspired to train as an actor by seeing Samuel Phelps as Hamlet. After paying to play Romeo with an amateur group in Soho he joined a touring company based on Sunderland in 1858 and adopted his stage name. His dedication was fanatical. In three years he played over 400 parts in 330 plays. The theatre historian Arthur Colby Sprague wrote that 'no other player of comparable rank, not even Edmund Kean, remained so long unrecognized; no other, when recognition came, was so widely or destructively criticized'.[1] Slowly he worked his way up to leading roles, finally achieving star status overnight at the Lyceum Theatre in 1871 with his sensational performance as Mathias in the melodrama of *The Bells* which he was to continue to play frequently throughout his career. As he drove home in a carriage that night his wife, Florence, by whom he had two sons, asked him if he intended to go on making a fool of himself in this way for the rest of his life. He stopped the carriage, got out, and blotted her out of his existence. He was to take over the management of the Lyceum in 1878 when Ellen Terry, with whom he had already acted, joined him as his leading lady, a significant artistic and personal partnership which was to endure for twenty-four years. He toured frequently with his own company in America and Canada from 1883 to 1904, giving up management of the Lyceum in 1898.

A professional man of the theatre to his fingertips, Irving ran the Lyceum with rigorous attention to detail, employing highly skilled set and costume designers, distinguished painters (including Sir Lawrence Alma-Tadema), and composers (such as Sir Arthur Sullivan) to enhance his visually elaborate productions in which he developed the spectacular methods of Charles Kean at the Princess's and of Edwin Booth in America. Like them, he often sacrificed text to pictorialism. Of his *Cymbeline* Shaw complained that 'every part is spoiled except the governor's'[2] (Irving wisely chose to play Iachimo, a more rewarding role than the play's ostensible hero Posthumus). He omitted almost half of *King Lear*, not much less of *Hamlet*, and cut more than 500 lines even from such a relatively short play as *The Merchant of Venice* (which occasionally, as with Booth, lost its last act so as to give Irving the final curtain). 'In a true republic of art', wrote Shaw, 'Sir Henry Irving would ere this have expiated his acting versions on the scaffold.'[3] And although he was often praised as an intellectual actor, his tastes were conventional. Shaw berated him for his lack of interest in Ibsen and other avant-garde dramatists (including Shaw himself).

Tall and thin, with bushy eyebrows and a long face, Irving was not conventionally handsome and walked awkwardly. It was even rumoured that he had a wooden leg. A young woman who tried to identify whether this was the left or the right leg came to the conclusion after seeing him act that it was both.[4] His voice was thin and rasping and his pronunciation highly idiosyncratic. Ellen Terry records an American journalist's attempt to represent phonetically his speaking of some lines of Shylock:

> Wa thane, eet no eperes
> Ah! um! Yo ned m'elp
> Ough! Ough! Gaw too thane! Ha! um!

Yo com'n say
Ah! Shilok, um! ouch! We wode hev moanies!

(Well then, it now appears you need my help. | Go to, then. You come [to me] and [you] say | '[Ah,] Shylock, we would have moneys.')

And far from denying the accuracy of the transcription, Terry defends 'the ejaculations, the interjections and grunts with which Henry inter-larded the text' on the grounds that 'they often helped to reveal the meaning of Shakespeare to his audience' more readily than would 'a perfect elocutionist'.[5]

Henry James too wrote of the 'strange tissue of arbitrary pronunci-ations which floats in the thankless medium of Mr Irving's harsh, monotonous voice'.[6] More sympathetically Max Beerbohm, in an obituary, wrote of the 'strange, suggestive voice that admirably attuned itself to the subtleties of Irving's conception of whatever part he was playing'.[7] Its individuality caused it to be frequently imitated both by professional music-hall entertainers and by amateurs such as the boorish Mr Burwin-Fosselton in George and Weedon Grossmith's *Diary of a Nobody* (1892), with the result that some of the alleged phonograph recordings of it are believed to be spurious, but the best authenticated, a performance of the opening soliloquy of *Richard III*, bears witness to the voice's harshness, to a growling delivery that ranges up and down the tenor and baritone registers and that incorporates distinctive pro-nunciations such as 'Yarrk' (for 'Yark'), 'warrr' (rhyming with 'bar' and with a rolling 'r'), 'mi' (for 'my'), a willingness to override line endings in the cause of expressiveness, and a sprightly jauntiness of delivery that privileges characterfulness over poetical values.

Self-awareness is essential in an actor. Irving was aware of his limitations, but succeeded in spite of them. Ellen Terry, in her enchanting memoirs, tells how when she was sitting opposite him in a train in America she asked him what he was thinking about. He replied, 'I was thinking how strange it is that I should have made the reputation I have as an actor with nothing to help me—with no equipment. My legs, my voice—everything has been against me.' But Terry thought differently. 'And I, looking at that splendid head, those wonderful hands, the whole strange beauty of him, thought "Ah, you little know!"'[8]

Along with his natural disadvantages Irving had mobile and expres-sive features, a sardonic sense of humour admirably suited to roles such as Richard III, Iago, and to some aspects of Hamlet, dignity, pathos, and—most important of all—a mesmeric control over his audience deriving at least in part from his dark eyes and intense gaze. Some of these qualities are apparent in the raffish, devil-may-care pose adopted in the strikingly informal though unfinished 1880 portrait by Jules Bastien Lepage (which Irving is said to have disliked). He was an interior actor who could convey a character's state of mind by gesture, facial expression, and intonation. And he had a perfectionist's attention to detail along with a highly developed sense of what would work in the theatre.

Irving's first great success in Shakespeare was as Hamlet, which he played first in Manchester in 1864, then at the Lyceum ten years later in a phenomenally successful run of 200 performances. Although the text was shortened by over 1,200 lines the performance, with long intervals for scene changing, lasted over five and a half hours. The production, marred by intrusive bursts of applause and backstage noises during scenes, had its absurdities. The critic Dutton Cook, whose review seems to suggest that he wished he had been almost anywhere else, wrote acerbically that there seemed to be no 'good reason why Hamlet should carry with him a flaming torch when he meditates the murder of his uncle at his prayers; a more likely way of informing Claudius of the danger threatening him could hardly have been devised'. Remarking that Irving's voice 'seems sometimes artificially treble in quality' and 'jerked out with effort', and that 'His bearing is deficient in dignity and courtliness, though not without a certain refinement of its own', he nevertheless grudgingly and somewhat surprisingly concluded that 'for those who care to see Hamlet played at all, here is a Hamlet who is always zealous and thoughtful; often very adroit; who spares no pains to please; who has at command a certain feverish impetuosity', and 'is, in short, as complete a representation of the part as the modern theatre can furnish'.[9] Others were more generous; William Winter wrote that the 'pervading spirit' of the performance 'was innate, ineffable loveliness of temperament contending with bitterness of feeling which has been engendered by wrong, outrage, and a frenzy of terror and doubt precipitated by preternatural visitation'. And he concluded that 'No other actor of our time has made Hamlet so entirely lovable.'[10]

Although Irving became a national institution, not all theatregoers could respond to his mannerisms, even eccentricities. His acting style was not primarily heroic or lyrical. He did not attempt Richard II and was relatively unsuccessful as Romeo, Othello, Coriolanus, and even Lear. His Macbeth (Ellen Terry said that in the last act he looked 'like a great famished wolf'[11]) split opinion. He was above all a character actor, intent on creating a sense of individuality through a patient building up of personality traits. Shaw (whose reviews of Irving were slanted both by his self-interest as a dramatist and by his love for Ellen Terry, whom he regarded—with some justice—as being unfairly treated by Irving) put it with his usual pungency when he wrote, in a review of *Richard III*, that 'Irving never did and never will make use of a play otherwise than as a vehicle for some fantastic creation of his own'.[12] He did however admit that 'the creations of Sir Henry Irving's imagination are sometimes—in the case of his Iachimo, for example— better than those of the dramatists whom he is supposed to interpret'.[13] Of Iachimo, Shaw wrote, 'It is a new and independent creation. . . . I witnessed it with unqualified delight: it was no vulgar bagful of "points," but a true impersonation, unbroken in its life-current from end to end, varied on the surface with the finest comedy, and without a single lapse in the sustained beauty of its execution.'[14]

For many playgoers Irving's greatest role was Shylock, which he played in the first production at the Lyceum under his own management in 1878. The play ran for 250 nights, and over his career Irving was to play Shylock more than a thousand times. He slanted the text both to make his own role more dominant and to increase sympathy for the character. Shylock, he told William Winter, was 'a bloody-minded monster—but you mustn't play him so, if you are to succeed; you must get some sympathy with him'.[15] One way in which he did this was to interpolate an episode after Jessica's elopement in which Shylock appeared on an unpeopled stage, 'lantern in hand, advancing, bent in thought' and as he drew close to the house—still unaware that it was not empty—the curtain fell. In later performances, he sometimes knocked at the door.[16] Henry James found the result sentimental. One of the most effective moments came at Irving's final, wordless exit after the trial. The critic of *The Spectator*, calling this 'Irving's finest perform- ance', judged that 'his final exit is its best point. The quiet shrug, the glance of ineffable, unfathomable contempt at the exultant booby, Gratiano, who, having got hold of a good joke, worries it like a puppy with a bone, the expression of defeat in every limb and feature, the deep, gasping sigh, as he passes slowly out, and the crowd rush from the Court to hoot and howl at him outside, make up an effect which must be seen to be comprehended.' And the critic continued, 'the thrill that passed over the house was a sensation to have witnessed and shared'.[17] But the dramatist Henry Arthur Jones paid Irving a double-edged compliment when he wrote that this exit, 'undoubtedly a great piece of acting... was, however, quite ex-Shakespearean, if not anti-Shakespearean. It illustrates a frequent habit and method of Irving—that of getting his greatest effects not in, and by, the text and obvious meaning of his author, but in his own extraneous bits of business.'[18]

Irving died suddenly in Bradford in 1905; his last words onstage, as Tennyson's Becket, were 'Into thy hands O lord, into thy hands . . .'. Greatly honoured in his lifetime, in 1895 he became the first actor to be knighted, and was buried in Westminster Abbey.

Figure 18.1. Ellen Terry as Beatrice, in *Much Ado About Nothing*: photograph, Lyceum Theatre, London, 1882. Reproduced by permission of the Shakespeare Birthplace Trust

Ellen Terry

1847–1928. *Principal Shakespeare roles*: Juliet, Portia, Beatrice, Ophelia, Lady Macbeth, Imogen, Cordelia, Queen Katherine, Volumnia, Mistress Page.

Like Dora Jordan before her, Ellen Terry, the most universally adored actress of the British stage, was all woman. Tall, slender (for most of her life), with long tresses of fair hair, full lips, a figure inclining to the buxom, and fine features, she moved with grace and radiated tenderness and joy. She appealed greatly to visual artists. Her youthful beauty was captured in paintings by George Frederick Watts, to whom she was briefly married at the age of 16, and in classic photographs by Julia Margaret Cameron. And John Singer Sargent's paintings of her as Lady Macbeth (not her greatest role) are among the finest of theatrical portraits.

Also like Dora Jordan, she belonged to an acting family: the Terrys peopled the British stage for several generations, as had the Kembles before them. At her Jubilee gala at Drury Lane in 1906 twenty-two Terrys appeared together in a scene from *Much Ado About Nothing*.

Though Ellen had little formal education, she possessed a natural intelligence which shines through every page of her delightful memoir *The Story of My Life*, and the apparent spontaneity of her acting was the result of diligent study and preparation. She writes that 'both my sister Kate and I had been trained almost from birth for the stage, and particularly in the important branch of clear articulation'.[1] And her prompt copies are heavily annotated with detailed notes on speech and movement. The results of her training can be heard in studio recordings made at the age of 64, when she was on a lecture tour in America in 1911. Their presentation appears to reflect her platform performance

Figure 18.2. Ellen Terry as Lady Macbeth: John Singer Sargent, oil painting made for her Jubilee programme in 1906, based on an earlier sketch. © National Portrait Gallery, London

rather than the way she would have spoken onstage. After a relatively rapid opening, the pace of Portia's 'quality of mercy' speech becomes slow, even elocutionary. Every syllable, even in function words such as 'the' and 'to', is given full value, antitheses are carefully pointed, consonants clearly articulated, vowels elongated and spoken sometimes with a tremolo that would have carried them to the back of the Lyceum gallery even if they sound artificial from a loudspeaker.

Extracts from Juliet's 'potion' speech and especially from Ophelia's mad scene (in which she speaks Laertes's cues) are far more theatrical, with a forward impetus that comes from occasional overriding of line endings. She takes a few liberties with the text in the interest of apparent spontaneity, omitting Ophelia's repeated 'Hey nonny nonny' while also sometimes repeating phrases, as in 'They say, [they say—they say]—he made a good end—[a good end!]', after which she interpolates a hysterically high-pitched laugh. The range of the voice is exceptionally wide, and she sings Ophelia's snatches of song with true beauty of tone, achieving a deeply touching sense of inwardness in grief. This is not naturalistic speaking, but in its imaginative identification of actor with character it creates a profound impression of emotional reality.

Ellen Terry's acting career lasted for sixty-nine years. She appeared first at the age of 9 as Mamillius in *The Winter's Tale* with Charles Kean at the Princess's Theatre in 1856, and soon afterwards popped up from beneath the stage on a mushroom as Puck in a spectacular production of *A Midsummer Night's Dream*. Though the German novelist Theodor Fontane found her 'intolerable, a precocious child brought up in the true English manner, old before her years',[2] Queen Victoria, a keen playgoer before Prince Albert died, thought she played the part 'delightfully'.[3] Kean's wife, Ellen Tree, was a kind though stern taskmistress, 'indefatigable in her lessons in clear enunciation'.[4]

Terry's developing career was interrupted by her short-lived marriage to Watts in 1864 and for another six years from 1868 to 1874 during which she lived with the architect E. W. Godwin. Their eccentric but brilliant son, known as Gordon Craig, who wrote books about both his mother and Henry Irving (whom he worshipped) became a highly influential designer, and their daughter Edith Craig was a designer and director too. Ellen's first big success came soon after she resumed her stage career and played Portia in a picturesque production of *The Merchant of Venice* in 1875 by Squire and Marie Bancroft designed by Godwin at the Prince of Wales's Theatre; in a perceptive notice, the enraptured critic of *Fraser's Magazine* wrote that 'As she moved through the changing scene, every new incident seemed to touch some new feeling; and each change of feeling expressed itself by voice, countenance, or gesture in a manner so lively and natural that it was felt at once to be both true in itself and in harmony with the rest.'[5] Ellen herself saw the production as a personal landmark; never before, she wrote, had she 'experienced that awe-struck feeling which comes, I suppose, to no actress more than once in a lifetime—the feeling of a conqueror. . . . Every one seemed to be in love with me!'[6] But Henry James was not. He was to write fastidiously of her Portia in 1880 that she 'giggles too much, plays too much with her fingers, is too free and familiar, too osculatory, in her relations with Bassanio'.[7]

Terry had played Kate to Irving's Petruchio in *Catherine and Petruchio*, Garrick's version of *The Taming of the Shrew* in 1867, and when he took over as manager of the Lyceum in 1878 he contracted her to play Ophelia to his Hamlet, inaugurating an immensely fruitful partnership which was to survive numerous stresses and strains for twenty-four years. At the Lyceum she played eleven Shakespeare roles—besides Ophelia and Portia, these were Desdemona, Juliet, Beatrice, Viola, Lady Macbeth, Queen Katherine in *Henry VIII*, Cordelia, Imogen, and Volumnia. To her deep regret Irving refused her the opportunity to play Rosalind, to which she was ideally suited—in her memoirs she writes rather as Rosalind speaks—because *As You Like It* offered no suitable role for him. (He should have tried Jaques.)

Her capacity for pathos stood her in good stead as Ophelia, but she was not a natural tragedienne. A reviewer wrote that she played Juliet 'with more tenderness, sweetness, and pathos than intensity of tragic expression'.[8] And Henry James blamed Irving for entrusting 'the girlish Juliet to the large, the long, the mature Miss Terry'.[9] As Lady Macbeth she appears to have been closer in style to Helen Faucit than to Sarah Siddons, playing for pathos rather than for the domination over her husband displayed by Charlotte Cushman. Her adoring son, Gordon Craig, attributes this to a desire to be loved—she allowed her audience to dominate her rather than wishing to dominate them. As a result 'one heard her saying under her breath to the British public: "Now, my dear, dear people, you won't *really* think I am a horrid woman like that, will you?"' So 'in the sleep-walking scene, you did not shudder at the thought beneath the words: "The Thane of Fife had a wife—where is she now?" You only felt: "Poor Ellen Terry—she is so sorry for the Thane of Fife's wife, and is wondering where she can possibly be now, poor, poor dear. What a *nice* woman!"'[10] She herself felt that Irving, with his gift for the uncanny, would have played the scene better than she did. At least the role gave John Singer Sargent the stimulus to produce two of the greatest ever theatre paintings, the hierarchical image of her with the crown above her head and wearing the famous dress shimmering with beetles' wings, and the unfinished but more dramatic sketch showing her emerging from the castle gates in a vivid swirl of movement.

It was the comedies that gave most scope to her individuality. She was to repeat the role of Portia many times both with Irving as Shylock and in other productions. She played Viola only in a Lyceum production of 1884 which went down so badly with some members of its first night audience that Irving, after numerous hostile interruptions during a curtain speech that suggests he was still inhabiting the character of Malvolio, petulantly complained, 'I can't understand how a company of earnest comedians [in the broad sense of actors] and admirable actors, having these three cardinal virtues of actors—being sober, clean, and [word-]perfect—and having exercised their abilities on one of the most difficult of plays, can have given any cause for dissatisfaction.'[11] Terry, however, came out of it well, Clement Scott writing that her Viola 'was set in a most enchanting key. It is tender, human, graceful, consistently picturesque, and with humour as light as feather down.'[12] Marie Corelli was inspired to write a (rather poor) sonnet about it.

Great actor though Irving was, Ellen Terry more than matched him in intelligence and in ability to communicate with some of the best minds of her time on their own level. She conducted an extensive and scintillating correspondence with Bernard Shaw, who despised much about Irving including his failure to provide for Terry the kinds of roles that Shaw thought she should be playing. In 1896 as she was preparing to play Imogen in *Cymbeline* Shaw wrote several long, intellectually flirtatious letters of encouragement and detailed advice in which he characteristically tried to rewrite her role in the manner that he, rather than the 'DAMNED fool Shakespear', would have written it.[13] (He was later to write an entirely new last act for the play.) Irving, he wrote, 'has no artistic sense outside his own person: he is an ogre who has carried you off to his cave, and now Childe Roland is coming to the dark tower to rescue you'.[14]

When Shaw came to review the production he indulged his spleen about Shakespeare in classic terms: 'With the single exception of Homer, there is no eminent writer, not even Sir Walter Scott, whom I can despise so entirely as I despise Shakespear when I measure my mind against his.'[15] But for once, as we have seen, he was able to write with generous admiration of Irving's acting of the role of Iachimo. 'Miss Terry', he wrote with tongue in cheek, 'had evidently cut her own part' (he had banged on endlessly about what he thought she should leave out) but Terry, 'who invariably fascinates me so much that I have not the smallest confidence in my own judgment respecting her', had played 'with infinite charm and delicacy of appeal'.[16] And another great writer who had often written derogatorily of Ellen, Henry James, found that 'her beautiful, melancholy boy's dress shows admirably that the more chance she has for freedom of motion the more easily she surmounts its dangers'. Her performance was 'naturally poetic' with 'delightful breadth and tenderness, delightful grace and youth'. For him, 'Miss Terry, as Imogen, grows younger and younger.'[17] She was close on 50 years old.

Ellen Terry left the Lyceum company in 1902, and soon afterwards went into management herself, mainly in order to help her son, Gordon Craig. At last she did a play by Ibsen, *The Vikings*, in which she was badly miscast; it failed, and a revival of *Much Ado About Nothing* was hastily prepared in an attempt to recoup finances. Beatrice had been perhaps her greatest and most popular role since she first played it in 1880. Now, aged 56, she triumphed again. Max Beerbohm wrote that 'there never has been, nor ever will be, so perfect a Beatrice as Miss Terry', and that 'Miss Terry never will be, nor ever has been, more perfect than as Beatrice. Beatrice, in all her sunniness and jollity; a tease, a romp; a woman with something beyond her generous womanhood—some touch of fairydom in her – here she is incarnate and unrivalled.'[18]

In spite of the dearth of older women's roles in his plays, Shakespeare continued to play a large part in Ellen's life in her later years. Her devotion was so great that she even undertook the tiny role of Francesca, who speaks only nine lines, in *Measure for Measure* in 1905. She had played a highly successful Mistress Page in *The Merry Wives of Windsor* with Herbert Beerbohm Tree in 1902, and undertook Hermione in *The Winter's Tale* for him in 1906. She gave (and published) lectures and readings of Shakespeare in America and Australia as well as England. Not until 1919 did she play the Nurse in *Romeo and Juliet*. By then her memory and eyesight were failing, and she sometimes pretended that the character was deaf so that her fellow actors could help her with her lines. She was created Dame of the British Empire in 1925—the first British actor to be so honoured—and died three years later.

Tommaso Salvini

Figure 19.1. Tomasso Salvini as Othello, Theatre Royal, Drury Lane, 1875. Reproduced by permission of the Shakespeare Birthplace Trust

1829–1915. *Principal Shakespeare roles*: Othello, Hamlet, Macbeth, Lear, Coriolanus.

During the earlier part of the nineteenth century certain American and English actors, including Ira Aldridge and Edwin Booth, played leading Shakespeare roles on the European continent in English along with native companies speaking the language of the country where the performances were given. Similarly in the later years of the century several eminent Italian actors played in America and in England using their own language along with supporting companies speaking English. Henry James described this as a system which 'has all the barbarism of an over-civilized age . . . grotesque, unpardonable, abominable'.[1] The practice invites an emphasis rather on virtuosity of performance in leading roles than on experiencing the content of the work being performed. It presents severe technical problems in that, for instance, star players need to be familiar enough with the language of their colleagues to pick up cues, and it can succeed only if the audience is at least reasonably familiar with the original text.

The same is true when the whole company plays in a language foreign to that of the country where it is acting. Max Beerbohm wrote of the great Italian actress Eleanora Duse's performances in London:

The technique of acting lies in the nice relation of the mime's voice, gesture and facial expression to the words by him or her spoken. Obviously, if those words are for you so much gibberish, you cannot pass any judgment on the mime's technique. You look on, and you see certain movements of the mime's face and hands, and you hear certain inflections of the mime's voice, but I defy you to know whether they are the right movements, the right inflections. You have to take them on trust.

The practice invites pretentiousness of response. Beerbohm wrote ironically of audiences who paid over the odds to be 'tremendously bored, tremendously edified' by such performances, and of critics whose reviews implied that they had a perfect understanding of Italian.[2]

The practice was popular all the same, and is revived from time to time. In 1930 a famous German actor, Alexander Moissi, played Hamlet in his own language in London at the same time as John Gielgud and Henry Ainley were both playing the role in the West End. There have been parallels on the operatic stage. In the 1940s at Covent Garden, for instance, productions employed multilingual casts partly in order to enable famous performers to sing their best-known roles without going to the expense of re-rehearsing an entire production. And in recent years it has become common for foreign-language productions of Shakespeare to be performed in England, most notably at Shakespeare's Globe in 2012 when thirty-seven of Shakespeare's plays were staged, each in a different language.

The first eminent Italian to perform Shakespeare in this way was Adelaide Ristori (1822–1906), who played Lady Macbeth usually in Italian but occasionally, and not very successfully, in English. She acted in America with Edwin Booth as Macbeth and toured Australia in a bizarre version of the play 'trimmed so as to bring the heroine into every possible prominence'.[3] Sometimes she gave the sleepwalking scene on its own as a kind of encore, rather as opera singers will frequently sing arias and duets out of their theatrical context. Another distinguished Italian actor, Ernesto Rossi (1827–96), played Hamlet, Lear, Macbeth, and Romeo with an Italian company at Drury Lane in

1876 and a few years later gave an unsuccessful Lear in Italian with an English-speaking cast in both New York and London. At one performance he even played the last two acts in badly broken English, provoking *The Athenaeum* to say, 'Signor Rossi quits our stage with a promise to return to our stage when he is able to act in English. For the performance of that promise we shall wait with resignation.'[4]

The greatest of the Italian Shakespearians was Tommaso Salvini (1829–1915). In many of the surviving photographs he looks, with his enormous handlebar moustaches, like a parody of a Victorian paterfamilias or an Italianate Lord Kitchener on a recruiting poster, making it difficult at first blush to take him seriously. And that impression may be compounded when we read Joseph Knight's account of how he played the murder of Desdemona: 'he seizes her by the hair of the head, and, dragging her on to the bed, strangles her with a ferocity that seems to take delight in its office . . . Nearing the end he rises, and at the supreme moment cuts his throat with a short scimitar, hacking and hewing with savage energy, and imitating the noise that escaping blood and air may together make when the windpipe is severed.'[5] This sounds like the worst excesses of Victorian melodrama. It shocked and offended some critics, and makes it understandable that certain British actresses declined the honour of playing Desdemona with him.

But such impressions are superficial. Salvini's physical appearance made a powerful impression on contemporaries. The Jewish-American poet Emma Lazarus wrote in an article published in the *Century Magazine* that

No man could be more perfectly equipped by nature for the tragic stage . . . his physical gifts are a frame of massive and harmonious proportions uniting an incomparable majesty of bearing with the utmost grace of movement, a handsome and singularly mobile face, and, most memorable of all, a voice of such depth and volume of tone, and such exquisite and infinitely varied modulation, that, having been once heard, it haunts the sense like noble music.[6]

The great Shakespearian scholar Mary Cowden Clarke, in her copy of this article now in the Shakespeare Birthplace Trust collections, endorses this judgement with the pencilled words 'most true M.C. C.'. Excellent critics praised Salvini's performances in the highest terms, making it clear that, in spite of the language problem and although he played in texts that were both translated and abbreviated, he was indeed one of the greatest of tragedians. Robert and Elizabeth Barrett Browning were impressed when they saw him as Hamlet and Othello in Florence in 1859, and after seeing his Othello in Genoa Mary Cowden Clarke described it in a letter to *The Athenaeum* as 'the greatest the world has ever seen'. His dramatic genius, she wrote, created productions 'so true to universal human nature that, even through the disadvantage of a translated version, they go straight to the hearts of men'.[7] And Salvini's great fellow actor Charlotte Cushman, after seeing him in the same role in Rome in 1870, said it was 'simply the greatest the world has ever seen'.[8] Three years later he embarked on his first American tour, playing both Hamlet and Othello, and in 1875 he brought his Othello to Drury Lane, playing usually three times a week, and giving a few performances of *Hamlet* in rivalry to Henry Irving later in the run. He also gave a modern tragedy well suited to his physical skills called *The Gladiator*, described by Henry James as a 'feeble and ridiculous piece'.[9] He added Macbeth to his touring repertoire in America in 1881, then King Lear in 1883, played all four roles at Covent Garden and in the English provinces in 1884, and introduced Coriolanus in New York in 1885. During his final tour of America in 1889–90 the only Shakespeare role he played was Othello, which he gave thirty-six times.

Salvini was clearly a technical actor in the sense that all his roles were meticulously prepared. However many times he had played a role he knew exactly what he would be doing and how he would be sounding from one performance to the next. Like any actor of strong individuality he had his detractors. Not every audience member capitulated to his passionate identification with the roles he played, his physicality, his extrovertly uninhibited displays of emotion. He was always in command, a virtuoso who expected all who acted with him to subordinate any ideas they might have to his own conception of his role. His Hamlet, played in a heavily adapted text, divided opinion. It had been poorly received in America. William Winter, who wrote that Salvini was 'one of the greatest [actors] that have ever lived',[10] nevertheless thought his inability to understand English disqualified him from playing Shakespeare roles, even Othello. He found Salvini's Hamlet technically admirable, but thought his 'massive frame, his leonine demeanour, his iron firmness, and his aspect of resolute overwhelming executive faculty combined to make him the literal opposite of everything that Hamlet is or means'.[11] Yet several eminent English theatregoers, including George Henry Lewes—an excellent judge of acting—and Robert Browning greatly admired it, and William Poel, who was to revolutionize Shakespearian production and performance, went so far as to say that Salvini's Hamlet was 'the only perfect one within living memory' and that the actor's 1875 performances were what caused him to devote his life to theatre.[12]

As Macbeth, Salvini wore costumes designed by the artist Gustave Doré who travelled to Scotland specially to research his designs. They included 'a spiked helmet with towering wings' which recalls the plumes of feathers worn by earlier actors in tragic roles. John Coleman mocked the white silver lamé robes of the third act and unkindly remarked that 'A delicately-jewelled filigreed waistbelt vainly attempted to restrain the rebellious region which obstinately persisted in asserting itself'.[13] Salvini used an exceptionally full text, even restoring the Porter and the Third Murderer, but even so, as was customary, brought down the final curtain as quickly as possible after the tragic hero's death.

The production as a whole seems to have been a bit of a shambles. Coleman wrote that in the banquet scene 'The half-empty stage was sparsely populated by pale, squalid guests, attired in tawdry costumes of all periods and all nations . . . . the ghost of Banquo, in the first instance, scrambled up from under a table, tumbled down again, and re-appeared from a front-trap, jerked up like a Harlequin.' And in the climactic battle, 'Some twenty or thirty supernumeraries in nondescript costumes came scrambling over the stage, in a kind of bungled mêlée, during which they exchanged an occasional crack on the head, or tumbled over one another, as the spirit moved them, with charming impartiality.'[14] Still, it is clear that Salvini had many impressive and original moments even in the ill-staged banquet scene, of which the *Boston Globe* critic wrote that 'The adjuration to the spirit to be gone, with the frenzy of motion and gesture, with horror and despair voiced in his words and depicted on his face, thrilled even the most blasé of theatre-goers. Here the actor towered above all who have essayed the part; here Salvini was Macbeth himself.'[15]

Salvini offered powerful and original interpretations of both King Lear and the rarely performed Coriolanus, but throughout his career Othello remained his signature role; his unusually well documented performance, which changed little over the years, is the subject of a whole book by Edward Tuckerman Mason who saw it many times and persuaded Salvini to add his own notes and comments. Aiming at racial and visual authenticity, he based his characterization on an actual Moor whom he had seen in Gibraltar and his costumes on fifteenth-century Venetian paintings of Moorish officers. Magnificent in presence, he was both powerful and beautiful. He performed with an eloquence of posture, gesture, facial expression, and vocal intonation that transcended the language barrier. Even those who felt that his uninhibited physicality as both warrior and lover exceeded the bounds of good taste had to acknowledge his technical excellence. In the earlier scenes sensuality, even uxoriousness as well as tenderness, was manifest in his dealings with Desdemona. The scenes in which she pleaded on behalf of Cassio were touched with high comedy, and when he quelled the brawling soldiers with 'Put up your bright swords—or the dew will rust them' (in Italian) he spoke the second part of the sentence with humorous irony which suggested an easy command of the situation. With his fellows he was always the commander, unsympathetic in his handling of Cassio, initially businesslike in his dealings with Iago, slower than many other Othellos to understand Iago's insinuations but fiercely violent as he caught him by the throat and dashed him to the ground in what the *Boston Globe* called 'the most terrifically realistic piece of acting ever seen'.[16] His violence towards Desdemona in the presence of Lodovico and the messengers from Venice shocked many spectators. He wept passionately as he repelled Desdemona in the 'brothel' scene, climactically pouncing on her, seizing her by the hair, and dragging her on to the bed. And finally he killed himself with the shocking realism described by Joseph Knight that I quoted at the start of this essay.[17]

TIMES OF CHANGE

Some of the great nineteenth-century actors I've been writing about confined their theatrical activities largely or wholly to acting. This is true of all the women. The ethos of the age did not encourage even the most independent-minded of them, such as Sarah Siddons, Charlotte Cushman, and Helen Faucit, to take a prominent part in theatre management. Some of the men, too, such as G. F. Cooke, Edwin Forrest, and Edmund Kean, were primarily actors. But as the century wore on, managerial and directorial functions came to play an increasingly large role in the responsibilities of leading actors in both England and America.

The development is associated with the rise of spectacular theatre. Elaborate productions require strong controlling hands, and leading actors liked these hands to be their own. Kemble, Macready, Edwin Booth, and Irving marshalled their forces around them, concerned that their greatness should not be dimmed by inadequate or under-rehearsed supporting casts, or by technical weaknesses. The later years of the century saw the rise of the actor-manager. In England, some actors, such as Samuel Phelps at Sadler's Wells from 1844 to 1862 and Charles Kean at the Princess's from 1850 to 1859, achieved eminence as co-coordinators of companies in which they played the leading roles rather than as great stars in their own right. A major influence on unified production and especially on the handling of crowd scenes came from Germany in the work of the Duke of Saxe-Meiningen's company, founded in 1861, which itself was influenced by performances in Berlin by Charles Kean and his well-disciplined company. The Duke's players, who visited England in 1881, placed a strong emphasis on coordinated ensemble playing, historical reconstruction, and the

handling of crowd scenes. Shakespeare production increased in grandeur of physical spectacle, reaching its apogee in the later years of the
century in the work of Henry Irving at the Lyceum and of Herbert
Beerbohm Tree at Her (later His) Majesty's Theatre from 1897 to 1915.
Tree, a considerable actor, was the first to be filmed in a Shakespeare
role. A brief clip which is all that survives of a few scenes from *King John*
from 1901 shows him taking an unconscionably long time a-dying as
the King.

London's actor-managers had counterparts in rapidly growing provincial cities: Charles Calvert—a disciple of Phelps—in Manchester
from 1859 to 1875 is a conspicuous example. And touring companies
continued to take Shakespeare to the provinces. Frank Benson, a
disciple of Irving, at one time ran as many as four of them simultaneously. With his wife Constance he played up and down the country,
but his career centred on Stratford-upon-Avon, where, in the Memorial Theatre which opened in 1879, he was in charge from 1886 to 1919
of twenty-eight spring and some six summer festivals, each lasting only
one or two weeks, producing all Shakespeare's plays except *Troilus and
Cressida* and *Titus Andronicus*.

Benson (knighted in 1916) was a considerable athlete; he put these
skills to use in a highly physical interpretation of Caliban, leaping
from bough to bough of trees on Prospero's island. Of his *Henry V*,
Max Beerbohm wrote, 'As a branch of university cricket, the whole
performance was indeed beyond praise. But, as a form of acting, it was
not impressive.'[1] Yet C. E. Montague, for long the theatre critic of
the *Manchester Guardian*, wrote with great admiration of Benson in
the conspicuously unathletic role of Richard II, describing his 1899
interpretation as 'brilliant in its equal grasp of the two sides of the
character, the one which everybody sees well enough, and the one
which nearly everybody seems to shun seeing, and in the value which it
rendered to the almost continuous flow of genuine and magnificent
poetry from Richard'.[2] A twenty-minute silent film made in the
Stratford Memorial Theatre in 1911 of scenes from Benson's *Richard
III*, the play's structure still influenced by Cibber's adaptation, is rev-
elatory as a visual record of the pictorial staging methods of the time,
but the actors are so obviously miming for the camera in the absence of
sound that it is difficult to assess the style or standard of acting. The cast
includes a live horse. Benson is notable too for putting on an uncut
Hamlet (known as 'the eternity version') which, in Wagnerian fashion,

lasted from 3.30 to 11.00 p.m. with a one-and-a-half-hour break for dinner. The critic of *The Athenaeum* found Benson 'but a colourless and an uninspiriting Hamlet'.[3]

Far more popular and successful in the role was Johnston Forbes-Robertson (1853–1937, knighted in 1913), a handsome disciple of Phelps with a beautiful voice who succeeded as Romeo with Irving's company and became the most highly admired Hamlet of his generation. He first played the role in 1897, when he was already 44 years old, and continued to do so till he was over 60. His performance was praised by Shaw in a review which is a classic of theatre criticism. In words that glance obliquely at Irving's speech habits, he wrote of Forbes-Robertson: 'He does not utter half a line; then stop to act; then go on with another half line; and then stop to act again, with the clock running away with Shakespear's chances all the time. He plays as Shakespear should be played, on the line and to the line, with the utterance and acting simultaneous, inseparable and in fact identical.' And he dies 'as we forgive everything to Charles II for dying, and makes "the rest is silence" a touchingly humorous apology for not being able to finish his business'.[4] (Charles had apologized for being 'an unconscionable time a-dying'.) This appears to have been a very gentlemanly Hamlet; in spite of playing an unusually full text which brought Fortinbras on at the end of the play for the first time for centuries, he omitted the words 'I'll lug the guts into the neighbour room.' A silent film made partly on location in 1913, when the actor was 60, offered a 59-minute condensation of the play; innovative for its time, it nevertheless shows the actors mouthing the words as if they were onstage.

Financial exigencies discouraged elaboration of staging in touring productions such as Benson's, and a movement away from the spectacle associated with the big London actor-managers, and with Booth in the United States, gradually set in. It had been oddly foreshadowed in a mock-Elizabethan production of *The Taming of the Shrew* put on at the Haymarket Theatre in 1844 which attempted to reproduce the conditions of Elizabethan performance. Paradoxically one of the leading spirits behind it was James Robinson Planché, designer of the costumes for a production of *King John* by Charles Kemble in 1823 which inaugurated the fashion for spectacular, historically oriented shows which came to dominate the English stage for close on a century.

But the Haymarket *Shrew* was a flash in the pan. The real revolution came with the advent on the scene of the eccentric amateur William

Poel who in 1881 directed and played the lead in a single performance at St George's Hall, London of the First Quarto text of *Hamlet*, given with no scenery or interval. The discovery in 1888 of the de Witt drawing of the Swan playhouse fuelled his enthusiasm. In 1895 Poel established the Elizabethan Stage Society with which for close on forty years he was to direct many early plays in pseudo-Elizabethan conditions. He showed how much could be gained by speaking the plays of Shakespeare and other early dramatists swiftly on unadorned open stages, avoiding the long pauses and textual rearrangements necessitated by naturalistic scenery.

The tyranny of naturalism, which often required textual rearrangement to facilitate scene changing, gradually gave way to more imaginative, sometimes symbolic methods, often using permanent sets on which scene changes could be suggested rather than represented. Gordon Craig's designs for his mother Ellen Terry's *Much Ado About Nothing* in 1903 were revolutionary in their simplicity. The church scene using 'nothing but candles and a corridor of draperies' lit by 'coloured shafts of light'[5] was, wrote Max Beerbohm, 'incomparably finer than any other attempt that has been made to suggest a cathedral on the stage'.[6] Later, Craig worked mainly abroad; his designs for a 1911 Moscow production of *Hamlet* by Stanislavsky used movable screens to both symbolic and practical ends. The production remained in the repertoire of the Moscow Art Theatre for many years; its Hamlet, V. I. Kachjalov, was still playing in it in 1940 at the age of 65.

The early years of the twentieth century also saw the rise of the director (formerly known as a producer) in the modern sense of the word; that is, one who oversees and coordinates every aspect of a production but does not normally act in it. Though Harley Granville-Barker was a disciple of Poel, for whom he had acted, he was by no means antiquarian in his approach to scenic design, and far more of a purist about texts. In his three productions at the Savoy Theatre from 1912 to 1914 he gave the plays almost complete in a theatre in which an attempt had been made to break down the distancing effect of the proscenium arch, building out an apron stage, and he encouraged rapid delivery of the lines without unnecessary interpolation of business. While not, like Poel, dispensing with scenery he formalized it, not permitting it to hinder the forward movement of the action. Unlike Poel, he engaged fully professional casts and rehearsed them rigorously. In later life he devoted himself mainly to writing his classic *Prefaces to*

Shakespeare, which give practical guidance that has been invaluable to generations of practitioners.

Granville-Barker was more aware than Poel of the need to translate understanding of the plays into terms attractive to modern theatre-goers. Similar movements occurred in America. The first two decades of the twentieth century represent a low point in Shakespeare performance there, but a sudden change for the better came when John Barrymore, who had made a reputation in modern plays, took the role of Richard III and later, with sensational success, Hamlet in productions designed by Robert Edmund Jones, who had worked with Granville-Barker and was influenced by Gordon Craig. The production of *Hamlet* in 1922 ran in New York for 102 performances, breaking (not without calculation) Booth's previous record by one. When it came to London in 1925 James Agate wrote of the set as 'the most beautiful thing I have ever seen on any stage. The vast arch at the back served as the battlements, and was hung with curtains for the indoor scenes, played on two platforms intersected by a flight of steps.'[7] The Ghost 'was represented in several scenes by a pale green wavering light'.[8] Barrymore, no less handsome than Booth, magnetic in presence, untrammelled by convention, brought new immediacy to the verse speaking. The young John Gielgud, who would soon afterwards score an even greater triumph in the role, wrote of it with admiration as a 'brilliantly intellectual performance' which was 'classical without being unduly severe'. Barrymore 'has tenderness, remoteness, and neurosis, all placed with great delicacy and used with immense effectiveness and admirable judgement'.[9] And Laurence Olivier, acknowledging that 'My Hamlets in later years owed a great deal to Jack Barrymore', wrote that he 'breathed life into the character, which, since Irving, had been lulled into arias and false inflections, all very beautiful and poetic, but castrated. Barrymore put the balls back.'[10] His later career was blighted, like those of some of his predecessors, by drink, but he played Mercutio in a Hollywood film of 1936.

Poel had a talent for spotting and training newcomers. His production of *Troilus and Cressida* of 1912, given in a mangled text, was historic for two reasons. It was the first fully staged production of the play on the English stage since Shakespeare's time. And it saw the professional debut of Edith Evans, soon to be recognized as the greatest English actress since Ellen Terry. As it happens, she is the first of the actors in this book whom I saw onstage (and whom I met in person).

Edith Evans

Figure 20.1. Edith Evans as the Nurse in *Romeo and Juliet* at the Shakespeare Memorial Theatre, Stratford-upon-Avon, 1961; photograph by Angus McBean. Angus McBean © Royal Shakespeare Company

1888–1976. *Principal Shakespeare roles*: Rosalind, Juliet's Nurse, Mistress Page, Queen Margaret, Emilia, Countess of Roussillon, Cleopatra, Volumnia, Queen Katherine.

Born in 1888, Edith Evans—oddly like Dora Jordan—was apprenticed to a milliner at the age of 15 but soon developed a passion for acting. William Poel, who spotted her playing Beatrice with an amateur company in scenes from *Much Ado About Nothing*, cast her as Cressida in his characteristically odd production of *Troilus and Cressida* of 1912 given both in London and, briefly, in the Shakespeare Memorial Theatre at Stratford. Poel undertook Pandarus himself and had some of the play's most heroic roles as well as the scurrilous Thersites played by women. For Edith Evans, this was the start of a long and illustrious career which was to last for some sixty years.

Tall, with wide-spaced, heavy-lidded eyes which she used to great effect and a highly idiosyncratic vocal delivery which was easily (and frequently) parodied, she was not a conventional beauty. James Agate, reviewing her as Millamant in 1924, wrote, 'if I wanted to hire a chit to carry a banner in a pantomime, I should not engage this artist'. But, he continued, 'if she does not possess rare beauty in the highest sense, then I know not that quality'.[1] She certainly had style: grace of movement, dignity, the capacity to portray aristocratic hauteur, memorably encapsulated in her classic performance of Lady Bracknell in Oscar Wilde's *The Importance of Being Earnest*, which is preserved on film and in sound recordings. She was above all a character actress in the sense that she conveyed delight in the idiosyncrasies, whether comic or touching, of the women she portrayed. She was not cut out by nature for the great heroic roles, though she played the old Queen Margaret in *Richard III* both at the Old Vic in 1926 and, late in life, at Stratford, and, memorably, Volumnia to Olivier's Coriolanus in 1959. In *Othello* she played Emilia, not Desdemona; in *Romeo and Juliet* the Nurse, not Juliet. She left characters such as St Joan, Lady Macbeth, and Medea to her great— and very different—contemporary Sybil Thorndike. In tragedy the wayward, often comic Cleopatra was more in Dame Edith's line, at least in the early scenes of the play. She played the role during a stint at the Old Vic in 1925–6 and with Godfrey Tearle in 1946. Kenneth Tynan (aged 23) wrote snidely about it while admitting that 'Expertly she gave us the coarse hoyden of the early acts'.[2] More sympathetically, J. C. Trewin wrote, 'Still matchless in the early wheedlings, rages, languishing ("Now I feed myself with most delicious poison"), hers was not a Cleopatra for fire and air.'[3] But to say that she did not triumph in every role she undertook is not to say that she lacked versatility. She was a master technician who could hold an audience in the palm of her hand through verbal nuance, variety of facial expression, and subtlety of gesture.

After her professional debut as Cressida her career developed fairly slowly. In 1917 and 1918 she toured in scenes from Shakespeare's comedies with Ellen Terry, then almost at the end of her career. She achieved great success in Bernard Shaw's *Back to Methuselah* in Birmingham in 1923, and went straight on to play Mistress Page in *The Merry Wives of Windsor* at the Lyric Theatre, Hammersmith, when Herbert Farjeon wrote of her as 'that rare thing, an actress with both breadth and subtlety. She is that equally rare thing, an actress who can bring out the full literary flavour of every word.' She 'quickens every syllable, recognizes in a choice epithet something as three-dimensional as a living being, reveals new wonders unsuspected and never to be forgotten'. Ellen Terry, playing the same role, had been 'more electric, more gallivanting, possessed more animal magnetism. But Miss Evans', he wrote, 'is more in period, more sweepingly dominant, and I verily believe, the better actress.'[4]

In the following year she established herself as the mistress of Restoration comedy as Millamant in Nigel Playfair's production of Congreve's *The Way of the World* again at the Lyric, and then demonstrated her professionalism by joining the Old Vic for a short but packed (and ill-paid) period in order to increase her Shakespearian experience. She tested her versatility by playing thirteen very different roles in rapid succession, most successfully Rosalind in *As You Like It*. Of this performance James Agate wrote that 'this gracious artist' rode on the 'bubbling seas of Renaissance wit . . . like some fair frigate out of the Book of Romance'.[5] Herbert Farjeon asked, 'Has there ever, I wonder, been an actress more sunnily in love?'[6] And Lilian Baylis told Sybil Thorndike, 'You must come at once and see her—even her toes twinkle like Rosalind. Didn't they say about Ellen Terry that a star danced when she was born—that's true of Edith's Rosalind.'[7] She was to play the role again in 1937 with Michael Redgrave, with whom she was having a love affair, which may well have added an extra dimension to their scenes together. A student at the Old Vic theatre school, Diana Graves, described watching her from the wings as she prepared to go onstage in a manner that illuminates the part that imagination can play in a great actress's self-transformation into the character she is playing.

I used to watch her waiting for her cue, night after night, dressed in her shirt and knee-breeches, transforming herself in a matter of seconds into a sparkling, adorable young creature. Her chin would go up, her eyes begin to shine, her body became spring-like and resilient, and full of confidence in her beauty and gaiety, she would sweep on to the stage to meet her dear love with such lightness that I used sometimes to wonder if her feet actually touched the stage at all.[8]

Sound recordings of speeches from the play show how entrancingly she could realize the poetry of Shakespeare's prose. A connoisseur of language, exceptionally responsive to nuances of expression, she could inflect words with the skill of a great instrumentalist. Laurence Kitchin wrote that 'she made transitions and variations not even sketched by other performers yet embedded in the lines'.[9] To do this is to turn acting into a creative art. Many years later I was present at a reading that she gave in Hall's Croft, Stratford-upon-Avon, with

Christopher Hassall. Introducing passages from *As You Like It* she said, 'We did this at Marlborough College recently. We told the boys we knew we were far too old for the parts, but they must just listen and shut their eyes. And do you know'—the inimitable but often imitated voice soared along with her eyebrows in simulated amazement—'they did.'

It was at the Old Vic in 1926 that she gave the first of several performances of a role with which she became peculiarly identified, the Nurse in *Romeo and Juliet*. She played it again in a semi-professional Oxford University Drama Society production of 1932 directed by John Gielgud with Peggy Ashcroft as Juliet and in a West End production of 1935 in which Gielgud and Olivier switched roles as Romeo and Mercutio. This, wrote James Agate, 'was all that an evening in the theatre should be—exciting, moving, provocative. Here in conjunction were the flower of Shakespeare's young genius and the best of young English acting talent.' 'To crown all,' he wrote, 'remains Miss Evans's Nurse, knocking the balance of the play into a cocked hat, just as would happen if the Porter were the centre of *Macbeth*. She ruled the entire roost . . . . It was a grand performance and the pathos of it should have taught young playgoers what pathos was in younger days.'[10] And W. A. Darlington, critic of the *Daily Telegraph*, wrote that she was 'as earthy as a potato, as slow as a cart horse, and as cunning as a badger'.[11] Dame Edith also played the role in New York and, finally, in Peter Hall's RSC production in 1961. This used a revolving stage which could be perilous. For one of her entries she was preceded by the actor playing Peter who lit her way with a torch, lest she should be precipitated off the edge of the revolve like an ill-placed needle on a gramophone record.

My most vivid memories of Edith Evans's Shakespearian roles are of her season at what was still the Shakespeare Memorial Theatre in 1959. Tyrone Guthrie's *All's Well That Ends Well* was one of the most brilliantly accomplished productions I have seen, Chekhovianly beautiful in the Roussillon scenes, farcically irreverent in those set in Florence. It was so technically finished that Guthrie was said to have given the actors the day off before the first night. Playing the Countess, the role that Shaw had described as 'the most beautiful old woman's part ever written',[12] Evans was all tenderness and grace as she spoke 'Even so it was with me when I was young' to Zoe Caldwell's Helena. And in the closing scenes she sparkled in bejewelled grandeur.

Her versatility was demonstrated in her performance during the same season as Volumnia to Olivier's magnificent Coriolanus. At the age of 71 she was a little taxed by some of the character's fiercer moments, but Mrs Siddons herself could not have been more formidable as, drawing herself up to her full height, she spoke of her anger at the commoners' banishment of her son:

> Anger's my meat: I sup upon myself
> And so shall starve with feeding. Come, let's go.
> Leave this faint puling and lament as I do,
> In anger, Juno-like. Come, come, come.

The phrases shot out of her with mounting intensity, every word given its full value, with a climax on 'Juno-like'. It was terrifying.

During this season Dame Edith gave a talk in which she discussed her approach to the role. When she accepted the part, she said, she had not read the play. But she had a preconceived idea that Volumnia was 'a bloodthirsty old harridan'. How, she asked—glancing at the Theatre's Artistic Director, Glen Byam Shaw, who was in the audience—'could I possibly be a bloodthirsty old harridan?' She had been invited to remember that Volumnia 'lived somewhere about the fourth century BC. That was something—there was no need to excuse her for not having heard about turning the other cheek.' And she went on to discuss how she had attempted to discover, and to play, the woman in the character. It was a help that in her first scene Volumnia brings her sewing, and she and the other women sit on stools. 'That's a friendly little opening, isn't it?' What she says is strong meat—'but they're *sewing*!' She found Volumnia's womanliness in her love for her son, 'a very arrogant boy' who 'displeases—what do you call it?—the Labour Party.' She pleads with him not to antagonize the plebeians. He should get power first and then he can antagonize them as much as he likes. She spoke about the actress's need to find in the words she has to speak a reality that is meaningful to herself. 'When she meets her son after his triumph she is almost too excited to be coherent. "What is it— Coriolanus must I call thee?" In other words, "What's this thing they have pinned on you, darling? The VC?"' And, she said, when the mother sees her son again after his banishment and on her return to Rome, 'her raiment and state of body ought indeed to show what her life has been since Coriolanus' exile'. The talk offered an illuminating insight into the working processes of a great actress.

Only a few months before she died, Dame Edith paid a final visit to Stratford to give a solo reading at the Shakespeare Institute. I had the responsibility of looking after her. Before going on for the first part she asked me to stop her if she went on for more than twenty minutes. In fact over half an hour passed before I plucked up my courage to break the spell, and by then she had read a poem by Alexander Pope twice without appearing to notice that she had done so. In the interval we sorted out her papers, and she said she'd been up till the early hours putting them into order. The second part of the recital passed without untoward incident and of course she was warmly applauded. As she prepared to leave, her chauffeur, William, drew up to the front door in her ancient Rolls-Royce, walked round to the passenger door, and brought out a footstool which he placed carefully on the road. Dame Edith gathered up her skirts and made a stately entry into the car as I waved her off.

Sybil Thorndike

Figure 21.1. Sybil Thorndike as Volumnia, with Laurence Olivier as Coriolanus, Old Vic, London, 1938. culture-images/Lebrecht

1882–1976. *Principal Shakespeare roles*: Queen Margaret, Gertrude, Lady Macbeth, Emilia, Queen Katherine, Volumnia, Hermione.

In 1951 Edith Evans acted with Sybil Thorndike in a long-running West End success, *Waters of the Moon*, by N. C. Hunter. Edith played a grand lady, Sybil a more humble character. Legend has it that after the play had run for a year the management offered Dame Edith a brand-new outfit from a fashionable designer, and that in accepting she suggested that dear Sybil should have something too—perhaps a nice cardigan.

True or not, the anecdote epitomizes the popular perception of the difference between the two great dames—Edith a patrician star of the West End, like the haughty Lady Bracknell, or the bejewelled Countess of Roussillon, or the dominating matriarch Volumnia; Sybil the more homespun, proselytizing socialist and pacifist happy to tour Welsh mining villages or America or Australia or the Far East, for whom Shaw wrote the role of St Joan, which she played repeatedly and with immense success, and who excelled in such 'heavy' parts as

Euripides' Hecuba, Phaedra, and Medea and the mad psychopaths of Grand Guignol as well as Shakespeare's Lady Macbeth.

But such a dichotomy does less than justice to these great actors' versatility. Sybil is unimaginable as Cleopatra or Millamant, and Edith never essayed Lady Macbeth, but both of them succeeded as Shakespeare's Emilia, Volumnia, Queen Katherine (in *Henry VIII*), and Queen Margaret. And Edith could play humble characters: in 1949— the year in which she scored one of her biggest hits as the aristocratically imperious and erotic Lady Pitts in James Bridie's *Daphne Laureola*—she gave a deeply moving performance as an old Welsh peasant woman in Emlyn Williams's film *The Last Days of Dolwyn* (1949), while Sybil played a Grand Duchess in Terence Rattigan's *The Sleeping Prince*, upgraded to a Queen Dowager in the film version, *The Prince and the Showgirl* (1957).

Thorndike was a woman of indefatigable, indeed exhausting energy, both mental and physical, throughout her long life. Like Dame Edith she was not conventionally beautiful, though her blue eyes could blaze with a passion that was intellectual rather than physical. Married early in her career to a successful actor and director, Lewis (later Sir Lewis) Casson, who shared her political views and directed numerous plays in which she appeared, and by whom she had four children, she nevertheless had, as she freely admitted, a strongly masculine streak in her personality. 'There's something in me', she said, 'which is male. I'm not attractive in a feminine way at all and I've known that all along. I've got an enormous number of men friends, but none of them fell in love with me. And a woman on the stage needs to make men fall in love with her. Otherwise she's terrifically hampered. The reason it didn't hold me back is that I recognised it and played very big, huge parts that required a lot of masculinity, as in the Greek plays.'[1] She longed to play Hamlet, but never did so.

An early mentor was the actor-manager Ben Greet, a follower of William Poel. She attended Greet's acting school after a wrist injury compelled her to abandon her ambitions to become a professional pianist. With Greet between 1904 and 1907, while in her early twenties, she performed widely in America and Canada in three separate tours. His company travelled thousands of miles by train, acting wherever they could find an audience. Playing with irrepressible if sometimes undisciplined enthusiasm Sybil undertook well over 100 small parts. In *Macbeth* alone she played at various times Malcolm, Donalbain, all three witches, Lady Macduff, the Bleeding Child, and the offstage cries of women who signal Lady Macbeth's death.

Returning to England, she worked for a while with amateur companies, and was lucky to catch the attention of Bernard Shaw who recognized her potential but deplored her lack of discipline. He allowed her to understudy the role of Candida on a provincial tour while secretly hoping that she would not be required to play it, and talked to her about some of the great actresses he had known. They were kindred spirits, and he became a lifelong friend.

Greet continued to influence Sybil's career when, early in the First World War, he invited her to play Adriana in *The Comedy of Errors* at the Old Vic, run under the eccentric but dedicated management of Lilian Baylis. Here during the next four years she was to develop her art in a wide range of Shakespearian roles which she played often with outstanding success. They included not only Lady Macbeth—which she was to repeat frequently in later years—Beatrice, Portia in *The Merchant of Venice* (a play she hated), Imogen, and Puck but also in the later years of the war male roles including Prince Hal, Lear's Fool, Ferdinand in *The Tempest*, Lancelot Gobbo, and Rugby in *The Merry Wives of Windsor*. The critic James Agate considered that it was during this period that she developed into a great actress.

She and her brother Russell, also an actor and author of a once-popular series of novels about a smuggler called Dr Syn, jointly published substantial tributes to Lilian Baylis soon after she died, in 1937. Sybil's, written in a characteristically breathless and impetuous style, paints a vivid picture of the primitive conditions under which the actors had to work amid the stresses of war and the perils of air raids. She shared a dressing room 'About twice the size of a telephone booth—perhaps three times—large Elizabethan dresses hung on all the walls; it was impossible for two of us to put on dresses at the same time—a shelf for our make-up, and—luxury—a gas fire with no protection—terribly dangerous, but the fireman was a pal.' Because of the war male actors were in short supply, and Baylis had to ask women to play men's parts. 'You won't mind, dear, will you? Because, after all, there should be no sex in acting – you ought to be able to understand men as well as women.' Sybil loved playing men anyway: 'I've always been jealous of the men in Shakespeare, for every good woman's part there are ten good men's.'[2]

Off the beaten track, the Old Vic was an unfashionable theatre to which professional critics paid little attention. As a result performances there at that time are inadequately recorded. Even the amateur play-goer Gordon Crosse, who attended over 500 Shakespeare perform-ances over a period of more than sixty years, from 1890 onwards, and wrote about them in voluminous diaries from which substantial selec-tions have appeared in print, did not go to the Old Vic until the beginning of 1918. At least this enabled him to write of Thorndike, whom he described as 'the greatest Shakespearean actress, after Ellen Terry, that I have seen',[3] in some of the roles that she did not play later in her career. Of her Fool in *King Lear*, he wrote that 'her halting gait, hanging lip, and nervous demeanour suggested the half-witted youth perfectly, and the childish pleasure the Fool took in his little jokes and snatches of song completed a brilliant piece of acting'.[4] She herself wrote illuminatingly, 'I made the Fool look like an egg—blank—no eyebrows, nothing but the shape of a face that could reflect Lear's moods.'[5] In her earlier years it seems unlikely that she could have stood still for long enough to play Hermione but Crosse writes that in the statue scene 'the vision of Sybil Thorndike radiating calm beauty, spiritual as well as physical, was an abiding memory'.[6] This sounds like an anticipation of her St Joan.

Spirituality must have been evident too in 1925 when, soon after her initial triumph as Joan, she played the comparatively small but reward-ing role of Queen Katherine in *Henry VIII* at the large Empire Theatre in one of her earliest West End appearances. Directed by Lewis Casson and designed by the eminent artist Charles Ricketts, this was acclaimed as a visually gorgeous production provoking comparison in its stage pictures with the paintings of Holbein. Gordon Crosse wrote, 'For a perfect effect produced with the utmost economy of space and means I have seen nothing equal to the Coronation procession. With true artistic sense Miss Thorndike as Katherine disdained extraneous aids and relied solely on her acting. Her make-up and dress showed the Queen if, like Tennyson's spinster, not "downright plain", at any rate severely unattractive.'[7] *The Times* spoke of her face as one that could 'render every shade of emotion',[8] and the *Era* described her as 'mag-nificent in her stillness and grief'.[9] Commenting on her appearance, Agate wrote that 'Her features may not launch ships for light-hearted capture; let them show moral anguish and whole navies will flock to her succour. Her voice is not for balconies and conquests, yet in suffering it moves you to shattering depths of spiritual pity.... Any-thing more noble, more dignified, more womanly, or more truly heroic than this Katherine would be impossible to conceive.'[10]

Lewis Casson had to take over from Ben Greet, who was ill, as director of an uncut *Hamlet* of 1926 in which Sybil played Gertrude, and the dress rehearsal was such a mess that Lewis and she—both devout Christians—felt a need to say the Psalm for the day; it turned out to be Psalm 87, which includes the words 'The Lord shall rehearse it...The singers also and trumpeters shall he rehearse: All my fresh springs shall be in thee.' Sybil considered that the subsequent perform-ance was 'electrifying', and the playwright St John Ervine found her Gertrude 'the most striking interpretation of the part' he had seen.[11] Agate however thought she was miscast: 'one felt that she would have set that court to rights in no time, and done it cheerfully'.[12] It is easy to believe that she lacked the sultry sensuality that other actresses have brought to the role. But her personal qualities of passionate forthright-ness in defence of perceived injustice stood her in good stead when she came to play Emilia to Paul Robeson's Othello at the Savoy Theatre in 1930. Though she admired Robeson, she was aware of his limitations as a classical actor: 'He was potentially a fine actor, but he hadn't the technique of acting, so he had to do everything *really*. He poured with sweat with the effort of it all.'[13] Robeson received a rapturous first-night reception but the production, using a badly cut text and poorly lit, was marred by racial prejudice. James Agate thought Sybil was only 'workmanlike',[14] but for Herbert Farjeon hers was the only perform-ance with any real zest in it, and the scholar George Rylands wrote approvingly that she 'played Emilia as comfortable and coarse, almost as the Wife of Bath, in rich tones redolent of plum cake and porter'.[15]

Tyrone Guthrie was to write that

Of the actors whom I have seen the two who...best combine protean skill with 'star quality' are Laurence Olivier and Sybil Thorndike. Both are more than equal to the long haul and are able, when required, to assume immense nobility, majesty and grandeur. Both excel in the expression of powerful passion. Both can be hilariously funny. Both take almost too much pleasure... in looking, sounding and behaving as unlike their 'real selves' as possible.[16]

Sybil had known Olivier since he was a boy; his performance of Brutus in *Julius Caesar* at the age of 10 convinced Lewis and her that he was a born actor; he was to say that he looked on her as a 'surrogate mother'.[17] She was to play his mother, Volumnia, under Lewis's direction in Olivier's first *Coriolanus* at the Old Vic in 1937 in a performance which, Agate wrote, 'has the full authentic sweep'.[18] The critic of *The Observer* felt that she was drawing on her experience of playing Greek tragedy: 'Wallowing in grief and trailing trains of crape is something this gracious actress knows all about. She just turns on the Hecuba tap, and there you are!'[19]

Guthrie brought her together with Olivier again in 1944 when, the Old Vic theatre having being put out of action by the war, he formed a company to perform a challenging repertory under its name at the New Theatre (now the Noël Coward Theatre) in St Martin's Lane. Sybil was cast as Aase to Ralph Richardson's Peer Gynt, Catherine Petkoff in Shaw's *Arms and the Man*, and in the comparatively small role of Queen Margaret to Olivier's sensationally successful Richard III. Here she was able to draw on her experiences of Grand Guignol as well as of Greek tragedy. Audrey Williamson wrote, 'Sybil Thorndike played Margaret with an agued intensity; her hands, quivering with age and a nervous passion, gave the half-mad queen an added terror, and she delivered the curse as if the woman's wandering mind had become transfixed, for a moment or two only, with a poisonous and prophetic hatred.'[20]

Actors who, like Edith Evans, preferred to confine themselves to the West End tended, as now, to be tied down to playing their roles only in a single production with a limited time span. The fact that Sybil Thorndike loved touring both in England and overseas meant that she was able to play some of her best parts repeatedly over a long period of years in the manner of great nineteenth-century actors such as Charlotte Cushman and Henry Irving. She gave her first Lady Macbeth in 1915, and went on playing the role, on and off, for close on forty years. Ben Greet asked her to play it at the Old Vic as an entirely evil character, but Lilian Baylis said that 'she loved her husband, and wanted him to get to the top of the tree, and I expect you feel that way too, and if it wasn't that you go to Communion I dare say you'd do all sorts of wicked things to help Lewis!' So 'Lady Macbeth didn't seem to me any more the great tragic evil queen, but only a woman like myself.' Greet also wanted her to wake up during the sleep walking scene before saying 'to bed, to bed', but Sybil protested, 'I can't wake up!...If she woke up then she'd die of shock.'[21] In Paris in 1921 she played the role wearing Ellen Terry's costumes, including the beetle wing dress, and felt that doing so calmed her and enabled her to deal with a bad loss of memory on the part of her Macbeth. The play lived up to its reputation as a source of disaster in 1926 when 'dreadful things kept occurring, reaching such frightening proportions one night that Lewis called me into his room and said, "Sybil, the Devil does work in this play—there is Horror behind it—we must do something positive against it", and together we read aloud the 91st Psalm'—which includes the words 'Thou shalt not be afraid for the terror by night'—'which quieted and strengthened us and made us feel normal again'.[22]

Shaw sat in on rehearsals for this production, advising her not to soften on the 'Now screw your courage to the sticking place' speech, but to 'scold like a fury'.[23] Agate wrote that 'within the actress's physical means' her performance was perfect.[24] But writing in 1938, she said, 'I've never got her quite right yet, but that's because she's so big and human and heart-breaking that she eludes, unless one is the same size oneself.'[25] In the early years of the Second World War, after the destruction by bombing of several West End theatres as well as their home, she and Lewis took the play on tour to Welsh mining villages, travelling by bus followed by a large furniture van carrying the accessories, and playing to widely appreciative though often unsophisticated audiences and prefacing the play with a prologue demonstrating its relevance to the times. Indomitably she wrote, 'we'd never enjoyed *Macbeth* so much!'[26]

I saw Sybil Thorndike several times, but never in Shakespeare. Aged 17, when I heard that she was coming to Hull in J. B. Priestley's *The Linden Tree* in 1947, I felt as excited as if I had heard of the approach of Mrs Siddons. Towards the end of her life she came to Stratford with Lewis for a poetry reading. The sound of that great voice filling the hall in Tennyson's *The Lady of Shalott* is with me still.

Charles Laughton

Figure 22.1. Charles Laughton as Bottom in *A Midsummer Night's Dream*, Shakespeare Memorial Theatre, 1959; photograph by Angus McBean. Angus McBean © Royal Shakespeare Company

1899–1962. *Principal Shakespeare roles*: Angelo, Henry VIII, Macbeth, Bottom, Lear.

It is not always easy—possibly it is not even necessary—to distinguish between great Shakespeare actors and great actors who have played Shakespeare. Charles Laughton may belong to the second category. Born in the Yorkshire seaside town of Scarborough, where his parents ran one of the best hotels, he was in his mid-twenties when, against parental opposition, and having acted only as an amateur, he undertook a course lasting a mere nine months at the Royal Academy of Dramatic Art in London. At the end of it he won the prestigious Bancroft Gold Medal. It was presented to him by Sybil Thorndike, with whom he was soon to play Creon in Gilbert Murray's translation of Euripides' *Medea*.

Laughton rapidly established a significant presence on the West End stage, demonstrating his versatility by playing a wide range of leading roles in plays by, among others, Gogol, Chekhov, and Ibsen as well as appearing as Mr Pickwick in an adaptation of *The Pickwick Papers* and in the premiere of Sean O'Casey's *The Silver Tassie* (1929). He soon attracted the attention of the developing cinema industry, first making a few insignificant films, some of them silent, in England along with his wife, Elsa Lanchester. In 1931, after appearing for the first time on the New York stage, he travelled to Hollywood where, among other roles, he played Nero in Cecil B. DeMille's *The Sign of the Cross*. He was to spend much of the rest of his life in Hollywood, but one of his best films, *The Private Life of Henry VIII*, was directed in England by Alexander Korda. Still remembered especially for the episode in which the King greedily devours a whole chicken before a sycophantic bunch of courtiers, throwing the carcass over his shoulder as he opens negotiations for his next marriage, his performance may have provided the impetus for his casting as Henry VIII in the play by Shakespeare and Fletcher directed by Tyrone Guthrie for the Old Vic Company in November 1933. This production marked the beginning of the first of Laughton's two stints of playing Shakespeare.

He was already acknowledged as a major actor. When he first appeared on Broadway, in 1931, the critic John Mason Brown had analysed his qualities with acute perception.

Mr Laughton's face is one of the most expressive masks that I have ever seen in the theatre. His hands and feet and his whole body are ever the willing and expressive instruments of the things he has to say. He does not say the lines, he thinks them. They can be seen gathering like clouds in the eyes. He can be cross with peppery violence, carnal with a grossness that is repellent, merry with the expansiveness of Falstaff, cruel with a hideousness that is sickening and afraid with a whimpering terror that is almost unendurable. He is the most remarkable character actor that New York has been privileged to see in years.[1]

For all this, Laughton was not an obvious choice as star of the Shakespeare-oriented Old Vic. He is reported as saying, 'I am going to the Old Vic to learn how to speak.'[2] His status required that he be given leading roles, but he had previously played only one part in a verse play, that of Creon who speaks no more than fifty-four lines in Gilbert Murray's version of *Medea*. Neither his appearance nor his talents obviously qualified him for either romantic or heroic roles. His gravelly voice lacked both lyricism and rhetorical power. He was blubber-cheeked and had heavy-lidded eyes and sensuous thick lips. But although he himself said that his face resembled an elephant's behind, this was self-caricature. His features were exceptionally mobile and could express a wide range of emotions. Large of build even in his early years, he was nevertheless capable of agile movement.

His stage Henry VIII disappointed Agate, who found him deficient in kingliness. 'This Henry is hardly ever royal; his bonhomie and his bad temper are alike low-born. Also, he is not ripe enough in years.'[3] Still, there were compensations. 'Given Mr Laughton's interpretation, his performance must be hailed as virile and lusty and full of animal spirits.' And Gordon Crosse, who had not seen the film, wrote that Laughton 'represented the Henry of the play magnificently, and brought out the humour without clowning it as some actors do'. But his diction was faulty: 'even in his Tudor rage he should not have said "what appetite yer have."'[4]

Given Laughton's lack of confidence in his verse-speaking prowess it seems astonishing that he should have been offered—and even more so that he should have accepted—the role of Prospero, perhaps the most poetical in the canon. Agate, who disliked the play to start with, also disliked the scenery, the costumes, and most of the music, and found that Laughton 'made the old boy perform his hocus-pocus with a naughty little twinkle in his eye', and never for one moment suggested 'the potent wizard brooding in gloomy abstraction over the secrets of his art'. 'The power to terrify' was missing. This 'must be at least latent in the character; how else could the old josser keep the whip-hand over Caliban?'[5] Guthrie himself later confessed that his direction had been 'at once feeble and confused'.[6]

Macbeth was another significant piece of miscasting. Agate wrote, 'when Macbeth falls he must fall like Lucifer. Mr Laughton was never within measurable distance of any kind of grandeur.' He was vocally deficient: 'Of this actor's voice we knew beforehand that he has very little, and that consequently the surge of passion in the soliloquies must reach us not as a great tide, but in driblets.'[7] The critic of *The Sketch* put it more pungently: 'he would be a great actor past question if he could keep his mouth shut'.[8] And his moon-like face was wrong.

But there were compensations. Laughton showed 'a complete intellectual grasp of the character, of which one felt that no nook or cranny had been left unexplored', wrote Agate. He filled the banquet scene 'with the most imaginative horror that I can remember, at the words "Avaunt, and quit my sight!" bouncing away from the ghost and landing half-way up the staircase like an indiarubber cat. This was followed by an exquisite essay in taking comfort; there was real heartache in "I am in blood stepped in so far", and "Come, we'll to sleep" was conceived as lullaby, the sad pair rocking breast to breast.'[9]

This may not have been a complete realization of the role of Macbeth, but it is nevertheless a performance that I should dearly like to have seen.

It was as Angelo in *Measure for Measure* that Laughton came into his own. He had a costume which, his biographer Simon Callow writes, 'turns Laughton into a terrible black bird, or, as many observers felt, into a bat, while his features are full of dark malignant horror'.[10] And the *Daily Telegraph* critic, W. A. Darlington, wrote that 'When the actor shows us Angelo in the scene where he bargains with Isabella, brooding over the girl like a lustful black bat, he gives a glimpse of such murky depths in the man's nature that we no longer despise him for his sins. Instead we admire him that he fought his temptations so long.'[11] The actress Fabia Drake found this scene so overwhelming 'that an inner, awful excitement generated itself throughout the audience'. For her, Laughton's Angelo was 'one of the four truly great performances in a long lifetime of theatregoing'.[12] (Simon Callow, quoting this, does not say what the other three were.)

After his Old Vic season Laughton was to appear in no Shakespeare play until 1959, at the Shakespeare Memorial Theatre. Not without a certain sleight of hand, this was designated the 100th season—the theatre had opened eighty years previously, but there had been more than one playing period in some years. Casts were starry. Besides Laughton the company was led by Laurence Olivier, Paul Robeson, and Edith Evans. The season opened with *A Midsummer Night's Dream*, in which Laughton played Bottom under the direction of Peter Hall, who became artistic director of the company in the following year. Numerous excellent actors who later became stars, including Albert Finney (Lysander), Vanessa Redgrave (Helena), and Ian Holm (outstanding as Puck) played other roles. The production was to be revived with major cast changes several times, and a shortened but substantial version, lasting well over an hour, is preserved on a unique archive film made as a documentary for American television but never completed or shown. It opens with Laughton genially showing viewers round Stratford. The play was filmed in the theatre from platforms built out over the stalls, not during a public performance. It is something of a hybrid, with Laughton in particular often speaking directly to camera, but it is of special interest as the only surviving film of the actor in a Shakespeare role. With tousled ginger hair, a voluminous beard (inappropriate given Bottom's offer to play the role in a false beard, but grown especially for the Lear that he was to play later in the season), and a rustic accent, he is a chubby teddy bear of a Bottom, innocent in his vanity, conscious of intellectual superiority to his adoring fellow workmen, and lovable in the pleasure he takes in his acting skills. His shifting facial reactions, filmed in close-up, to Peter Quince's insistence that he must play Pyramus—'for Pyramus is a sweet-faced man, a proper man as one shall see in a summer's day, a most lovely gentle-manlike man' (1.2.79-81)—precisely exemplify in their transitions from crossness through doubt to flattered and wholehearted acquies-cence John Mason Brown's statement 'He does not say the lines, he thinks them. They can be seen gathering like clouds in the eyes' which I quoted earlier.[13] Kenneth Tynan, in a notice that is overall curmudg-eonly, nevertheless accurately hits off aspects of the performance when he writes that Laughton 'takes the audience into his confidence', and 'blinks at the pit his moist, reproachful eyes, softly cajoles, and suddenly roars'.[14] In the theatre in 1959, the jack-knife paroxysms with which he portrays Pyramus' death throes clearly parodied Olivier's death scene in *Richard III*, a metatheatrical allusion which gained in point from Oli-vier's presence in the company. It was a performance of great joy and gusto.

Laughton's Lear, his last stage role, directed by the outgoing artistic director Glen Byam Shaw, was less successful, perhaps in part because the actor was so desperately anxious to achieve greatness in a play that meant a great deal to him and which he saw as the culmination of his career. Misguidedly he had his wife sit in the stalls with a copy of the First Folio on her lap and with instructions to tell him whenever a word was capitalized so that he could emphasize it, in the mistaken belief that this would provide a hotline to Shakespeare's intentions. The limita-tions that had been apparent when he played Macbeth nearly thirty years previously marred this performance too. His voice, wrote Alan Brien in a perceptive (if somewhat overwritten) analysis published in *The Spectator*, 'lacks diapason and the whole poetic orchestra has had to narrow its range to follow a soloist who is a three-note virtuoso'. The storm scenes fatally lacked power even though the director muted the sound effects. But,

In the second half, safely and securely enthroned at the centre of his madness, Mr Laughton suddenly unveiled his powers. Sitting on a haycart from an Arcadian pastoral, gowned like Madame Arcati [in Noël Coward's *Blithe Spirit*], crowned like the Queen of the May, his heavy rubber face dead and cratered like an abandoned planet, he spoke his 'every inch a king' speech with enormous, defenceless tenderness and restful, affectionate irony. The King Lear whom we had never seen onstage was unearthed fragment by fragment, the remnants of his greatness were gradually discovered in this 'ruined piece of nature.' This was superb acting. It arrived just in time to save the legend of Charles Laughton for a new generation.[15]

Figure 23.1. Donald Wolfit as Hamlet; Shakespeare Memorial Theatre, 1936–7. © Lebrecht Authors

Donald Wolfit

1902–68. *Principal Shakespeare roles*: Hamlet, Richard III, Malvolio, Ulysses, Cassius, Shylock, Claudius, Macbeth, Othello, Iago, Lear.

Both as an actor and in the circumstances in which he performed, Donald Wolfit was a throwback. His acting style was more akin to that of Tommaso Salvini, or Herbert Beerbohm Tree, or even perhaps Edward Alleyn, or Richard Burbage himself than to those of his more refined contemporaries such as John Gielgud or Alec Guinness. And the fact that he acted for much of his career with a touring company under his own management links him with the nineteenth-century tradition exemplified by Edmund Kean, Ira Aldridge, and—at least in his earlier days—Henry Irving, and extending as far back as the strolling players of Shakespeare's time. He excelled in large-scale rhetorical roles, including Ben Jonson's Volpone, Massinger's Sir Giles Overreach, Marlowe's Tamburlaine, and, above all, Shakespeare's tragic heroes. Self-centred to the point of egocentricity, touchy and easily hurt, he was not at home in companies directed by anyone other than himself.

Of average height, heavy jowled and with large bushy eyebrows, a full head of swept-back hair, and a sturdy figure inclining to stoutness even as a young man, Wolfit was no matinee idol. His voice, darkly baritonal by nature but capable of wide range, with pure vowels, emphatic consonants, and a tendency to use vibrato for emotional effect was, like the Guinness with which he would lubricate it during performances, rich to the point of fruitiness. Not an intellectual actor, he had exceptional powers of conveying a sense of imaginative identification with the roles he played.

Born into a working-class, provincial family with no theatrical interests, Wolfit nevertheless had early ambitions to become an actor, developing a passion for Shakespeare through reading the plays rather than seeing them. In 1920, at the age of 18, after a brief spell of school teaching, he joined a touring company led by the Irish actor-manager Charles Doran which played in provincial theatres. During his first season Wolfit was cast as Biondello in *The Taming of the Shrew* and other roles, mostly minor but including Sir Andrew Aguecheek and Fluellen. Shakespeare dominated his career till 1953 when he acted Falstaff in *Henry IV Part One* in London. By then he had played well over seventy Shakespearian characters, mostly with his own company of touring players. After that he abandoned Shakespeare for the last fifteen years of his life except for a few radio broadcasts and some recital work.

Wolfit made his way slowly up the professional ladder by acting in both classic and modern plays in provincial repertory theatres mixed with occasional London engagements until 1929, when he joined the Old Vic company, then under the direction of Harcourt Williams. It was the season that saw John Gielgud's early triumphs as Richard II, Macbeth, Mark Antony, and above all Hamlet. But Wolfit, too, received high praise in a slightly less starry run of parts. Agate wrote that 'Macduff was magnificently given by Mr. Donald Wolfit',[1] and the critic of *Truth* admired his Claudius more than Gielgud's Hamlet: 'for me the best performance of the evening was Donald Wolfit as Claudius'.[2] In this role, writes his biographer the playwright Ronald Harwood, Wolfit 'discovered his own style of acting, a style that would depend on a mighty inner power which was to swell to such enormity [*sic*] that the actor would have difficulty in containing it'. His line of parts during this season, writes Harwood, 'was like a well-planned training session for the real thing. Tybalt allowed him to exploit villainy; Lorenzo gave free rein to his poetic gifts; in Cassius he explored venom and bitterness; playing Macduff he was obliged to portray a man of action in turn horrified at the death of Duncan and shattered at the murder of his own family.'[3]

It was after he had played Cassius, a performance variously described by critics as 'fiery', 'tempestuous', 'impetuous', and 'vehement',[4] that he, not Gielgud, was presented with the laurel wreath awarded by the galleryites to the actor who had most pleased them throughout the season. This mark of approval from the less fashionable segment of the audience appeased his social insecurity; he writes in his autobiography that it 'hung on my sitting-room wall until it fell to pieces, the proudest trophy of my life'.[5] But, to Wolfit's bitter disappointment, it was Gielgud, not he, who was invited to remain with the company for the following season. Wolfit and Gielgud were opposites both in temperament and in talents. Wolfit, the elder by four years, robust, homophobic, aggressively masculine, was jealous of the more fastidious, willowy, and discreetly but enthusiastically gay Gielgud and resentful of his early triumphs; although they acted together in one of Gielgud's biggest and longest running early successes, *Richard of Bordeaux* written by the pseudonymous Gordon Daviot in 1933, they remained on uneasy—even on Wolfit's part hostile—terms with one another till Wolfit died.

Wolfit moved from playing Claudius—never a Gielgud role—to Hamlet, thus implicitly challenging Gielgud, first in Ben Greet's enterprising staging of the corrupt First Quarto text, which they believed to be based on Shakespeare's first draft of the play and to be in some ways superior to the later texts, in a production for Shakespeare's Birthday in 1933. But his big chance in the role, and a defining moment in his career, came three years later when Ben Iden Payne (whose daughter, Rosalind Iden, was later to become Wolfit's leading lady and, eventually, his third wife) invited him to join the company of the Shakespeare Memorial Theatre. At first his run of parts did not include Hamlet, but the play was added to the repertoire halfway through the season, by which time Wolfit had scored a hit in the slightly improbable role of Ulysses, man of thought rather than of action, in the first performances at Stratford of *Troilus and Cressida* since Edith Evans had played Cressida there in William Poel's 1912 production. Wolfit, who bizarrely described it as 'a strange botched play to which Shakespeare gave his great verse, but was probably largely written by Dekker', nevertheless felt that 'the part of Ulysses has the authentic ring' and wrote that 'the beauty and profundity of his speeches on Degree and the Ingratitude of Time [*his capital letters*] called up all the reserves in me which I had learned from Poel and earned me golden opinions'.[6]

Wolfit's description of preparations for *Hamlet* is revealing of theatre conditions at this time. Exceptionally, nine weeks were available for rehearsals, and during this period Payne and he

worked over all the cuts which had perforce to be made to bring the play within the compass of even three hours and a half. A new duel with sword and main-gauche [left-hand] dagger was arranged by Madame Perigal and rehearsed twice a week. Costumes were chosen from the vast Elizabethan wardrobe and fitted in ample time and the dress-rehearsal took place several days before the first night.[7]

Wolfit's account of that first night both reveals the genuine and passionate dedication which he brought to his Shakespearian perform-ances and implicitly tells us much about his interpretation of the role:

I did my best and was swept away on the wings of the play. I knew the hurdles, the long sequence of great scenes which rush towards one from the play scene until the departure for England and culminating in 'How all occasions do inform against me' as Hamlet sees the army of Fortinbras marching below him. Then the long break which Shakespeare always devised for his leading tragedian in every play and the return, gentle but bitterly philosophical to the graveyard; the cry of tortured rage at the heroics of Laertes; the leap into the grave beside the body of Ophelia so that the brother and lover can tear at each other across her lifeless form; the resigna-tion of 'If it be not to come it will be now, the readiness is all'; and on to the tumult of the final scene.[8]

He put all he had into it, attempting to convey to the audience 'the great struggle in Hamlet's soul... with every fibre of my heart and brain'. It was a success. John Masefield, the Poet Laureate, wrote to him, 'I was much impressed by your Hamlet which seemed to me to catch in every line a vital point which no actor save yourself seems to have seen, that is, that Hamlet was, and knew that he was, in deadly danger at every turn.'[9] But, Wolfit says, none of the favourable com-ments pleased him more than that of *The Times*'s critic who found it refreshing 'to see for once the producer's ascendancy broken and Shakespeare made vivid and vital by an actor who has the freedom and the power to meet full face the challenge of a tragic part'.[10] There speaks the future actor-manager protesting against the increasing ascendancy of the role of the director, exemplified during this Stratford season by Theodore Komisarjevsky in whose disastrous London pro-duction of a heavily rewritten *Antony and Cleopatra* in the following year—it lasted for only four performances—Wolfit had the misfortune to play Antony opposite the Russian-born Eugenie Leontovitch. Notoriously, her speaking of the lines

> O withered is the garland of the war,
> The soldier's pole is fall'n! Young boys and girls
> Are level now with men

was cruelly parodied as

> O wilderdee degarlano devar
> Desolderspo less falln; yong boisenguls
> Alefellnow wimen.[11]

Wolfit was re-engaged at Stratford for a second season with a largely new set of roles, along with a repeat of Hamlet, but the time had come for him to become his own master. All through the early part of his career he had been saving and planning in the hope of founding a theatre company dedicated primarily to performing Shakespeare and other classical plays with, of course, himself as its star. And on 11 October 1937 the Donald Wolfit Shakespearean Company opened in Malvern, its leader playing Hamlet, Macbeth, and Shylock twice and Petruccio once within six days. It made a profit. 'The heavenly trumpets blew in my ears... everyone was paid and the world was mine', Wolfit exulted.[12]

For the remainder of his career all Wolfit's Shakespeare performances were given under his own management and with a company of actors chosen by himself. He relished the freedom to play the great roles whenever and however he liked. But the autonomy that acting only with his own company gave him was not entirely good for him or his art. If only to save money he tended, in the manner of the old actor-managers, to surround himself with inferior colleagues, and the exigencies of touring imposed damaging limitations on scenery and costumes. Though he shone all the more brightly by comparison with his fellow actors, he too often lacked both the stimulus that would have been provided by a strong all-round company and the discipline that a good director could have instilled in him. There was more than a touch of Dickens's magniloquent Vincent Crummles, in *Nicholas Nickleby*, about him. He could be selfish, upstaging his colleagues. At his worst, his speaking could be orotund to the point of fruitiness. His acceptance of applause when, clutching the edge of the curtain with an obeisance that threatened to pull it to the ground, he would declare, with Hamlet, 'Poor as I am, I am even poor in thanks', was a performance in itself.

But there was another side to him. He had a passion for Shakespeare, and a determination to communicate this widely. For fourteen years, like Frank Benson before him, he toured extensively in the English provinces and occasionally overseas while also sometimes playing in

London. But unlike Benson he ran only one company—with himself at its centre. I am thankful that he gave me my first experience of Shakespeare on the stage when, as a schoolboy, I saw him in Hull during the 1940s. (Admittedly my main memory of his Othello is of him opening his eyes while lying onstage having a fit and gazing around the theatre, clearly anxious to see how full the house was.) During the Second World War he and his company braved the bombs in London to give hour-long lunchtime performances of selected scenes.

Inevitably given the circumstances in which he played, Wolfit sometimes became stale and gave of less than his best, but when his acting caught fire it could rouse even the most discerning judges to extraordinary rhapsodies of praise. Of his Richard III in 1942 Agate wrote:

Mr Wolfit does more than frighten the other actors; he terrifies the playgoer . . . His final 'A horse! A horse! my kingdom for a horse!' is agony made vocal. The spectator, no longer concerned whether Richard is a good king or a bad, is appalled at this cry of a man about to die on his feet. Baffled enjoyment of his well-laid schemes, vengeance on Richmond, the fury of the trapped animal— all these are merged in the hoarse scream which still rings in my ears.[13]

After he had played Macbeth the poet Edith Sitwell wrote, 'The greatness of your heart-shaking Macbeth will remain with us all our lives.'[14] Though he was dissatisfied with his early performances of Lear, he worked on the role with such success that after seeing him play it in London in 1942 James Agate, in a review headed 'Every Inch King Lear', wrote, 'I say deliberately that his performance on Wednesday was the greatest piece of Shakespearean acting I have seen since I have been privileged to write for the *Sunday Times*', to which he had been appointed in 1923.[15] London accepted Wolfit at last, and Edith Sitwell came up trumps again: 'The cosmic grandeur of your "King Lear" left us unable to speak. . . . Surely this stupendous revelation of the redemption of a soul (to see only one aspect of the play) is one of the greatest *religious* works ever born from the heart of man. And equally surely, even when Shakespeare himself was there to advise and to fire, there can have been no greater performance.'[16] Ronald Harwood, who based his play *The Dresser* on his experiences with Wolfit in this capacity, devotes a chapter to describing the performance in his biography of the actor.

In 1947, towards the end of his career as a Shakespeare actor, Wolfit at last teamed up with a worthy partner. He put on *Othello*, and, 'consumed as he was with resentment', as Harwood writes,[17] chose for the first time to play Iago. His Othello, a refugee German actor, Frederick Valk, who had taken Czech nationality, was in the Wolfit mould, 'possessed of a deep, growling voice, rich and resonant, a massive turret of a head and the body of an armoured tank'.[18] The young Kenneth Tynan, later Wolfit's bitter enemy, was knocked back and celebrated the event in the purplest of prose: 'I have lived for two hours on the red brink of a volcano, and the crust of lava crumbles still from my feet.'[19]

Always his own worst enemy, in 1953 Wolfit, having triumphed as Tamburlaine directed by Tyrone Guthrie at the Old Vic, lost his chance of crowning his career in a major production of *King Lear* by behaving so badly that he was compelled to resign from the company. He got his longed-for knighthood in 1957, and when he died Guthrie, while regretting that his was essentially the art of a star performer, said that otherwise 'he was almost without fault as an actor'.[20]

Ralph Richardson

Figure 24.1. Ralph Richardson as Falstaff in *Henry IV, Part One*: Old Vic Theatre, London, 1944. University of Bristol/ArenaPAL

1902–83. *Principal Shakespeare roles*: Falconbridge, Bottom, Henry V, Falstaff.

Three of the greatest English actors of the twentieth century—Donald Wolfit, John Gielgud, and Ralph Richardson—were all born in 1902; their careers intertwined at various times with each other's and with those of other leading actors, especially, in Richardson's case, that of Laurence Olivier. Each had his own distinctive talents, related inevitably to their physical and vocal characteristics. The most idiosyncratic, and so, perhaps, the most limited in range, was Ralph Richardson.

Like Olivier, Richardson came from an untheatrical background. Developing the ambition to become an actor as an impecunious teenager after seeing Frank Benson play Hamlet on tour in Brighton, he paid for lessons with the manager of a local theatre company out of a legacy from his grandmother, and became an odd-job man with the company both before and behind the scenes. Before he was 20 years old he played both Banquo and Macduff—an unusual double—in a single production of *Macbeth*. This aroused in him an enthusiasm for Shakespeare, and after a few months he joined Charles Doran's touring company with which both Wolfit and Edith Evans were gaining early experience. Here he played a wide range of Shakespeare roles, mostly minor but including Malvolio, and Mark Antony in *Julius Caesar*, before joining Barry Jackson's Birmingham Repertory Theatre company in 1925. There he made his mark in a modern-dress production of *The Taming of the Shrew* by playing Tranio with a Cockney accent and thus, according to the critic Horace Horsnell, turning a relatively small part into a star role. He began to make a reputation for himself on the London stage in modern plays, and his Shakespearian career resumed in 1930, when he played Roderigo to Robeson's Othello and then joined the Old Vic as a colleague of John Gielgud.

Not especially handsome, certainly not heroic in build, and lacking Gielgud's innate lyricism and Wolfit's extrovert dynamism, Richardson was by nature what is known as a character actor. He had a special talent for playing ordinariness. Described by Sheridan Morley in the *Dictionary of National Biography* as looking 'like a respectable bank manager possessed of magical powers',[1] he could use his eyes to mesmeric effect and had a highly idiosyncratic vocal delivery which compelled attention. Endowed with a quirky sense of comedy (and eccentric in personal behaviour as well), he scored some of his greatest successes in strongly characterized non-Shakespearian roles including Ibsen's Peer Gynt and Rostand's Cyrano de Bergerac, and in plays by Chekhov, J. B. Priestley, and—later in life, acting alongside John Gielgud—by Harold Pinter and David Storey. He also enjoyed a successful film career.

Richardson's career as a Shakespeare actor is by no means a sustained success story. At the Old Vic from 1930 to 1932 as a kind of second string to Gielgud he played a remarkable range of roles, developing his talents as he did so. At this time each production was rehearsed for only a few days, and given for not more than a month. James Agate, in more than one review, astutely identified Richardson's especial strengths. Reviewing *King John* in 1931, he wrote that playing Falconbridge—a much more eye-catching role than the king—Richardson, 'who a year or two ago was good in a shambling sort of way, has discarded loutishness and an oafish gait and transmuted these into the sterling of forthrightness and honesty. His Kent'—in *King Lear*—'was superb and his Falconbridge is as good. He has a direct and manly pathos and can fill any role that needs vitality and command.'[2] That he could also transcend ordinariness and invest it with touches of poetic magic even in a prose role is clear from Agate's praise of his performance as Bottom in *A Midsummer Night's Dream*:

In the fairy scenes he abandoned clowning in favour of a dim consciousness of a rarer world and of being at court there. This was new to me, and if Mr Richardson [still under 30 years old] had not the ripeness of some of the older actors, his acting here was an agreeable change from the familiar refusal to alternate fruitiness with anything else. Most of the old players seem to have thought that Bottom, with the ass's head on, was the same Bottom only funnier. Shakespeare says he was 'translated', and Mr Richardson translated him.[3]

This is creative acting, discerning possible depths under the surface of the lines and plumbing them to their full potential. Commenting on this interpretation in relation to the history of the play as acted, the scholar Trevor Griffiths writes: 'no one before Richardson, and no one after him either, guessed that there was in this weaver so deep a well of abused poetry, such an ineradicable vision of uncomprehended wonder'.[4] That is a fine tribute to Richardson's acting even though it does less than justice to Benjamin Britten's deeply imaginative setting of Bottom's dream in his great opera.

Richardson repeated the role at the Old Vic in 1937 when, says Audrey Williamson, 'His waking from his "most rare vision", with the dew of wonder on him, was exquisite drollery'.[5] A pleasure of attending a performance at the present Old Vic theatre is to see hanging in one of the corridors a photograph of Richardson in the weaver's workshop.

One of Richardson's more surprising successes at the Old Vic in 1931 was as Henry V, when he presented the character, writes Agate, 'as a human being and not as a mailed fist, eating, sleeping, and thinking in armour'.[6] This sounds like an anticipation of Branagh rather than of Olivier. More predictably, he was highly praised as the plain-speaking Enobarbus and as Kent to Gielgud's first Lear. He did less well as Iago in 1932 when, says Agate, he grew 'more and more honest as the play proceeded' and 'convinced us that he couldn't hurt a fly, which was very good Richardson but indifferent Shakespeare'.[7] Herbert Farjeon, too, finding him 'the most honest Iago ever exhibited', wrote 'Mr Ralph Richardson is too radically agreeable to be cast for any but the most sympathetic parts'.[8] But there were counter-opinions: the critic of *The Times* found, 'we have seldom seen a man smile and smile and be a villain so adequately'.[9] By the end of his first Old Vic stint Richardson was fully established as one of the best Shakespeare actors of the day.

In his next London Shakespeare role, as Othello with Olivier dominating as Iago (see Chapter 26), he split the critics. Agate called it 'an almost total failure' while praising highly his delivery of the speech to the Senate and his playing of the last act.[10] Raymond Mortimer, while praising his 'skill, dignity, and taste', found a fatal absence of heroic qualities: 'the tragedy dwindles into a thriller about a villain who ruins an amiable and well-bred simpleton'.[11] Audrey Williamson used the performance as the basis for what seems like an astute summing-up of Richardson's Shakespearian qualities: 'his voice is by nature a prose voice, and when he achieves poetry (he often does) it is by the force of his will and imagination alone'.[12]

The high point of Richardson's Shakespearian career came in 1944 with the forming of a new Old Vic company which he led with Olivier. The two men were both close friends and intense rivals. During the company's first season Richardson triumphed as Peer Gynt, and loyally played the non-starring role of Richmond to Olivier's Richard III. For the following year they decided, unusually at that time, to play both *Part One* and *Part Two* of *Henry IV* in conjunction, with Richardson as Falstaff in both plays and Olivier as Hotspur in *Part One* and Justice Shallow in *Part Two*. Richardson played an enormously fat Falstaff, helped by a costume skilfully designed so that he could move with a physical agility that matched the quickness of the character's wit. 'As the great belly moved,' wrote Tynan in a glowing review, 'step following step with great finesse lest it overtopple, the arms flapped fussily at the sides as if to paddle the body's bulk along.'[13] He was dignified and gentlemanly, 'Sir John first, and Falstaff second'. Gordon Crosse noted the skill with which he played the character's volte-face when his lies are discovered, 'going up stage and turning with a roar of laughter at "By the Lord I knew ye . . ."'[14]

In Part Two, writes Audrey Williamson, he moved to 'a still deeper understanding which could catch the sombre illumination of "Do not bid me remember mine end" and suggest, as Falstaffs do rarely, the attraction of the man for the Prince as well as the considerable brain behind the wit'. Richardson's 'greatness . . . in the part', she writes, 'was a greatness of spirit that transcended the mere hulk of flesh'.[15] I kick myself for not having paid my half-crown and climbed the steps to the gallery to experience this performance.

This was the peak of Richardson's career as a Shakespeare actor. At Stratford in 1952 he predictably failed with the lyricism of Prospero, and, just as he had been unable to open up into the poetry and passion of Othello, so as Macbeth, directed by Gielgud, he seems to have been completely unable to enter imaginatively into the character's nightmare. 'He let line after line fall flat, without shape of phrase, dramatic drive, or quite simply, conviction', wrote Philip Hope-Wallace in the *Manchester Guardian*.[16] And Tynan, merciless as ever, declared himself 'unmoved to the point of paralysis'.[17] Richardson's return to the Old Vic company to play Timon of Athens in 1956 was equally uninspiring. In 1964 for the Shakespeare quatercentenary he undertook a successful overseas tour in which he played Shylock for the first time and returned to one of his greatest roles, Bottom. It is a paradox that this sometimes great actor achieved his most poetical effects when he was speaking prose.

John Gielgud

Figure 25.1. John Gielgud as Hamlet, Theatre Royal, Haymarket, London, 1944. Gwen Watford Collection/Lebrecht Music & Arts

1904–2000. *Principal Shakespeare roles*: Romeo, Mercutio, Hamlet, Richard II, Oberon, Benedick, Angelo, Cassius, Macbeth, Lear, Leontes, Prospero.

John Gielgud was born in the same year as Wolfit but into a very different background. Theatre was in his blood, and he had a privileged upbringing. His mother, Kate, was a member of the Terry family who provided the English stage with bright stars, above all his adored great-aunt Ellen, from the middle of the nineteenth century onwards. From early days he was able to cultivate wide artistic interests, in books, ballet, music, painting, and especially, nurtured by family connections, theatre of all kinds. As a schoolboy he played Shylock in scenes from *The Merchant of Venice* and, aged 12, Mark Antony in selections from *Julius Caesar*. Living in London, where he attended the prestigious Westminster School, and encouraged by his parents, he was able to take full use of the opportunities the capital offered for artistic experience of many kinds, including going to see eminent relatives onstage.

At first he wanted to become a stage designer, like his cousin Gordon Craig, but when he realized that this would have called for technical skills which were beyond him he turned towards acting as a profession. Towards the end of his school career he took lessons from a celebrated teacher, Rosina Filippi, who laid especial stress on the importance of good speaking, and instead of going on to university as his parents wished, at the age of 17 he entered a drama school run by Frank Benson's wife, Constance. To his dismay she identified a weakness that he spent many years trying to conquer when she said 'Good heavens, you walk exactly like a cat with rickets!'[1]

Slim and elegant throughout his exceptionally long working life, Gielgud was by nature fastidious of appearance and gesture, though possessed of exceptional mental energy. He was good-looking in a slightly effete way, and had a distinctly bulbous nose; as a young man he wore his hair long but went bald relatively early in life. Famous for beauty of speech, he had inherited what is sometimes called 'the Terry voice', a musical resonance of perfectly controlled vocal quality guided in his case by keen intelligence and deep understanding of his lines and responsiveness to the dramatic situation. To modern tastes his speaking on early recordings is susceptible to a charge of self-indulgence, the voice wobbling from time to time with a vibrato like that of an old-style string player. He shows however an extraordinary ability to contain great richness and range of verbal nuance within the verse structure, using subtle fluctuations of pitch and tempo to create the sense of a mind at work, the words newly minted from within the man who speaks them.

Gielgud was by nature a lyrical actor, excelling in primarily poetic roles such as Richard II, Oberon, Prospero, and above all Hamlet. It is impossible to imagine him onstage as the strenuously heroic Richard

III, the warrior Henry V (though recordings of speeches from the play made during his Old Vic period show that vocally he could do the role full justice), or Coriolanus; unsurprising that one of his rare failures in Shakespeare was as Othello; and unexpected (not least to himself) that he succeeded in the physically taxing role of Macbeth in two different productions.

The foundations of Gielgud's career as a great Shakespeare actor were laid during two extraordinary, ill-paid seasons at the Old Vic from 1929 to 1931 which were also central to the career of Donald Wolfit. During this period Gielgud, still in his late twenties, undertook for the first time a high proportion of the star Shakespearian roles that he was to go on developing in later productions. He had already played Romeo, at the age of 20, with praise for beauty of voice and emotional commitment but harsh criticisms from some reviewers on the grounds of effeminacy and of awkwardness of movement. Ivor Brown complained that he was 'scant of virility' and that his 'body from his hips down never meant anything throughout the evening. He has the most meaningless legs imaginable.'[2] His legs were to remain a constant source of embarrassment.

At the Old Vic in 1929 his Romeo was popular with audiences but Gielgud himself felt that he lacked the technique for this linguistically intricate role. In 1932 an invitation to direct the play in a semi-professional production for the Oxford University Dramatic Society launched him on a second, parallel career as director. Christopher Hassall played Romeo, the young Peggy Ashcroft Juliet, and Edith Evans the Nurse. In Gielgud's subsequent West End production of 1935, also with Ashcroft and Evans, Laurence Olivier took over first as Romeo, then, switching roles with Gielgud, as Mercutio. As I said in writing of Edith Evans (Chapter 20), this became a classic production, praised by Granville Barker as 'far the best bit of Shakespeare I've seen for years',[3] even though Gielgud and Olivier took diametrically opposed approaches to the speaking of verse. Olivier sought realism, while Gielgud took a more lyrical, classically based approach. As Mercutio, wrote Agate, Gielgud built the role out of the Queen Mab speech, delivering it exquisitely, and saying the character's dying words, 'A plague o' both your houses', 'with a smile which is all a benison'.[4] When he took over from Olivier as Romeo, Agate, admitting that he again 'carves the verse . . . exquisitely', asked 'is this Romeo ever really in love with anybody except himself?'[5] But Gordon Crosse thought it 'certainly the best of the more than twenty Romeos I have seen, in passing from the moody youth, through the happy, eager lover, to the fully developed man of the later Acts'.[6]

During the 1929 Old Vic season Gielgud had the first of his early triumphs as Richard II, a role that he was to repeat under his own direction at the Queen's Theatre, London, with a strong company in 1937 and in Rhodesia in 1953, and which (like other roles) he also recorded. This all-verse part gave ample scope to his lyrical gifts. Agate, comparing the 1937 version with the Old Vic performance, wrote, 'His present performance lays greater stress on the artist without losing any of the kingliness. His reading has gained in depth, subtlety, insight, power. The last act is not only the peak of his achievement to date; it is probably the best piece of Shakespearean acting on the English stage today.'[7] And, unselfishly—by contrast with many of Wolfit's successes—it was a company achievement; Ivor Brown wrote, 'the chief note of his first venture [into management] is the teamwork and the giving of distinction to routine elements or seemingly inconsiderable parts by shrewd casting and rich performance. Mr Gielgud is not only a fine actor himself, but a source of fine acting in others.'[8]

At the Old Vic in 1929–30, more great roles followed with the relentless dedication to sheer hard labour that Lilian Baylis exacted from her actors—a poetic and witty Oberon, a fine Mark Antony in *Julius Caesar*, and an unremarkable Orlando. Then Gielgud's versatility was put to its strongest test so far with Macbeth, in which Ivor Brown, who had found him lacking in virility as Romeo, now found that his acting had 'ripened into a fine masculinity'.[9]

It was natural that Hamlet should soon follow, and this (along with Prospero) became the role with which Gielgud was to be most closely identified. At the Old Vic in 1930 he was required to rehearse both a full and a shortened text simultaneously. The critics saw the full version, and, like the audience, were bowled over. In his curtain speech on the last night, Gielgud said he hoped his performance would get better—not a remark that one would have expected from his Claudius, Donald Wolfit. This was a fresh, youthful, tender, passionate, noble interpretation. On a second visit Agate wrote, 'His performance is subtle, brilliant, vigorous, imaginative, tender, and full of the right kind of ironic humour. It has elegance of body and elevation of mind; it is conceived in the key of poetry, and executed with beautiful diction. I have no hesitation whatsoever in saying that it is the high water-mark of English Shakespearean acting of our time.'[10] All this from a young man aged 26. The production transferred to the West End, in the shortened version, and Gielgud was to play the role again numerous times, in England, America, Canada, at Elsinore, and finally in a tour of the Far East in 1945–6, when he thought he was becoming too old for it, though numerous actors from Betterton onwards have played it when they were older.

Back at the Old Vic from 1931 to 1932 the great roles continued to come thick and fast: a 'fiery, youthful, impetuous Hotspur',[11] Prospero, Malvolio, Antony in *Antony and Cleopatra*, Benedick, and—the ultimate test—King Lear. He was, he later wrote, entirely unsuited to Antony, 'but I padded my doublet and wore a false beard and shouted and boomed, and achieved some sort of result'.[12] Nevertheless it was a critical success, the *Manchester Guardian* critic writing that 'he fully discovers that subtle sensual quality, that Renaissance refinement on barbarism, which makes him the most exciting of all Shakespeare's Romans'.[13]

He never played Hotspur, Antony, or Malvolio again, but Prospero was to be a key role for him for an astonishing sixty more years. Though the character's age is indeterminate, he has a teenage daughter, so when Gielgud first played it he was young for the role, but in its wealth of poetry (along with the light demands it makes on an actor's legs) it was ideally suited to Gielgud. He played it again in 1940 at the Old Vic, in Stratford and London in 1957, and at the Old Vic yet again in 1974, directed by Peter Hall. In his delightful book *An Actor and His Time*, published in 1979, Gielgud writes: 'In all four productions of the play I have acted in . . . I never looked at Ariel. He was always behind me or above me, never in front of me. I tried to see him in my mind's eye, never looking at him physically. It heightened the impression of Ariel as a spirit.'[14]

He also wrote, 'I have always wanted to make a film of *The Tempest*.' He approached numerous directors, without success, but the opportunity came when, after he had made his last stage appearance in any role, he broached the subject to Peter Greenaway, with whom he had made a television film about Dante. The outcome was the relentlessly uncommercial and highbrow, visually stunning postmodern film *Prospero's Books*, which appeared in 1991 and in which Gielgud, who appears naked in the opening sequence along with a multitude of similarly exposed extras, speaks not just Prospero's lines but most of the rest of the text and, as the film historian Kenneth Rothwell (not an admirer) writes, 'outdoes himself as a singer of verse, his already mellifluous but stagy voice being unnaturally amplified and resonated through the sophisticated electronic recording equipment'.[15]

After Prospero at the Old Vic, the relatively lightweight but delightful and popular Benedick, to be repeated several times, and then the mighty Lear. For Gielgud himself the most important of the four productions of the tragedy in which he appeared—Old Vic 1930 and 1940, Stratford 1950, London 1955—was that of 1940. Ostensibly it was directed by Lewis Casson, but Granville-Barker's attendance at just ten days of rehearsals was, wrote Gielgud, 'one of the great experiences of my career'. They had read the part together in advance, when Barker had said, 'Well, you've got two lines right. Of course, you are an ash and this part demands an oak, but we'll see what can be done.' At rehearsals, 'we hung on his every word'. 'To me he was like a masseur who forces you to discover and use muscles you never knew you possessed.'[16] Barker's advice drew from Gielgud a volatile performance full of irony, responsive to every shift in Lear's constantly changing moods, spiritually serene in the reunion scene and profoundly moving in death. When he played Lear at Stratford in 1950, co-directing himself with George Devine, he self-destructively invited the avant-garde American/Japanese sculptor Isami Noguchi to design the sets and costumes. His biographer Jonathan Croall writes that 'His face surrounded by dense white horsehair, Gielgud wore a crown resembling an upturned milking stool, and a cloak full of holes, which symbolically grew larger as Lear's mind disintegrated. At the dress parade he kept saying "I'm terribly worried, George. I look like a gruyere cheese."'[17] Few critics resisted the temptation to quote Lear's words 'I do not like the fashion of your garments . . . Let them be changed.'

Even after Gielgud had undertaken so many of the great roles during a relatively short period in his Old Vic years, some peaks remained unconquered. Shylock is a role that is always liable to provoke controversy. His performance in a production of 1938 that he co-directed with Glen Byam Shaw had a mixed reception, perhaps because he refused to let the role dominate the play. In 1950 at Stratford again he undertook new roles, Angelo in *Measure for Measure*, directed by the young genius Peter Brook—who also designed the sets, costumes, and lighting as well as writing the music—and Cassius in *Julius Caesar*. Brook found ways of challenging Gielgud without upsetting him, to such an extent that the critic T. C. Worsley wrote that 'with his Angelo he makes a break—it may be a complete break—with his past . . . there are no traces of the romantic gestures, no echoes of the youthful tones'.[18] His Cassius, too, was passionately vehement, tough, and intense. Though at this point in his career he disliked filming, he agreed to play the same role in Joseph Mankiewicz's film of 1953. All responses to acting are personal; Kenneth Rothwell, in his outstanding study of *Shakespeare on Screen*, is throughout antipathetic to Gielgud, remarking that as Cassius he 'predictably and characteristically stresses verse over sense, tending to "sing" the lines'[19] but this is a minority view; Croall is more representative of reactions to the film when he writes that Gielgud's 'fierce, steely performance brims with confidence, and the tent scene with Brutus is subtle and riveting'.[20]

Peter Brook directed Gielgud in another new role, that of Leontes in *The Winter's Tale* in a visually beautiful production of 1951. Exceptionally—and I think mistakenly—Gielgud played Leontes as jealous from the start of the play, but it was a darkly intense interpretation. Some years later, in 1957, he gave the first performances of a one-man show, *The Ages of Man*, based on a Shakespeare anthology compiled by George Rylands, which was to serve him well for the next ten years (and was recorded both in sound and for television.) It was a great showcase, full of plums from his repertory. When I saw it at Stratford I found his delivery of Leontes's great speech ending in 'nor nothing have these nothings | If this be nothing' (1.2.286–98) so passionately riveting that I was almost torn out of my seat at the back of the stalls. Gielgud could be as viscerally exciting with his voice as Olivier with his body.

Gielgud's success as Leontes encouraged him to think that he might tackle the no-less-jealous Othello, as he did in a return to Stratford in 1961. It was a mistake. Franco Zeffirelli, the director, designed beautiful but cumbersome and wobbly sets of operatic grandeur which took so long to manipulate that on the press night the two intervals seemed to last for ever. Gielgud spoke the address to the Senate beautifully but could not encompass either Othello's martial qualities or his descent into animalism. Dorothy Tutin, who played Desdemona, said 'I practically had to throttle *myself*.'[21] As the evening wore on, his confidence visibly drained away. In one scene his beard came loose and, lacking the presence of mind to rip it off altogether, he played the rest of the scene with it dangling from his chin. The infection spread. Towards the end

Ian Bannen as Iago got confused and said 'He's almost slain, and Cassio dead—no, sorry, Roderigo's dead.' (At least that's how I remember it. Croall says it was 'Cassio's slain—at least he's almost slain.'[22]) The evening was redeemed only by the exquisite tenderness with which Tutin and Peggy Ashcroft, as Emilia, played the 'willow' scene.

Gielgud's last Shakespearian stage role was Julius Caesar at the National Theatre in 1977, but he played King Lear yet again in a studio recording with an all-star cast made to celebrate his ninetieth birthday, in 1994, and went on acting till almost the end of his long life.

Laurence Olivier

Figure 26.1. Laurence Olivier as Coriolanus, Shakespeare Memorial Theatre, Stratford-upon-Avon, 1959: photograph by Angus McBean. Angus McBean © Royal Shakespeare Company

1907–89. *Principal Shakespeare roles*: Richard III, Romeo, Mercutio, Hotspur, Shylock, Henry V, Justice Shallow, Mark Antony, Hamlet, Lear, Iago, Othello, Macbeth, Titus Andronicus, Coriolanus.

Some actors turn their roles into themselves, others transform themselves into their roles. If Gielgud—who, wrote Michael Billington, 'rarely stooped to impersonation'[1]—belongs to the first category, Laurence Olivier most certainly belongs to the second. Simply to glance at photographs of him in a succession of the parts he played is to gain the sense of a protean actor of extraordinary external transformative power, a master of both physical and psychological make-up, able to seem older or younger, even taller or shorter than he really was. This is nowhere more apparent than in the images of him as the virile, ginger-headed Hotspur in *Henry IV Part One*, and the aged, quivering Justice Shallow in *Henry IV Part Two*, both of which he played in a single season for the Old Vic Company at the New Theatre at the age of 37, and still more so in his double bill of Sophocles' *Oedipus* along with Mr Puff in Sheridan's *The Critic* during the same season.

Facial make-up, including putty for the nose, wigs, posture, costume, vocal manipulation—he is said to have worked for six months to
lower his voice by an octave for Othello—all played their part. He was
a virtuoso, an actor of high intelligence and fanatical dedication who
prepared his roles with a perfectionist's passion and unremitting physical courage. But he hid himself behind the parts he played. Although
he published fascinating books called *Confessions of an Actor* and *On
Acting*, his writings about his art—ghosted in part, it would appear—are
more concerned with technique than with interpretation, and often
flippantly self-concealing. His greatness lay in his art, not in what he
said about it.

As well as being an actor on both stage and screen, Olivier was also a
director, an innovative film-maker, and an administrator. Over the
years he became the leader of his profession—a knight in 1947, the first
director of the National Theatre in 1962, the first, and so far only, actor
to become a baron of the realm in 1970, and in 1981 the first of only
two so far to become members of the Order of Merit—the other is
John Gielgud.

Son of a priest with histrionic abilities, Olivier showed precocious
signs of acting talent as a young pupil at a London boys' school where a
surprising number of great actors dropped in to see the boys perform.
Ellen Terry, after seeing him in *Julius Caesar* at the age of 10, wrote in
her diary, 'The small boy who played Brutus is already a great actor';[2]
Forbes-Robertson also expressed admiration. After playing Maria in
Twelfth Night the following year, the slightly less small boy undertook
Katherine in *The Taming of the Shrew*, this time winning the approba-
tion not only of Ellen Terry but also of Sybil Thorndike—a family
friend—who later said that his was 'the best Katherine I ever saw'.[3] In
1922, still aged only 14, he played Kate again in the Stratford Memorial
Theatre when his school was invited to take part in the Shakespeare
Birthday celebrations.

On leaving school three years later he auditioned successfully with
the great voice teacher Elsie Fogerty for a place at the Central School of
Speech Training and Dramatic Art, where he vied with Peggy Ashcroft
for top honours. After playing small parts in London theatres, he gained
valuable experience at the Birmingham Repertory Theatre, where his
roles included Paroles and a modern-dress Macduff, in 1926–7, and
soon became a successful West End actor in modern plays, but his first
major Shakespeare role came in 1935 when he and Gielgud played

both Romeo and Mercutio in the same production, exchanging roles in midstream.

Of slightly more than average height, athletic build, and clearly defined features, Olivier was handsome enough even without the aid of artifice to play romantic leads on both stage and screen, achieving stardom in the films of *Rebecca* and *Wuthering Heights*. His voice was by nature a light baritone, and lacked the musicality associated especially with Gielgud. His delivery could be clipped, but characteristically he varied it from role to role. His speaking of Richard III's opening lines, 'Now is the winter of our discontent', famously parodied by Peter Sellers, is not typical; Olivier wrote that, while seeking a voice appropriate to this character, 'it came to me: the thin reed of a sanctimonious scholar. I started putting it on at once. It arrived and set the vision going: thin and rapier-like, but all-powerful. Somewhere between the bridge of the nose and the sinuses at first.'[4]

Skilful though he was at varying his delivery, his inherent vocal characteristics played a part in defining his repertory. As I have said, some critics found him unmusical as Romeo, especially by comparison with Gielgud, and it is hard—though not, I find, impossible—to imagine him in such primarily lyrical roles as Richard II, Oberon, or Prospero, or in psychologically complex, inwardly probing ones such as Brutus or Leontes, none of which he played professionally. Yet having said this, one has to acknowledge that he made a success of the most introspective of all Shakespearian characters, Hamlet, and that he took us deep into the inward recesses of unselfknowing Coriolanus.

The accusation sometimes made that Olivier turned verse into prose is an unconscious tribute to the virtuosity with which, in his maturity, he achieved an impression of naturalism while making full use of Shakespeare's verse structures; he trained himself rigorously to acquire the vocal control required for some of Shakespeare's more complex speeches, and analysis of recordings is enough to show his respect for rhythm and line endings. He didn't sing Shakespeare's verse, but he used and moulded it with the skill of a great orator. He could be vibrantly heroic, as in the war speeches of Henry V, but also irresistibly seductive, as with Lady Anne in *Richard III*. If he had a fault, or at least a limitation as an actor, it is that the self-conscious artifice of his acting drew attention to itself in a way that caused spectators to undervalue his penetration into the minds and hearts of the characters he portrayed.

Like Gielgud before him in 1929–31, Olivier played a sequence of great Shakespeare roles at the Old Vic in 1937 and 1938, when he was 30 years old, and in doing so gained greatly in stature as a Shakespearian. Full of ambition, he wanted, he wrote, 'to be completely different in every performance' of the season.[5] First came a highly extrovert, full-text *Hamlet* directed by Tyrone Guthrie which, though it divided critical opinion, was a popular triumph. Actor and director, influenced by Freudian theory as expounded by Ernest Jones, sought to portray a Hamlet driven by an Oedipus complex, but for some critics Olivier's extrovert athleticism, finding an outlet in an astonishing nose-dive of exultation at the climax of the play scene and a daringly adventurous duel at the close, distracted attention from the character's inwardness.

The acrobatic, farcical Sir Toby Belch that followed appears to have done more for Olivier's ego than for the play; heavily made up, he was, wrote the critic of *The Times*, 'now and then recognizable only by a gleam of teeth'.[6] And his Henry V began shakily because he distrusted what he saw as the jingoism of the role, though his performance grew in stature during the run and later formed the basis for the highly successful wartime film. In the *Macbeth* that followed in a gimmicky, heavily stylized production by Michel Saint-Denis, Olivier was so heavily made up that his then wife, Vivien Leigh, said, 'Larry's make-up comes on, then Banquo comes on, then Larry comes on.'[7] He himself wrote, 'I had a huge false face on: a nose that went down straight from the forehead, a false chin and a putty forehead with vast eyebrows. The idea was to make something real through a highly poetic and unreal approach.'[8] James Agate, praising 'some magnificent vocal effects', presciently wrote, 'Mr Olivier will probably play this part twice as well when he has twice his present years.'[9]

For Iago to Ralph Richardson's Othello in 1938, Olivier and Guthrie turned again to Ernest Jones who, he writes, contended

that Iago was subconsciously in love with Othello and had to destroy him. Unfortunately there was not the slightest chance of Ralph entertaining this idea. I was however determined upon my wicked intentions, in cahoots with Tony [Guthrie]; we constantly watched for occasions when our diagnosis might be made apparent to the discriminating among the audience, though I must say I have never yet discovered any means of divulging something that is definitely *subconscious* to any audience, no matter how discerning they may be. In a reckless moment during rehearsals I threw my arms round Ralph and kissed him full on the lips. He coolly disengaged himself from my embrace, patted me gently on the back of the neck and, more in sorrow than in anger, murmured 'There, there now; dear boy; good boy...' Tony and I dropped all secret connivance after that.[10]

Richardson was badly miscast as Othello. Agate described his performance as 'an almost total failure', and thought that Olivier played Iago as a 'super-subtle dilettante, looking upon the murder of another man's spirit not only as a fine art, but as a highly amusing one to boot'.[11] Olivier himself, more straightforwardly, wrote that because Richardson was 'boring' he played Iago 'entirely for laughs'.[12] *Coriolanus*, directed by Lewis Casson at the end of this season with Sybil Thorndike as Volumnia in a more sober fashion than the productions of Guthrie and Saint-Denis, provided Olivier with another great role which, like Macbeth, he was to take on again even more successfully later in his career.

Olivier was in America at the start of the Second World War and, except for a disastrous New York production of *Romeo and Juliet* in which he starred with Vivien Leigh, his stage career went into abeyance, interrupted both by filming and by National Service until 1944. The Old Vic Theatre, badly damaged in air raids, was not to reopen until 1951, but in 1944 Olivier along with Richardson was invited to form a new Old Vic company playing at the New Theatre in St Martin's Lane. The desire to demonstrate versatility is clear again from his diverse choice of roles: he played Richard III, Hotspur, Justice Shallow, and, aged 39, directed himself as King Lear. In his racy, unbuttoned book *On Acting* he provocatively describes Lear as 'an easy part'.[13] But this performance too split opinions. Alan Dent called it a 'tremendous achievement',[14] but Kenneth Tynan, in his self-consciously brilliant book *He That Plays the King*, was not over-impressed. It was, he wrote, 'an absorbing display, but in no way a great Lear'.[15] And, naughtily, 'it merely introduced us to a few wholly unexpected facets of the private life of Mr. Justice Shallow'.[16]

I first saw Olivier during the Old Vic season of 1949, from a seat in the gods, in a revival of *Richard III* which had opened in 1947. It was a formative experience. As was the custom then, the theatre orchestra played till curtain up. We settled down, a spotlight shone, and he emerged, humpbacked, at the right of the stage from a door which, with a complicit glance at us, he locked behind him. He loped forwards, and 'Now is the winter of our discontent...'. We were off, and I was hooked for life.

His virtuosity was well served by this role. Like many great actors of the past—Kean, another great Richard III, is the most obvious parallel—he excelled in mercurial transitions which could be brilliantly comic. Tynan describes the virtuosity with which he reacted when the newly executed Hastings's head was brought to him in a bag: 'he peeps in with wistful intentness, looking almost elegiac—then, after a pause, hurriedly turns the bag as he realizes he has been looking at the head upside down'.[17] He switched dazzlingly from affability to contempt as, enthroned, he stretched out his hand and brought Buckingham to his knees with 'I am not in the giving vein'. Mock-humility turned in an instant to exultant self-satisfaction as he fooled the Mayor of London into supporting his cause. He was daringly athletic as he slid rapidly down a bell-rope in glee after this success. And, lying on his back, his legs waving in the air like a great black beetle, he crowned the performance with horrifying death throes.

After the Old Vic seasons Olivier went into management himself and set up a season at the St James's Theatre which, in 1951, showcased both himself and his wife, Vivien Leigh, in Shaw's *Caesar and Cleopatra* and Shakespeare's *Antony and Cleopatra*. Critics suspected that he subdued his own performances to boost her success, but I have two abiding memories of his Antony. One is of his complex manipulation of sympathies in his sudden tenderness towards his household servants as he foreshadowed his defeat, making even Enobarbus 'onion-eyed' (4.2.35); this was interior acting of great potency. My other memory is of a piece of subtly contrived stage action; in his attempt to kill himself, with apparent clumsiness he caused his sword to fly from his hands on to a level where he strove in vain to reach it in order to give himself the *coup de grâce*, and so had ignominiously to call on the guard to 'make an end' (4.15.105) of him.

Four years later, in 1955, Olivier returned to the theatre in Stratford-upon-Avon where as a boy he had played Katherine the shrew, this time as Malvolio in a production of *Twelfth Night* directed by John Gielgud. Tynan vented his customary spleen on the unfortunate Vivien Leigh, comparing her verse-speaking as Viola to the sound of 'steady rain on a corrugated tin roofing', while finding Olivier's Malvolio 'a diverting exercise, but scarcely the substance of Sir Laurence's vocation'.[18] That vocation found full flowering, however, a few months later when Olivier returned to Macbeth in a production by Glen Byam Shaw. By now his formidable technique was at the service of his interpretative powers. He later wrote, 'I was the right age for the production at Stratford, and at my peak: no mask-like make-up was required.... I had the bellows and I understood the play.'[19] The critics agreed. T. C. Worsley wrote that he 'made every syllable, every consonant and vowel do its maximum of work, and had appreciated every nuance of the weight and feel of the words'.[20] And for J. C. Trewin, Olivier 'presented frighteningly the death of a soul: the lingering suicide of this man with a warrior's bearing that slackened to shoulders hunched beneath the giant's robe as he spoke out his heart in those images of darkness and death'.[21] In the same season, aided and abetted by Peter Brook, he followed his Macbeth with a *Titus Andronicus* which showed that, given sympathetic treatment, this early tragedy, flawed and dated though it is, can form the vehicle for a central performance of profound emotional intensity. The critical reaction was one of universally astonished acclamation. 'Olivier', wrote Trewin, 'had thought himself into the hell of Titus; we forgot the inadequacy of the words in the splendour of their projection.'[22] This was creative acting which released previously unsuspected energies from a neglected text.

Olivier's second Coriolanus was directed by Peter Hall in 1959, the same season that Charles Laughton as Bottom was parodying his death throes as Richard III.[23] The warrior hero is often thought of as forbiddingly austere, an inhuman fighting machine, but Olivier, while not shirking the man's physical heroism, humanized him with touches of comedy and revelatory moments of self-understanding. His arrogance was so extreme as to be comic in itself. I hear still, after half a century, 'The fires i' th' lowest hell fold in the people', with a great vocal leap on the last syllable. And he achieved a stunning effect by silently mouthing rather than voicing the final word in 'mildly be it then, mildly' in response to Volumnia's plea that he moderate his anger. He held a long, long silence with profound intimations of inner conflict as, holding Volumnia's hand, he yielded to her entreaties on behalf of his family and of Rome. In the final moments his voice soared with immeasurable contempt in ''tis there | That, like an eagle in a dovecote, I | Fluttered your Volscians in Corioles', elongating 'I' in a way that threw devastating emphasis on 'Fluttered', the syllables crashing against one another like squawking birds. And he died with a return to the old athleticism. Beleaguered by his enemies, he was forced up the stage steps to the rostrum on which he had made his initial entry and from which he had denounced the citizens in 'You common cry of curs'. Aufidius' soldiers advanced upon him and toppled him over backwards so that he swung by the heels, dangling in the air as Aufidius stabbed him in the belly before he was lowered to the stage. We leapt half out of our seats.

A great if politically incorrect Othello in 1964 and a meticulously detailed, unusually sympathetic Shylock of 1970 achieved in the face of illness and stage fright completed Olivier's Shakespearian roles onstage. He died in 1989, and was honoured with a memorial service in Westminster Abbey which was so theatrical an occasion that Gielgud reported a friend as saying that it should have been held in Drury Lane.

To see Olivier act Shakespeare was an event in one's life. 'Like Garrick, Kean, and Irving before him', wrote Michael Billington, he 'lent glamour and excitement to acting so that, in every theatre in the world, an Olivier night raised the level of expectation and sent spectators out into the darkness a little more aware of themselves and having experienced a transcendent touch of ecstasy'.[24]

Figure 27.1. Peggy Ashcroft as Queen Margaret in *The Wars of the Roses*, Royal Shakespeare Theatre, Stratford-upon-Avon, 1963: photograph by Tom Holte. Tom Holte Theatre Photographic Collection © Shakespeare Birthplace Trust

Peggy Ashcroft

1907–91. *Principal Shakespeare roles*: Queen Margaret, Kate, Juliet, Titania, Portia, Rosalind, Ophelia, Desdemona, Emilia, Cleopatra, Queen Katherine, Countess of Roussillon.

Rather like Sybil Thorndike, Peggy Ashcroft was not only a great actress but also a woman of high intelligence and passionate social commitment, devoting herself especially to the cause of nationally subsidized theatre companies. More conventionally beautiful and less resolutely monogamous than Dame Sybil, she entranced audiences over a long and developing career during which she played many Shakespeare roles and also served as a member of the Advisory Directorate of the Royal Shakespeare Company. Also like Dame Sybil she came from a middle-class family with artistic, especially literary, leanings. Her mother was a keen amateur actress who would have taken up the stage as a career if that had been socially acceptable.

As a girl Peggy fell for Ralph Richardson after seeing him perform Mark Antony and Henry V with the Charles Doran Company. She read avidly about the theatre, taking a special interest in Henry Irving and Ellen Terry, while also devouring both the plays and the music and theatre criticism of Bernard Shaw. (So, incidentally, did I.) Under the influence of an inspirational teacher she (like Olivier) played Shakespearian roles, including a Shylock modelled on Irving's, in school productions. At the age of 16 she even turned down the role of Hamlet because she insisted on leaving school early to train for the stage at Elsie Fogerty's acting school. Her fellow student Laurence Olivier vividly described her appearance at this time: 'Her eyes were strong, very dark, almost almond-shaped but by no means always kindly. Her looks were those of a serious person; her nose was right for her face, sizeable with an even, downward curve. Her voice was predictably remarkable; its pitch was that of a richly skilled bass-baritone.'[1] (If she really had the vocal tones of a Bryn Terfel it must soon have risen greatly in pitch.) Each year students of the school were required to declaim from the stage of the Albert Hall to the Royal Box. 'Out of that', writes Michael Billington in his excellent biography, 'must have come one of the most priceless gifts for an actor or actress: a voice that can hit the back of a theatre effortlessly.'[2]

In her younger years she was suited primarily to the lighter side of the Shakespearian repertory, the romantic heroines (along with Juliet), Ophelia, and Titania; as the years passed she succeeded in weightier roles, including Cleopatra, Emilia, Paulina, and, outstandingly, the Queen Margaret of the early histories, later mellowing into Queen Katherine and, finally, the Countess in *All's Well That Ends Well*. She never played the more anguished heroines, Isabella and, more surprisingly, Helen, or the heaviest roles such as Goneril, Constance, Gertrude, Lady Macbeth, and Volumnia, though on the evidence of her Queen Margaret they would not have been outside her range, at least in her later years.

While she was at drama school she read Stanislavsky's newly published *My Life in Art* (1924) and was inspired both by his teaching about acting and by his passionate commitment to a company ideal. She was profoundly influenced too by seeing low-budget productions of Russian plays in translation directed in a tiny suburban theatre by Theodore Komisarjevsky, who would later become her second husband. His company included both John Gielgud and Charles Laughton. At the age of 18 she made her professional debut at the Birmingham Repertory Theatre, playing opposite her childhood hero Ralph Richardson in James Barrie's *Dear Brutus*. Her early links with most of the other great British actors of the early part of the twentieth century were completed when she played a one-line role in Nigel Playfair's 1927 Hammersmith production of *The Way of the World* which brought stardom to Edith Evans.

I saw and admired many of Peggy Ashcroft's later performances in Shakespearian and other roles. Of average height and with a youthfully slim figure which filled out gracefully in her mature years, she could radiate warmth and charm. Her highly distinctive voice, somewhat upper-class in accent by nature and controlled by immaculate precision of diction, had a bell-like purity that could encompass a wide range of emotional states from tenderness to ferocity. A fine reader—she was a founder member of the Apollo Society, chaired by her friend George Rylands, which organized recitals of poetry and music initially for wartime audiences—she was equally responsive to the rhythms of verse and of prose. The passion that she demonstrated both in her private life and in her public support of causes that she supported communicated itself easily through her acting. She commanded attention through movement and gesture as well as through voice and facial expression. Even her silences were eloquent: she was a great listener.

Her first professional Shakespeare role was as Desdemona to Paul Robeson's Othello, in 1930, when she was only 22. The production, which left much to be desired, was marred by technical problems on its press night, but Gielgud later wrote that 'when Peggy came on in the Senate scene it was as if all the lights in the theatre had suddenly gone up. Later, in the handkerchief scene, I shall never forget her touching gaiety as she darted about the stage, utterly innocent and light-hearted, trying to coax and charm Othello from his angry questioning.'[3] Two years later she played her first Juliet, in the Oxford University Dramatic Society production directed by Gielgud which was to form the basis of the London production three years later starring himself, Laurence Olivier, and Edith Evans as well as Peggy. In the meantime, from 1932 to 1933, like Olivier, Gielgud, and Edith Evans before her, still in her mid-twenties, she undertook the treadmill of playing a succession of major Shakespeare roles—ten of them, including Cleopatra, Imogen, Juliet again, and Rosalind—in low-budget productions with limited rehearsal time for three-week runs at Lilian Baylis's Old Vic. The strain showed and she received some poor notices, Farjeon for instance describing her Portia as 'weak work'[4] (though according to Michael Billington it was 'intelligent, refined and refreshingly natural'[5]); even so, Laurence Kitchin was able to write in romantic retrospect that 'Ashcroft's performances had the effect of very sweet woodwind interludes in a robust symphony'. She had 'a kind of distilled essence of sex which humanized the lyrical heroines, who seem too hearty or too knowing when the average actress attempts them'.[6]

It was Gielgud's 1935 restaging of *Romeo and Juliet* in London that established Peggy Ashcroft as a star. Peter Fleming wrote enthusiastically:

There is a triumphant beauty in Miss Peggy Ashcroft's Juliet, a passion not to be gainsaid: from the first we tremble for the child who challenges with such a love the inauspicious stars. Technically her performance is perfection: there is no one like her for conveying the sense of a difficult passage without, so to speak, being caught in the act. She does more than make Shakespeare's expression of Juliet's thoughts seem natural: she makes it seem inevitable.[7]

Her rapport with Gielgud bore more fruit in later years. Among other roles she played the Queen to his Richard II in 1937, Portia to his Shylock in 1938, Ophelia to his 1944 Hamlet, and Titania to his Oberon in 1945. She took over from Diana Wynyard as Beatrice to his Benedick in revivals of his 1949 production of *Much Ado About Nothing*, which became a classic, each of them in top form in their scenes together so that, wrote Worsley, 'they set off each other's best points, call out in each other the highest art'.[8] And as Cordelia to his Lear in 1950 she showed how much she could do with silence; 'She has,' wrote Worsley in the *New Statesman*, 'more than any other actress, the power of touching us simply by her posture and the atmosphere she distils. The change from anxiety to a flooding relief here is beautifully done. Her "no cause, no cause" is marvellously dropped like two reassuring tears of forgiveness.'[9]

Paired with Redgrave at Stratford in 1953 she returned for the last time to the role of Portia. Michael Billington's account of her playing of the trial scene demonstrates her thoughtful approach to the text. She 'had plotted its progress with due care'.

Peggy says that when Portia comes on she knows exactly what the quibble will be and she has been told that she must try to let Shylock recant. She gives Shylock three opportunities or three loopholes in which to change his mind. He rejects them. She brings him to the point of admitting that he wants to murder Antonio. Then, having opened the trap for him, Portia strikes with 'Tarry a little, there is something else.' As Peggy remarks, 'There are those who think Portia is extremely cruel both to Shylock and Antonio, but I see her as an extraordinary mixture of legality and humanity.'[10]

Tynan wrote lyrically of her performance as 'the jewel of the evening', praising the new-minted quality of her verse speaking and the wit, good manners, and compassion with which she invested the role.[11]

Reviews of her subsequent Cleopatra to Redgrave's Antony show that while most critics felt that she did not encompass every facet of the complex character, she surpassed expectation at many points of her performance. Worsley wrote, 'Miss Ashcroft could always be counted on to do the long close beautifully, and high and lonely in her purple she conducted it with a rare feeling for the tragic poetry. Less foreseeable was the variety she injected into her moods and the range she found in the earlier scenes, the humour, the languor and the heat.'[12]

Her capacity to accept a challenge was demonstrated in 1960 when, aged 52, she played Kate to the 26-year-old firebrand Peter O'Toole's Petruccio in John Barton's witty yet richly romantic production of *The Taming of the Shrew*. Their quarrel scenes crackled with both sexual tension and nervous energy, carrying us along with the delighted expectation of the unexpected that is one of theatre's highest pleasures. A great moment came on their journey back to Padua when, apparently subdued to her husband's will, she apologizes to old Vincentio for addressing him as a woman.

> Pardon, old father, my mistaking eyes
> That have been so bedazzled with the . . .

Turning her head, she then spoke 'sun' with a cheeky upward inflexion as if seeking her husband's agreement that it was indeed not the moon while at the same time making it perfectly clear that they were now in full accord. In the final scene Petruccio sang patiently and played on his lute as he waited to see if, against all expectation, she would not only win his bet for him but seal the love that had grown between them by appearing at his command. Peggy Ashcroft made a radiantly beautiful moment of her perfectly timed entry to make a public avowal of her transformation before speaking her long speech as a declaration not of submission but of fully trusting love. Under feminist influences *The Taming of the Shrew* has become an unfashionable play, but this interpretation of the lovers made it, for me, completely acceptable as a fulfilled romance, enhanced by the production's emphasis, by using the full Christopher Sly framework, on the shrew story as romantic dream.

In this same season, with true company spirit, she undertook two roles which, though of the second rank, might have been written for her. Laurence Kitchin wrote of her Emilia to Gielgud's ill-judged Othello, 'She knows what all this is about, verse, character, place in the crisis, all of it. For me this is the definitive Emilia.'[13] And in *The Winter's Tale* she invested Paulina, who can be shrewish, with a rare depth of humanity.

The greatest challenge was still to come. In 1964 the Royal Shake-speare Company celebrated the four hundredth anniversary of Shake-speare's birth by putting on *The Wars of the Roses*, a sequence of three plays audaciously but triumphantly adapted, abbreviated, and restruc-tured from the then rarely performed early histories along with *Richard III* by John Barton, who controversially contributed some 1,400 lines of his own composition. Performed sometimes as a sequence in a single day, this was epic theatre, and Dame Peggy, playing Queen Margaret from the young, beautiful—and rapidly adulterous—bride of Henry VI to the aged crone of *Richard III*, gave an epic performance, virtuosic in its development from youthful sexiness to aged despair. J. W. Lambert traced the character's progress:

Young and beautiful, wary and passionate, she is won by the Earl of Suffolk for his king and for himself. Frustrated and impatient she moves like a gadfly among the beef-witted lords of England, breaks out, takes the field against them, and in a terrifying scene baits the captured Duke of York, slaps him across the face with a napkin soaked in his own child's blood . . . and, barely tolerated, old and dismayed, haunts the infinitely haunted court of Richard, her very fingers gnarled with loathing; an appalling portrait, drawn with fierce sensual splendour, of the feminine principle at work in a masculine world.[14]

And Philip Hope-Wallace, describing it as 'a most marvellous perform-ance', admired 'the energy of it for a start: things fairly began to *buzz* every time she came on. It was as if the whole play and everyone on stage took a charge of electricity. Then, the sheer protean range . . . It was one of the most gradually "growing" performances I have seen.'[15] It was powerfully supported by Donald Sinden's Duke of York; an onstage recording of the great scene in which she taunts him about his young son's death has been commercially issued.

This was the climax of Dame Peggy's Shakespearian career. Two more roles were to come. In 1969 she returned to Stratford with Donald Sinden again, playing Queen Katherine to his Henry VIII. Garry O'Connor wrote that she endowed 'each moment of humble and downtrodden Queen Katherine's progress to a dignified end, with an emotional truth which is the crown of great technical achievement; there is, in each line, a life-time's work'.[16] And finally, in 1981, she crowned her career—like Edith Evans before her and Judi Dench after—with the Countess in Trevor Nunn's picturesquely nat-uralistic, Edwardian production of *All's Well That Ends Well*. As always, the role was freshly thought through. She made a success of one of the play's most difficult scenes, the Countess's interview with the clown Lavatch. Guthrie had funked this altogether in his great production of 1959. Here, I wrote in *The Times Literary Supplement*, Nunn had Geoffrey Hutchings perform him

as a physically deformed appendage of the Countess's household, sweeping the floor, occasionally entrusted with messages. Peggy Ashcroft exquisitely defines an indulgent tolerance of his winking and blinking presence, treating him as a simpleton with his own kind of shrewdness and power to amuse. For once, and with her help, his set-piece on 'O Lord, Sir' becomes genuinely comic. The precision of Dame Peggy's characterization shifts the balance of her role away from poetic generality to personal expression. 'Even so it was with me when I was young' is not (as Edith Evans made it) a meditation but a statement. This is a practical woman, warm in her sympathies but capable of ironic detachment, most moving in the little scene with her Steward (Bert Parnaby) in which she expresses the dilemma of her divided affections and confesses her grief.[17]

Shakespeare and the Old Vic remained with her to the end: as the finale of the gala performance given in that theatre to celebrate her eightieth birthday she spoke Rosalind's Epilogue to *As You Like It* before disappearing into the wings.

Figure 28.1. Michael Redgrave as Richard II, Shakespeare Memorial Theatre, Stratford-upon-Avon, 1951: photograph by Angus McBean. Angus McBean © Royal Shakespeare Company

Michael Redgrave

1908–85. *Principal Shakespeare roles*: Orlando, Richard II, Hotspur, Macbeth, Prospero, Antony, Benedick, Hamlet, Lear, Berowne, Claudius.

Born of theatrical parents, and destined to become father and grand-father to distinguished actors, most famously his daughter Vanessa, Michael Redgrave, unlike his greatest contemporaries, was university-educated. His handsome father, Roy, played Hamlet at the Britannia Theatre, Hoxton, in North London, where he was billed as 'the Dramatic Cock of the North', in the 1890s. He died in Australia before reaching the age of 50. Michael's mother, known professionally as Margaret Scudamore, was an actress who became a member of the Stratford Memorial Theatre company in 1921, when the 13-year-old Michael was allowed to walk on, showering the newly crowned Henry V with rose petals at the climax of *Henry IV, Part Two*.

As a boy at Clifton College in Bristol he showed early talent as a pianist and writer as well as an actor, winning his mother's admiration as Lady Macbeth. At the end of the sleepwalking scene, she wrote to him, 'You not only seemed to be asleep, you bowed your head just before the end of the scene and your head seemed to droop as though you were tired to death—a lovely bit of business.'[1]

At the age of 18 he made his first professional appearances in a non-speaking role in two matinees of *The Taming of the Shrew* directed by Ben Greet. While on an educational trip to France he was immensely impressed by seeing the great actor Louis Jouvet in his signature role, Dr Knock, in the satire by Jules Romains; Jouvet's ideas about acting were to have a profound influence on him. At Cambridge he glittered as both writer and athlete and attracted the attention of the glamorous young don George Rylands, six years his senior, who for many years was to exert a major influence on British Shakespeare production through his teaching and his productions for the Marlowe Society— at that time an all-male institution—and his influential friendships with many undergraduates, male and female, who took up theatre as a profession.

Rylands, who placed great emphasis on the importance of fine verse speaking, coaxed the initially reluctant Redgrave into playing Edgar in his production of *King Lear*, saying that if he did so he would 'get to know Shakespeare . . . in exactly the same way you would get to know Mozart by playing first violin in a symphony'.[2] Redgrave had a great success in the role, but after leaving Cambridge worked for a couple of years as a schoolteacher at Cranleigh, near Guildford, where he directed a number of productions. In the first, *As You Like It*, he played only the tiny role of Hymen but made a sensational entrance 'down the central aisle, dressed from head to foot in gold with a golden make-up including glittering golden sequins on his eyelids and followed by a retinue of near-naked golden putti'.[3] Still at Cranleigh he directed and starred in productions of Milton's *Samson Agonistes* and of *Hamlet* and *The Tempest* which attracted attention far beyond the bounds of the school while also undertaking some semi-professional acting with the Guildford Repertory Company. His final production as a teacher was a *King Lear*—starring himself, of course—which won golden opinions from such good judges as George Rylands, G. Wilson Knight, and William Poel. By now Michael was poised to take off on a professional career as an actor, and after an inconclusive audition for Lilian Baylis— who told him he waved his hands around too much—at the Old Vic, joined the Liverpool Playhouse in 1934.

Exceptionally tall at 6 feet 3 inches, athletically elegant, handsome in a British public school, Rupert Brooke style with regular features, wide-set, bright blue eyes, and a light, flexible voice, Redgrave possessed natural attributes that directed him towards lyrical, poetical, and wittily comic roles rather than to the harshly villainous or heavily tragic end of the repertoire. Like Gielgud, he was not a Richard III, a Titus Andronicus, or a Coriolanus. Nor would he have been a natural for the inner torments of Angelo or Leontes. He played Romeo only in a single charity matinee performance of the balcony scene and never undertook Mercutio, a role to which, with his mercurial intelligence and bravura elocutionary skills, he would have been ideally suited.

Redgrave was sometimes criticized for over-intellectuality. Certainly he thought long and hard about his art, and was exceptional in his capacity to formulate his ideas. His book *An Actor's Ways and Means*, based on lectures given at the University of Bristol, offers rare insights into the actor's craft. He distinguishes—not entirely pellucidly— between two kinds of actor, 'those who play primarily for effect and those who, whether by instinct or method, seek for cause before making their effect'. Elaborating on this he cites Jouvet, who had greatly impressed him in his youth, as distinguishing between the words *acteur* and *comédien*. The former

represents the 'personality actor', the man who can be relied on to go on and give a performance which may help the play to unfold its story, but who in so doing moulds a character in lines set by his own. The *comédien* . . . is the actor who, by sinking his own personality or by, as it were, translating or in some cases exceeding it, brings, according to Jouvet, something of the same creative process to bear on his part as the author has brought to the creation of the character.[4]

This difficult distinction becomes clearer, I think, when Redgrave speaks of a forgotten actor who 'was so complete an artist that he could appear in two leading parts in the same play without the audience knowing of it'. This, I take it, is what Jouvet would have called a *comédien*. Redgrave then speaks of such actors as 'protean', remarking that 'Signing away that intensification of their own personalities, we remember them not as one person but as many'.[5] I take it that he wished to class himself as a *comédien*, a protean actor, and perhaps that as a result he would not be surprised to find that he has come to be regarded as less of a 'star' than others of his generation. Yet it is inordinately difficult to apply these distinctions to other actors whose work I am discussing. I have written that Guthrie described both Olivier and Thorndike as 'protean'. And my guess is that Redgrave, at least, would have regarded Wolfit as an *acteur*, someone who was always recognizable even behind thick layers of make-up, and Edith Evans, like himself, as a *comédien*. One could make quite a party game of trying to fit the other actors of this book into one or other of these categories.

Redgrave played two Shakespeare roles—Horatio and Malvolio—in Liverpool before moving on to the Old Vic in 1936. There he under- took second-string roles—Ferdinand, King of Navarre, in *Love's*

Labour's Lost, Laertes in *Hamlet*, and Bolingbroke in *Richard II*—in plays in which he would later star with great success. He made a good initial impression as Ferdinand before scoring his first big hit as a rapturous, physically commanding Orlando—also often considered an unreward-ing role—to Edith Evans's Rosalind. Audrey Williamson, chronicler of the Old Vic, writes that 'He made the youth a handsome, well-spoken stripling, with a strong measure of charm and enough virility to force one to believe him when he said he felt the spirit of his father grow strong within him'.[6] Soon afterwards he won high praise as Laertes to Olivier's Hamlet, achieving a real sense of relationship with his father, Polonius, and fighting a thrilling final duel with Hamlet. It was in this production that Olivier, one Saturday night, presciently announced at curtain-call to a thrilled audience, 'A great actress has been born. Laertes has a daughter!', thus heralding Vanessa Redgrave into the world.

Having played second string to Olivier in *Hamlet*, Redgrave went on to do the same with the other reigning young star, Gielgud, by playing Bolingbroke in his picturesquely designed and strongly cast production of *Richard II*. Again, physically impressive and no less eloquent in the character's silences than in his speeches, he showed that he too had star quality.

Soon after this, in 1938, he demonstrated his comedic skills as Sir Andrew Aguecheek, giving the only well-received performance in an ill-designed and generally unsuccessful production of *Twelfth Night* directed at the Phoenix Theatre by Michel Saint-Denis. After this, there was a long period during which, making a reputation as a film star as well as serving in the Royal Navy, he played no Shakespeare. The return came in 1947 when, for the first time since his teaching days, he took on one of the major tragic roles. His Macbeth at the Aldwych in 1947 had a mixed reception. Accounts of the staging, with three additional witches on stilts and a 'special effects empty chair with a movable arm'[7] standing in for Banquo's ghost in a clumsily staged banquet scene, make it sound distinctly odd. Criticism of his verse speaking, usually much admired, may result from the fact that, accord-ing to Redgrave's biographer, Alan Strachan, he 'had consciously roughened his voice as part of his concept of Macbeth as a violent man in a barbaric society'.[8] Ivor Brown wrote that he left 'Macbeth the poet almost unnoticed',[9] and the critic of *The Times* complained of 'the monotonous hoarseness of his speech'.[10] According to Tynan,

'Mr Redgrave did all that lungs of leather and power of movement could do for Macbeth, but it was not enough.'[11] But T. C. Worsley, a thoughtful critic, praised this as 'a designed production, an attempt to give a considered and rounded version of a play, instead of a series of virtuoso performances of parts'. And he found that 'Mr Redgrave within the limits that he sets himself—and they are proper limits—gives a performance that commands our acceptance, fine and finished, with the gradations exactly marked, and movingly rendered'.[12] Well over sixty years on, I have two main memories of this production. One is of Redgrave seated on a table and violently smashing his boot into the face of the kneeling 'cream-faced loon' who brings him news that the English army is advancing upon him. The other is of Ena Burrill, as Lady Macbeth, coming into view from my seat at the top of the gallery feet first as she descended the bedroom stairs in the sleepwalking scene.

The heyday of Redgrave's Shakespearian career came from 1949 to 1958, during which he played a succession of great roles, both comic and tragic, first in London, then in Stratford-upon-Avon. At the age of 42 he came inevitably if rather late to the role of Hamlet at the Old Vic in a rather unsatisfactory production by Hugh Hunt. Still slim, handsome, dignified in bearing and athletic in movement, looking rather like J. P. Kemble in the portrait by Lawrence, he presented, wrote Audrey Williamson, 'a golden-haired and romantic prince, with the height and natural grace of royalty and the effect, not of an unseasoned and sensitive student, but a man of ripened youth and maturity of mind'.[13] His speaking of this role won nothing but praise, Worsley writing of his 'absolute mastery of the vocal line. . . . It is an exemplary performance as a piece of verse-speaking, without tricks, mannerisms or affectations, but immensely various, always absolutely true, always perfectly in tune.'[14] The actress Joan Plowright, then a student, compared his speaking favourably with Olivier's in the film version (unaware of course that Olivier would later become her husband), writing, 'He took the famous "To be or not to be" well down near the front of the stage, and so quietly and simply . . . he had his hands behind him and just brought his right hand forward at the end to make one significant gesture which was the more beautiful for being the only one.'[15] (Clearly Lilian Baylis's advice about his hands had taken effect.) This was an intelligent, rational Hamlet, lacking perhaps the ultimate sense of mystery but immensely rewarding all the same.

For the Stratford-upon-Avon season of 1951 the newly appointed Artistic Director, Anthony Quayle, himself a fine actor, conceived the plan, unusual at the time, of staging the four plays of Shakespeare's second history cycle, with himself as Falstaff, as a sequence on a permanent set designed by Tanya Moiseiwitsch. He invited Redgrave to play Richard II, Hotspur, and the Chorus in *Henry V*, to direct *Henry IV, Part Two*, and in addition to play Prospero in the last play of the season. Redgrave's gilded, effete Richard II seems to have looked back in its appearance to his youthful Hymen in *As You Like It*. Playing up the text's openness to a homosexual interpretation, writes Strachan, he made the keynote of his performance

shame, the self-abasement of a once arrogant man forced to admit to his few remaining followers that he is, after all, as human as they, his voice unforgettably cracking after a daringly long pause between the confession 'I live with bread like you, feel want, taste grief' and the half-statement, half-plea of 'need friends'. He filled the pause with a world of emotion—hurt, bewilderment and shame—in another of those startlingly piercing moments of self-recognition that marked some of his greatest performances.[16]

Richard David described his Hotspur, played with a Northumbrian accent, as 'the greatest performance of his Shakespearean career', describing it as 'gallant, vigorous, and yet relaxed'.[17] In Michael Benthall's *Tempest* Prospero was onstage at the start (a mistake, in my opinion) and Redgrave won universal praise for what Worsley considered 'one of his very best performances', distilling 'an extraordinary human warmth and a dominating largeness of heart'.[18]

Stratford was the scene of more successes in 1953, starting with a full-blooded Shylock presented, wrote Harold Hobson, 'with overwhelming theatrical bravura',[19] followed by a triumphant Antony to Peggy Ashcroft's Cleopatra. It is a difficult role; we see little of Antony in action, and his death scene is decisively trumped by Cleopatra's; but Redgrave overcame its difficulties. He looked superb; 'with his height and physique, breastplate open to reveal a broad, bronzed chest, tousled auburn-gold hair and beard, he looked', writes Strachan, 'like something out of a Veronese allegorical painting'.[20] And Ivor Brown described this as 'a powerful, soldierly Antony, towering in arms as the descendant of Hercules should and burning with desire as the dissipated Roman must'.[21] It was followed by a climactic Lear, described by Strachan as 'a sometimes near clinical study of senility in the workings of his lower jaw or the way in which his body, straining to draw his broadsword, failed to match the force of his fury when Lear turns on Kent'.[22] Ivor Brown judged it 'a triumph for Michael Redgrave, a triumph gradually, carefully achieved and made certain at the close'.[23] And the actor-scholar Robert Speaight found that 'time and again we are caught up by the sweep and the surprise of great acting'.[24]

In 1958 Redgrave brought his gifts for high comedy back to Stratford as a dandyish Benedick, with Googie Withers as a well-matched Beatrice, in a charmingly designed if lightweight production of *Much Ado About Nothing*, sunnily set in 1850s Italy with crinolines and parasols. More adventurously, at the age of 50 he returned to the role of Hamlet, giving a deeply considered rethinking of the role in an uninspiring production. And finally he had a personal success as Hamlet's Uncle Claudius to Peter O'Toole's Hamlet in Olivier's sadly misconceived opening production of the National Theatre, in 1963.

♛

Paul Scofield

Figure 29.1. Paul Scofield as King Lear, Royal Shakespeare Theatre, Stratford-upon-Avon, 1962: photograph by Angus McBean. Angus McBean © Royal Shakespeare Company

1922–2008. *Principal Shakespeare roles*: Don Armado, Falconbridge, Richard II, Mercutio, Hamlet, Lear, Timon, Coriolanus, Prospero.

Paul Scofield was not an actor who could easily disguise himself. Quite early in his career the critic J. C. Trewin wrote of 'those high cheekbones, the forehead deep-lined beneath thick curling hair, the eyes dark under burdened brows, a tense nobility of profile'.[1] And it wasn't only the craggily handsome, Rembrandtesque face, wrinkled and furrowed as it grew older as if with untold depths of experience. Whatever the role, his voice was unmistakable too—gravelly with a nasal twang, baritonal but ample in range, subtle in inflection, capable of resonance and an almost other-worldly tenderness, the consonants precisely articulated even to the point of creating infinitesimal pauses between words. The gait—influenced, it appears, by a slight foot deformity—was unmistakable too, a long-legged 'loping stride', as Trewin put it.[2]

Yet for all Scofield's idiosyncratic distinctiveness he grew into an actor of exceptional range and transformative power, capable of projecting the eccentric comedy of a Don Armado, the introspection of Richard II and Hamlet, the blunt aggression of Coriolanus, and the tragic depths of Lear and of Timon of Athens.

Though theatre was not in his genes, he was drawn to acting from his schooldays, playing Juliet when he was 13, Rosalind soon afterwards, and Prince Hal when his voice had broken ('it is not mended yet', quipped Trewin many years later[3]). After training as an actor from the age of 17, first in Croydon then at the London Mask Theatre, where one of his teachers was Sybil Thorndike's younger sister Eileen, he became a professional at the age of 19, playing a wide range of roles, large and small, in repertory and touring companies. A defining career moment came when he joined Barry Jackson's Birmingham Repertory Company in 1944, not least because here he met the precocious genius Peter Brook, three years his junior, who was to direct many of his most important performances in plays by Shakespeare and other dramatists. The first of these was the scene-stealing role of Falconbridge, the Bastard, in *King John*; Trewin wrote of 'the extraordinary personal magnetism, the loping stride, eyes in which one could trace the growing thought, vocal gusts that almost startled the speaker'.[4]

In the following year Barry Jackson became director of the Shakespeare Memorial Theatre in nearby Stratford, and took Scofield with him. The Festival had been in the doldrums; Jackson's appointment was seen as a determined, and in the event successful, attempt to turn it round. In a punishing schedule reminiscent of Lilian Baylis's Old Vic, six Shakespeare plays along with Marlowe's *Dr Faustus* were presented within a five-month season; Scofield was in all of them. He made his mark. Of his opening performance in a shortened *Cymbeline* directed by Nugent Monck, T. C. Kemp wrote in the *Birmingham Post*, 'Paul Scofield makes much of Cloten, a character that could so easily be shown as nothing more than a clodpoll. Mr Scofield most ably suggests that the man has a life and mind of his own.' And, encouragingly, 'Intelligent performances of this kind are the sort of thing many of us are looking for under the new order at Stratford.'[5] Peter Brook's Watteauesque *Love's Labour's Lost* triumphantly reclaimed this great but previously neglected comedy for the repertory, and Scofield as Don Armado, wrote Trewin, 'managed to humanize a part that had been deemed almost unactable'.[6] Only as Henry V was he less than entirely successful, being found wanting in declamatory force, more convincing as the man than as the king.

Looking back over the season, Philip Hope-Wallace identified Scofield's ability to inhabit his characters while remaining himself, fancifully resorting to canine imagery as he wrote admiringly of his 'greyhound Lucio and bull-terrier Cloten with a Don Armado faintly reminiscent of an overbred and beautiful old borzoi'. The actor 'showed a most unusual gift for getting under the skin of half a dozen breeds, while retaining undiminished the full force of his own personality. He has a most marked flair for comedy of a certain kind and instantly gets on to terms with his audience in a way that speaks the born actor.'[7] Alan Dent was inspired by his Lucio to write, 'How the scene quickens whenever he crosses the stage. Here, undoubtedly, is that exciting thing—a fine actor in the making. He comes on apace like a chestnut-branch in bud.'[8] And Trewin, summing up the season, wrote, 'The Festival produced one new actor of first merit; Paul Scofield has an uncommon quality of attack and a leaping intelligence. . . . his Malcolm was the best in Stratford memory; only Henry V found him less than commanding.'[9]

This must have been most encouraging for an actor still in his early twenties, and it is not surprising that he was kept on at Stratford for the following two seasons both to repeat his Don Armado and to undertake a range of new roles. As Mercutio in Peter Brook's iconoclastic, sun-drenched, textually adventurous *Romeo and Juliet* of 1947 he was, wrote the 23-year-old Kenneth Tynan—'a great dramatic critic in the making' according to James Agate[10]—'not the noisy bragger who usually capsizes the play and then leaves it to founder, but a rapt goblin, ruddy and likeable (his pensive delivery of the Mab speech, with demoniac masquers grouped around him, crowns the scene with authentic faery)'.[11] Trewin too remembered the speech: 'One thinks of him now, stretched upon the stage in the torchlight, a great caped cloak flung about him, arm raised and eyes rapt as he let the speech flower into the silence of those grotesquely-visaged masquers.'[12] His biggest role this season was as the hero of the rarely performed *Pericles*, severely abbreviated, in which, wrote the critic of the *Manchester Guardian* (hedging his bets about the collaborative nature of the text), 'he dominated the production from start to finish; his command of the lines and usually Shakespearean music is instant and unmistakeable'.[13]

In 1948 his gift for eccentric comedy found an outlet in the role of the Clown in *The Winter's Tale*, 'a rare jewel of a character performance', wrote Agate's protégé Alan Dent: 'You feel that the oaf has a mind and a soul if only he could find them.'[14] Laura Knight portrayed him in this role from a vantage point in the wings. In addition to Troilus and Roderigo he was given his first chance to play Hamlet, though in a production designed primarily for Robert Helpmann, the great actor-dancer, with whom he alternated in the role. Not all who saw it liked the nineteenth-century costumes which, wrote one critic, made Scofield look like Nicholas Nickleby.[15] Worsley, noting that the production was designed for Helpmann's 'vivid, quicksilver conception', remarked that Scofield, 'the alternative Hamlet, had the difficult task of fitting himself into it. This much talked-of young actor certainly has gifts, youth, looks and, above all, attack.' But 'The pace was too much for him, and where Mr Helpmann brought it off by clever timing and subtle variations in pace, he too often simply scampered.'[16] Tynan, however, preferred Scofield's Hamlet to Gielgud's, Wolfit's, Alec Clunes's, and Jean-Louis Barrault's, and wrote presciently, 'I know that there is now in England a young actor who is bond-slave to greatness, and can stand beside the other exciting young men (Mr Benthall, Mr Ustinov, Mr Quayle) who are going to make our theatre in the coming decade a thing of great pride and fruition.'[17]

By now Scofield was ready for the West End, where Brook directed him again, this time playing twins in a two-year run of an exquisite production of *Ring Round the Moon*, translated by Christopher Fry from a play by Jean Anouilh. His next major excursion into Shakespeare was under the direction of John Gielgud, for whom in 1952 he played first the relatively undemanding role of Don Pedro in his immensely popular production of *Much Ado About Nothing* at the Phoenix Theatre in London. Gielgud—maddeningly if endearingly indecisive as a director—also directed him as Richard II at the Lyric Theatre Hammersmith. Gielgud's own greatness in this role seems to have had an inhibiting effect. His biographer, Jonathan Croall, writes, 'Scofield was constricted rather than released by the role, giving an intelligent but remote performance, that lacked the soaring, self-pitying lyricism of Gielgud's.'[18] Tynan, in a letter to Cecil Beaton, wrote, 'Everyone seemed to be sleep-walking, even Scofield.'[19] Three years later he gave his second Hamlet, directed this time by Peter Brook, in a Phoenix Theatre production which made a historic and triumphant visit to the Moscow Art Theatre, the first English company to perform in the city since 1917. But the triumph was not unequivocal. In a fascinating analysis, Tynan opens by describing why 'no living actor is better equipped for Hamlet'. 'On him the right sadness sits, and also the right spleen; his gait is a prowl over quicksands; and he can freeze a word with an irony at once mournful and deadly.' But, though the outline of the role is impeccable, 'what is surprising is the crude brushwork with which he fills it in.' He complains of mechanical gabbling, of a face which is 'a mask devoid of pathos', of excessive and self-conscious artifice in declamation.[20] Still, the production was a popular success with a London run of 124 performances.

After playing an inadequately documented Coriolanus in Napoleonic costume at Stratford Ontario in 1960, Scofield returned to Stratford-upon-Avon and to Peter Brook's direction in 1962 for what has come to be seen as the greatest Shakespearian performance of his career. His King Lear was a hard-won triumph. Brook's challenging production, variously described as Brechtian and Beckettian, defied tradition, both braving and, in some quarters, incurring unpopularity in its bleak austerity. When, for example, he caused Lear's knights to behave in the debauched and riotous fashion that Goneril complains of instead of interpreting hers as a false accusation, and allowed their master to encourage them, he was consciously breaking with tradition in a manner that reduced sympathy for the king. Scofield, shaping his interpretation to Brook's overall vision, gave an austere reading of the role, understated in suffering, denying to both the character and the audience the emotional release afforded by actors who rage more extrovertly against the coming of the dark. Gravel-voiced, crop-haired, bent with age (though the actor was only 40) but fully invested with the authority that Kent ascribes to him, this was a Lear who evoked sympathy in spite of himself. 'Lay him to rest,' wrote Tynan, 'the royal Lear with whom generations of star actors have made us reverently familiar.'[21] But the effect of Scofield's austerity on many members of the audience was no less devastating than the overt emotionalism of a Wolfit.

Lear was followed, logically enough, with the rarely played *Timon of Athens* in an inventive production also at Stratford of 1965 by John Schlesinger which made the most, in the play's well defined first half, of its social comedy. As Timon's sycophants began to show themselves in their true colours following his fall, Scofield charted his bewildered progress to disillusionment with touching skill. His speaking of 'To Lacedaemon did my lands extend' made us conscious of geographical vastness. His tirade against Athens at the opening of the second part as he tore off his garments bit like vitriol, the four syllables of 'detestable' in 'thou detestable town' spat out in individual gobbets. His slanging contest with Paul Rogers's well-matched Apemantus was exhilarating in its vehemence, and he found a withdrawn, other-worldly music for

> Timon hath made his everlasting mansion
> Upon the beachèd verge of the salt flood,
> Who once a day with his embossèd froth
> The turbulent surge shall cover.

Scofield had a West End success as Prospero in a production of *The Tempest* that originated at the Leeds Playhouse in 1974, but neither his Stratford Macbeth of 1967 nor his National Theatre Othello of 1980, with an ill-matched Iago from Michel Bryant, rivalled his earlier Shakespearian performances. He stars in Brook's fine 1970 film of *King Lear*, which is independent of the stage production, and appears briefly but memorably as the King of France in Branagh's film of *Henry V* (1989) and as the Ghost in Zeffirelli's *Hamlet* (1991). A modest man, he refused a knighthood twice, but was appointed Companion of Honour in 2001.

Figure 30.1. Donald Sinden as Malvolio in *Twelfth Night*, Royal Shakespeare Theatre, Stratford-upon-Avon, 1962: photograph by Joe Cocks. Joe Cocks Studio Collection © Shakespeare Birthplace Trust

Donald Sinden

1923–2014. *Principal Shakespeare roles*: Duke of York, Benedick, Malvolio, Othello, Lear, Henry VIII.

Donald Sinden was one of the most versatile of actors. A popular star of films both comic and serious and of stage comedy and farce, he succeeded too in Shakespeare roles ranging from Benedick to King Lear, Malvolio to Othello, and from the Duke of York in the early Histories to King Henry VIII. And his essay on playing Malvolio published in *Players of Shakespeare 1* (edited by Philip Brockbank, 1985) is a classic exposition of the art of comic acting.

A strongly robust figure allied to a deep, powerful, and flexible voice with impeccable enunciation qualified him for heroic roles. Twinkling eyes, a ready smile, and an extraordinary ease of rapport with his audiences were especially valuable in comedy. He was a great company man, genial, warm-hearted, good-humoured, a fount of knowledge about the history of the theatre and a raconteur of genius as well as a wit in his own right. Like Falstaff—a role to which he was ideally suited and which—sadly for us and for him—was denied him by the vagaries of our current theatre system—he was both witty in himself and the cause that wit was in other men.

Sinden's acting career started with amateur performances in Brighton. After training at the Webber Douglas Academy of Dramatic Art he joined the Leicester Repertory Company in 1946. He became a colleague of the young Paul Scofield at Stratford later that year, understudying him as Henry V and playing Dumaine along with lesser roles including Arviragus in *Cymbeline*. His speaking in the dirge won praise from Trewin, but there was no question that the honours of the season fell to Scofield. In 1947, however, he scored an unexpected success as Romeo, taking over from Laurence Payne, when the Stratford company moved to London; he records, claiming to disbelieve it, that Sybil Thorndike said he was 'the best Romeo she had ever seen'.[1] (She had gushed similarly about Olivier as Kate.)

Not until 1963 did Sinden return to Shakespeare and to Stratford, where his gifts for comedy blossomed in the role of the Duke in a revival of Clifford Williams's fine production of *The Comedy of Errors*, one of the few that I have seen which genuinely treated this early masterpiece as a romantic comedy rather than a farcical romp. In the final scene, as the confusions of the action are unfolding, the explanation for them begins to dawn on the Duke.

> Why, here begins his morning story right:
> These two Antipholus', these two so like,
> And these two Dromios, one in semblance—
> Besides his arguing of her wreck at sea.
> These are the parents to these children,
> Which accidentally are met together.

Sinden had the imagination to speak these lines not as if he knew what he would say from the beginning of the sentence but phrase by phrase as the explanation for the day's slowly events dawned upon him. 'It was', wrote Trewin, 'a joy to watch Donald Sinden's face as the Duke, after so much baffled listening, suddenly knows that it is all coming right and tries to explain it to his dimmest courtier.'[2]

It is a far cry from the Duke of Ephesus to the Duke of York in the early history plays, but that is the role, in John Barton's adaptation of them as *The Wars of the Roses*, in which, playing against Peggy Ashcroft's magnificent Queen Margaret, Sinden was able most strongly to demonstrate his powers as a heroic actor. This was, wrote Worsley, 'a performance of great power and depth, and, in the last terrible scene of his humiliation, noble as well'.[3] And the ubiquitous Trewin, praising his 'control of consonants and vowels', wrote '"Anjou and Maine are given to the French," and the last flare before death, are both examples of full-scale speaking that we find today very seldom'.[4]

Sinden's two finest comic performances were both given in great Stratford productions by John Barton of *Twelfth Night* (1969) and of *Much Ado About Nothing* (1976). His illuminating essay on playing Malvolio tells how he based the character's appearance on Graham

Sutherland's painting of Somerset Maugham: 'The eyebrows, the mouth, the wrinkles—every one of them vertical, and that is what I must be: vertical—the knees close together, the hair very thin on top but grown longer in an attempt to cover the balding pate, above all the colour—yellow, jaundiced.' This was complemented by costume: 'black, only relieved by very narrow plain, white collar and cuffs', along with 'a period hat like a black flower pot', and gold chain of office. The apparent spontaneity of the performance was achieved by rigorous self-control. 'I am now one-hundred-per-cent Malvolio, but in a comedy I, the actor, must remain one-hundred-per-cent myself, standing outside my character, my ears out on stalks listening for the very slightest sound from the audience, controlling them, so that I am able to steer a "cue", "punch", or "tag" line clear of any interruption. If on any night Malvolio takes over, the precision, the immaculate timing, the control, suffer.'[5] And as he analyses the role moment by moment he assesses on a scale of 1 to 10 the force of the laughter that he hopes to raise at individual points of the action. One of the heartiest outbursts came when, finding that the time told by his watch differed from that on a sundial, instead of correcting his watch he tried to move the sundial. It was a good laugh because it epitomized the character's self-centredness. Sinden's capacity to engage with the audience was nowhere more apparent than in his reading of the letter supposedly written by Olivia but actually planted by Sir Toby and his co-conspirators. The entire theatre became momentarily complicit with him.

Sinden's Benedick to Judi Dench's great Beatrice in Barton's Chekhovian *Much Ado About Nothing* was no less brilliantly calculated. The actors' partnership was, wrote Roger Warren, 'the main triumph of the production. . . . Predictable, of course; but that didn't decrease the sheer delight of hearing those brilliant lines delivered with such panache and relish, but more important still with such awareness of the human realities they imply . . . All the great moments went off superbly, and all were related to character and situation.'[6] Michael Dobson describes one of those great moments:

Audiences remember how he would sometimes perform the whole of his soliloquy at the end of the second act—in which Benedick, tricked into believing Beatrice loves him, gradually abandons his former opposition to marriage—as though remonstrating with increasing vehemence with a single chosen spectator in the stalls. He would make a tremendous, emphatically nodding climax of the line 'The world must be peopled', as though this were a clinching riposte with which to convince his obdurate opponent, and would then stomp triumphantly off—only to return a moment later, visibly calming himself, to offer the same spectator amends with a placatory, face-saving 'When I said I would die a bachelor, I did not think I would live till I were married'. Dench recalls finding Sinden so funny and so perpetually unexpected that she would sometimes be laughing too much to make her ensuing entrance.[7]

And as Roger Warren's remark about 'human realities' implies, neither his Benedick nor his Malvolio was an emptily farcical interpretation. Indeed J. W. Lambert went so far as to describe the latter as 'an almost Ibsenesque figure, a lightless torch of puritan ambition, appalled when others fail to play the role he allots them, all too easily gulled into thinking that they will'.[8]

In the same season Donald Sinden also played King Lear in a production directed jointly by Trevor Nunn, John Barton, and Barry Kyle. Somewhat eccentrically, and not very helpfully to the actor, the setting and costumes were updated to the late nineteenth century in a manner that, Trewin wrote, 'shouts at the text'.[9] Irving Wardle described Sinden 'stomping in like the aged Hindenburg, chewing a cigar and creakily heaving himself into his seat in absurd top-boots'.[10] The boots disturbed Trewin too: 'Sinden is a grand actor who now has to present a crumbling Stonehenge in top-boots.' Nevertheless 'he can summon the thunder; no one, after this, will deny his right to be among our first classical actors'.[11] And Michael Billington praised his 'brilliant insights'. He 'conveys madness's strange blend of muddle and clarity, chilling the heart with his sudden recognition of Gloucester in the Dover scene'.[12]

Some years later, in 1980, Sinden undertook his last tragic role, playing Othello in a Stratford production directed by Ronald Eyre. Billington wrote of Sinden and Bob Peck, as Iago, 'acting together more unselfishly than any pair I can recall'. Sinden, he wrote, 'conveys the ecstasy of jealousy with splendid conviction. At one point he is reduced to emptying his wife's laundry basket and sniffing the sheets for evidence of copulation. And he carries the humiliation of Desdemona further than I have ever seen by threatening to tup her in front of Emilia and by hurling her contemptuously to the ground in front of the Venetian visitors.'[13]

In the last analysis it has to be said that Donald Sinden's greatness as an actor was more apparent in comic and heroic roles than in tragedy. Pathos did not come easily to him. Larger, and sometimes louder, than life, he dominated the stages on which he appeared with ebullience and great-heartedness. He was the greatest Falstaff who never played the role.

Richard Pasco

Figure 31.1. Richard Pasco as Jacques in *As You Like It*, Royal Shakespeare Theatre, 1973: photograph by Zoë Dominic. © Dominic Photography

1926–2014. *Principal Shakespeare roles*: Henry V, Hamlet, Don John, Buckingham, Orsino, Richard II, Philip the Bastard, Proteus, Bolingbroke, Jaques, Timon of Athens.

Richard Pasco started his career as a Shakespeare actor with Barry Jackson's Birmingham Repertory Theatre and went on to greater glory culminating in the performance of leading roles in nearby Stratford-upon-Avon. For him however the route involved a major detour via Bristol. In Birmingham his roles included the Duke of Suffolk in Douglas Seale's pioneering production of the Henry VI plays (from 1961) and the title role in *Pericles*. His career had been interrupted by war service, and it was not until 1965, when he was in his late thirties, that he made his mark at the Bristol Old Vic with roles that included Berowne, Henry V, and Hamlet, in which, wrote Trewin, he offered 'the classical performance of his life. Always he has thought his way in Shakespearean verse instead of skimming it hopefully; he has never robbed us of the sound in his quest for the sense: an intellectual actor, he is not afraid to use his voice.'[1]

Well-built, with regular features and large, luminous eyes, he was, as Trewin's comment indicates, remarkable especially for the beauty and range of his voice, the depth of understanding that he brought to the speaking of Shakespeare's language, and the fresh but truthful character-ization of the roles he played. Not a heroic actor, in spite of the early Henry V, he excelled in lyrical, romantic roles and in the portrayal of eccentric outsiders including Don John, Jaques, and Timon of Athens.

Pasco joined the Royal Shakespeare Company in 1969, bringing his own kind of distinction initially to a series of middle-ranking roles which included Polixenes to Judi Dench's Hermione in Trevor Nunn's production of *The Winter's Tale,* causing Trewin (again) to write that he 'brings his magnificent voice to the service of the R.S.C.'.[2] Trewin was not his only eulogist. Of Pasco's Buckingham in *Henry VIII,* Philip Hope-Wallace wrote in *The Guardian* that the character's 'great speech of farewell to life was delivered as well as I have ever heard it'.[3] Unselfishly taking over the role of Orsino in John Barton's long-running *Twelfth Night* to Judi Dench's Viola after the death of Charles Thomas, who originally played the role, on tour in Australia, Pasco brought out to the full the character's romantic self-indulgence. Gaunt and hollow-eyed in his first scene with Viola (2.4), he conveyed a sense of an unexplained passion which made it easy to believe that his wooing of Olivia was a substitute for his repressed longing for Cesario/Viola; the relief he felt when he discovered that Cesario was indeed a girl was the greater for this. David Isaacs wrote that he portrayed the character as 'an emotional masochist whose "You uncivil lady" and "O, thou dissembling cub!"' addressed to the disguised Viola when he believes that she/he has married Olivia 'are rapier-like thrusts which may scratch others but which are simultaneously deeper, self-inflicted wounds'.[4]

In Ronald Eyre's 1971 production of *Much Ado About Nothing* he brought originality of thought to the relatively minor role of Don John, suggesting that the character's apparently unmotivated malice in his plotting against Claudio sprang from submerged homosexual desire; his 'description of Hero as "A very forward March chick"', wrote Richard David, 'revealed enough spite and envy to fuel a hundred such plots'.[5]

Full stardom came in 1973, in John Barton's highly conceptualized—and, as usual with this director, textually adapted—production of *Richard II,* which was revived in considerably altered form in the follow-ing year and which attracted much attention, both academic and popular. Acknowledging that in Richard Pasco and his younger colleague

Ian Richardson the Royal Shakespeare Company boasted two great classical actors, both of them equally well fitted to play the King, Barton devised a way of enabling them to do so. In some performances Pasco played Bolingbroke, and in others Richard. The textual changes clarified, strengthened, and simplified Bolingbroke's role, even giving him an invented soliloquy made up in part of lines from *Henry IV, Part Two*.

Both actors were splendid verse speakers, graceful in movement with expressive gestures and masterly audience control. To see them within a short space of time as both Richard and Bolingbroke offered a fascinating opportunity to consider the contribution of an actor's personality and physique to the role he plays. Bolingbroke is often given to an actor of the second rank, and it was interesting to see it played by a star. The decision to cast these players in both roles also had interpretative implications. It is often said that Richard II is an actor, and the production consciously explored this aspect of the character, to the extent of making textual changes to do so. There was also a strong attempt to show close spiritual resemblances between Richard and Bolingbroke, which may have been helped by the casting.

But there were interesting differences between them. Pasco, taller and of bigger build, had the more 'committed', overtly emotional acting style. Irving Wardle wrote that his 'Richard excels in cold frivolity and philosophical dejection more than in storms of moral outrage. Within the production's terms what he does perfectly capture is the switching on and off of the public performance; gaily waving goodbye to the banished Mowbray with his staff of office, and shakily collecting himself when the impassioned John of Gaunt (Tony Church) drags him to the ground'.[6] And Michael Billington found that his Richard 'establishes from the start that the man is a mercurial tyrant rather than a medieval Lord Alfred Douglas, and he also ravenously seizes every opportunity for flamboyant show: at Flint Castle he invokes heavenly thunder on "God omnipotent is mustering in the clouds on my behalf", and literally descends like glistering Phaeton spreading his golden cloak like some giant bird. It is a richly exciting performance in that it acquires genuine dignity in defeat and that Pasco unashamedly uses his soaring top notes to extract musical value from the great central arias.'[7] Trewin too used the operatic analogy: 'Mr Pasco tastes every word as he moves from the contemplative smiling sun-king through the arias . . . to hear Pasco and Richardson in full career is to know what the English language in the English theatre should be.'[8] And then, when Pasco played Bolingbroke, 'Richard Pasco, now a contained and smouldering Bolingbroke, also speaks with his invariable authority.'[9]

Pasco followed this with another performance that turned what can seem merely a supporting role into a star part. The play was *As You Like It*, directed by Buzz Goodbody in a modern-dress production with Eileen Atkins as Rosalind. Pasco was cast as Jaques, and I remember him telling me that when he was discussing his interpretation with his director she had set before him two images: one was Joseph Severn's portrait of the young John Keats, the other a photograph of the raddled and careworn face of the ageing W. H. Auden. This was what she had in mind as the journey the character had undergone. Whatever the source of inspiration, the actor scored a personal triumph in a production which otherwise had a lukewarm reception. John Barber drew a comparison with Oscar Wilde, writing that the 'production will go down in history for Richard Pasco's Jaques, the wry looker-on as lovers quarrel and pun in the Forest of Arden. Becloaked, bespectacled, with thinning hair and bookish stoop, the first impression is of an arrogant dandy of the old Café Royal, parading a sour wit to conceal a secret trauma... This is a man with one skin too few, for whom the death of an animal is painful and the embrace of a lover a living torment. An unforgettable creation.'[10] Other critics evoked Chekhov: 'With Jaques', wrote B. A. Young, 'we enter the sphere of serious performance at the core of the production. Richard Pasco in a white suit, greying beard and steel-rimmed glasses has wandered in from Chekhov, he invests all his lines with a freshness that brings them leaping to life again.' Similarly Billington: 'The one triumph of the evening is Richard Pasco's brilliant Jaques, a stooping, sottish, almost Chekhovian figure in whom bitter self-hatred has turned to misanthropy.' He praised the actor's speaking not merely for musicality but for power of characterization and interpretative insight: 'I have never heard a better rendition of the Seven Ages of Man, which becomes not the usual grave philosophical discourse but the repugnant vision of a blinkered cynic.'[11] Similarly, J. W. Lambert, hailing the actor's 'unqualified triumph', wrote, 'He enriches the Ages of Man speech by making each age a self-contained antithesis, with a twist in the tail. He signals recognition of each predictable folly with a most delicate play of feature, points each deflationary line with a musical accuracy that is a joy in itself.' And he concluded with a remarkable compliment: 'he expands one's knowledge of human nature'.[12]

Richard Pasco's last Shakespeare role was Timon of Athens in a low-budget production of 1980 directed by Ron Daniels in the RSC's studio theatre, The Other Place. It is almost a one-character play, and one that makes heavy demands especially on the actor's vocal technique. Billington found that Pasco 'gives the tirades a mordant vivacity. With his red-rimmed eyes, patchwork costume, and habit of gnawing passionately on root vegetables, he is the picture of desolation.' The actor 'expertly offers a concerto of bile. . . . Mr Pasco's usual forte is golden virtue, but here he proves he can do stark hate and cornered despair. When he finally expires under a huge net, it seems a logical end from a character who finds life a mortal sickness.'[13] Irving Wardle wrote that the later scenes 'are the greatest test of verse speaking in the English repertory and anyone who has found them obscure or batteringly obsessive will discover new areas of gentleness, Swiftian wit and exultant music in this thrilling performance'.[14]

Richard Pasco was a great classical actor whose stage career in Shakespeare suffered from the vagaries of a theatrical system that often failed, and that continues to fail, to offer actors the opportunity to play in major productions roles to which they are ideally suited. If I were to play the casting game I should name Romeo, Brutus, Mark Antony in both *Julius Caesar* and *Antony and Cleopatra*, Oberon, Henry IV, the Chorus in *Henry V*, Pandarus, King Lear, Iachimo in *Cymbeline*, and Prospero as roles in which, at various stages of his career, he would surely have excelled had he been given the opportunity. For all this, his star burned brightly when given the chance to do so.

Ian Richardson

Figure 32.1. Ian Richardson as Richard II with Richard Pasco as Bolingbroke, Royal Shakespeare Company, 1973: photograph by Joe Cocks. Joe Cocks Studio Collection © Shakespeare Birthplace Trust

1934–2007. *Principal Shakespeare roles*: Richard III, Richard II, Bolingbroke, Antipholus, Master Ford, Berowne, Lucio, Coriolanus, Pericles.

Like many actors before him—Edith Evans, Laurence Olivier, Peggy Ashcroft, Ralph Richardson, and Richard Pasco among them—Ian Richardson (unrelated to Ralph) first began to make a name for himself at Barry Jackson's Birmingham Repertory Theatre. Born in Edinburgh of non-theatrical parents, he acted as an amateur in his youth and went into stage-management straight from school. Hoping to become a professional actor he took elocution lessons with the aim partly of eliminating his Scottish accent. After three years of war service he studied for a teaching qualification in Glasgow while also training as an actor. Joining the Birmingham company in 1958 at the age of 24 he was catapulted into the role of Hamlet with such success that a couple of years later he became a founding member of the Royal Shakespeare Company with which he acted for the next fifteen years, playing a wide range of roles. After this his only Shakespeare role was Mercutio, for Prospect Players at the Old Vic in 1979.

Of average height, slim, neatly built, he had well-defined features, with a rather long nose, which gave him a somewhat aloof expression; but his bright eyes twinkled and he had a ready smile. His voice was light and penetratingly clear, his diction almost pedantically crisp. Exceptionally fine breath control enabled him to shape long speeches with virtuosic ease, and high intelligence controlled and pointed them with clarity and wit. He moved lightly and economically, compelling attention through stillness and attentiveness to what was going on around him as much as through action of his own. Economy was a keynote of his acting. He kept you waiting for the big moments. I once heard him say that he aimed to make no more than five or six 'points' within a performance even of a long role. Peter Thomson, reviewing his Buckingham to Norman Rodway's Richard III in 1970, justly wrote, 'Richardson has a supreme ability to stand still. It gave him, in this production, all the sinister authority that Richard lacked.'[1]

Though he was not a heavyweight, he could succeed in certain tragic roles. The ability to convey high intelligence and biting irony which made him a brilliant Vindice—a Hamlet-like role—in Trevor Nunn's production of *The Revenger's Tragedy* would surely have enabled him to develop the high promise of his early Hamlet if he had been offered the role again later in his career. Both the lyricism and the growing self-knowledge of Richard II helped him to make of it one of his greatest successes. He was fitted to take on Richard III in a rather tricksy production at The Other Place because of the irony with which the King is portrayed, and some aspects of Coriolanus, which he also played, have this quality too. But neither John Barton's production of that play nor Richardson's performance was universally admired. Harold Hobson, for one, intemperately called the show 'inordinately protracted and ferociously boring', describing Richardson as 'stiff and petulant'.[2] But the play contains some of Shakespeare's most difficult writing, and Alan Brien, writing that Richardson gave 'a remarkable impersonation of a man who seems positively varnished under a veneer of upper-class correctness', praised especially his handling of the language. Richardson 'speaks that peculiar Coriolanian verse and grinding, abrasive language with sudden fluid spurts of oiled movement, with immense intelligence in a careful, metallic voice which never sacrifices sense to sound'.[3]

Among the characters of tragedy I can imagine him as Timon, too, but at no time in his career could he have achieved the degree of self-identification and the inwardness required for Titus, Othello, Macbeth, and Lear, and he probably had too much sense of humour to be a Romeo. He was at his best with characters who stand at a certain distance from themselves (and others), with the self-knowing eloquence of Berowne in *Love's Labour's Lost*, the deflating realism of Lucio in *Measure for Measure*, the comic bewilderment of the Antipholuses in *The Comedy of Errors*—he played both of them (though not in the same performance)—and the aristocratic superiority of Oberon.

He rapidly made his mark in Stratford. Peter Hall's first production as artistic director was a rather lacklustre *The Two Gentlemen of Verona*. Few parts in the entire canon are less potentially rewarding than that of Thurio, who at one point enters at the beginning of a scene only to be told instantly to leave. Yet Richardson, wrote Trewin, managed to make of him a character rather than a caricature;[4] a couple of years later the same critic, reviewing a *Macbeth* in which Richardson played Seyton doubled with other small roles, justly described him as 'an actor no one can help recalling, however minor his parts'.[5] In the second play of the 1960 season, *The Merchant of Venice*, which had Peter O'Toole as Shylock and Dorothy Tutin as Portia, he was hilarious as a costively self-conscious Prince of Aragon. Accompanied all the time by a dominating old battleaxe of a mother (played in fact by his young wife) he made his casket scene, wrote the critic of *Punch*, 'funnier than I ever remember it', playing 'with telling affectation' and taking 'so long making up his mind that no one can blame the girl holding the casket for dropping in a swoon'.[6]

His comic talent developed and revealed itself in other roles, too. His gift for physical comedy found expression in Master Ford, in *The Merry Wives of Windsor*, which he played both in 1964 and in 1968. He succeeded brilliantly in conveying the character's schizophrenic confusion as he took on the feigned identity of Master Brook, desperately trying to remember who he was supposed to be at any given moment. But although this was a virtuosic comic performance it had a heart, too. B. A. Young wrote that, 'proceeding from a nervous irritability in his first confrontation with Falstaff to an almost inarticulate rage that possesses him for almost all the rest of the evening', he gave 'a rounded portrait of a real man, a bourgeois husband wronged by his social superior and determined to show him up'.[7] As the complications of the action are unfolded and Ford's suspicions of his wife turn out to be totally unjust, he asks her forgiveness in lines that can easily be skated over or spoken jokily.

> Pardon me, wife. Henceforth do what thou wilt.
> I rather will suspect the sun with cold
> Than thee with wantonness.

Richardson, kneeling for forgiveness, brought real love and tenderness to this passage in a manner which in retrospect humanized the entire role.

As Proteus in a modern-dress, hippy *The Two Gentlemen of Verona* (1970) he was, by comparison with the actor playing Valentine, 'comparatively puny', wrote Peter Thomson in *Shakespeare Survey* 24, but 'made a virtue of it'. He 'finds a precise comic image of Proteus's search for physical grace when he throws his strapped bundle of "books for the voyage" over his shoulder in a gesture of careless abandon that Valentine might have admired but fails quite to restrain a wince when the strap brings them around in an arc to clobber him on the left buttock'.[8]

His gifts as both comic actor and verse speaker came together especially happily as Berowne in David Jones's 1973 *Love's Labour's Lost*. Thomson again, this time in *Shakespeare Survey* 27, acutely described the way in which the actor 'found a way—a pause, a smirk, a turn of the head—of bringing the audience into the wordplay without explicitly acknowledging their presence.... All his major speeches were explored for their legitimate vocal variety.' The touchstone of any performance of this role is Berowne's great paean in praise of love, beginning 'Have at you now, affection's men at arms', which Richardson 'began quietly', but 'reached a controlled climax only at "For wisdom's sake, a word that all men love..."' But the comic peak of the performance was reached with the tearing of his incriminating letter to Rosaline. He had come close to giving himself away in the lustful delivery of his reproach to the King... Now, in the attempt to preserve his secret, he not only tore the letter into tiny pieces but tried by whirling his arms like a possessed windmill to scatter the fragments.'[9]

The production in which he appeared which attracted most attention, both academic and popular, was John Barton's *Richard II* in which, as I have said in writing of Richard Pasco (see Chapter 31), he played the King in some performances and Bolingbroke in others. Richardson, less vocally resonant than Pasco, nevertheless brought to both roles all his customary incisiveness and command of vocal nuance. Audience members enjoyed comparing and contrasting the actors' respective merits in each role. Of the 1973 version, Richard David wrote,

To the great arias with which Richard meets the news of successive disasters Richardson gave a rapt abstraction that expressed, better than Pasco's more straightforward reading, that this is not mere posturing: a change is taking place in the King's inmost soul, as his destiny closes in on him. On the other side, Pasco's Bolingbroke, too, was a complex figure, determined enough but evincing just that quality of ruth whose absence from Richardson's literally ruthless baron made that a flatter portrait.

Nevertheless, David wrote,

In the first year I had preferred the version with Richardson as Richard and Pasco as Bolingbroke because it seemed less hackneyed than the utterly weak (if pitiable) Richard and the utterly ruthless Bolingbroke of the alternative casting. Richardson had a tensile strength and unpredictable flashes of authority that made his Richard anything but a natural victim. In the revival I preferred it the other way round, chiefly because Pasco's Richard had grown enormously in stature, becoming younger and stronger and showing for the first time that quality of leadership that alone can explain the utter devotion of Aumerle... Richardson's Richard, on the other hand, had hardened, so that what last year was inspired invention seemed this year to be mannerism and actor's fireworks.[10]

Richardson's distinctive qualities may at times have degenerated into mannerism, and like Sinden he occasionally went over the top in comedy, but he was a life-enhancing actor whose presence always lit up a stage and who could ignite fireworks whenever he chose to do so.

Judi Dench

Figure 33.1. Judi Dench as Titania in *A Midsummer Night's Dream*, Royal Shakespeare Theatre, 1962: photograph by Tom Holte. Tom Holte Theatre Photographic Collection © Shakespeare Birthplace Trust

1934– . *Principal Shakespeare roles*: Juliet, Adriana, Titania, Portia, Beatrice, Viola, Isabella, Hermione/Perdita (doubled), Volumnia, Countess of Roussillon, Lady Macbeth, Cleopatra.

Judi Dench, more than anyone else, has inherited the mantles of three other great Shakespearian Dames—Ellen Terry, Edith Evans, and Peggy Ashcroft—as the finest women performers of Shakespeare over the twentieth century and beyond. Her passion for Shakespeare—'the man who pays the rent', she has called him—goes back to schooldays in her home town of York, when she played Titania, Ariel, and the Queen in *Richard II*. Her subsequent professional career has been remarkably versatile. She has acted to acclaim in classic and modern plays covering a wide range of dramatic styles, in musicals, and in television situation comedies. But Shakespeare's plays have given her the greatest opportunities and provided the cornerstone of her repertoire.

Inevitably, given the theatrical conditions of the time, her career has been largely shaped by external forces. She has not, like an actor manager, been able to determine in which plays she would appear, but rather has responded to the needs of companies for which she has worked, such as the Old Vic, the Oxford and Nottingham Playhouses, the Royal Shakespeare Company, and the National Theatre. A regrettable result of the system is that she has not had the opportunity to play onstage roles for which she seems well suited such as Rosalind, Cressida, and, in later years, the Nurse in *Romeo and Juliet*, and that her Volumnia was given only in a limited number of performances in Chichester in 1992. Only three of her major Shakespeare roles can be seen on commercially available film—Titania in a version of the RSC 1962 production filmed, not very satisfactorily, on location at Compton Verney; Lady Macbeth in Trevor Nunn's great 1976 production at The Other Place in Stratford; and Adriana in his musical adaptation of *The Comedy of Errors*, also given in 1976. She is however a memorable and moving Mistress Quickly in Kenneth Branagh's film of *Henry V*, and can be seen and heard briefly but piercingly as Hecuba in his *Hamlet*. And she has made audio recordings of the Nurse with Branagh, and of Goneril to John Gielgud's King Lear.

The beginnings of Judi Dench's career were inauspicious. Her debut as Ophelia at the Old Vic in 1957, to John Neville's Hamlet, was harshly criticized, the critic Richard Findlater writing, 'The debut was, in my view, a debacle.'[1] When the production went on tour she was replaced by another fine Shakespeare actor, Barbara Jefford. But the challenge appears to have been salutary. Her subsequent performance as Juliet in Zeffirelli's 1960 Old Vic production both made her a star and taught her a lot about the balance in classical acting between psychological verisimilitude and the demands of poetic drama. The production's innovative nature caused it initially to receive bad reviews, with several critics complaining about neglect of the play's poetry; but its fortunes changed when Kenneth Tynan wrote that Zeffirelli had worked 'a miracle. . . . a revelation, even perhaps a revolution, . . . so abundant and compelling was the life on stage that I could not wait to find out what happened next'.[2]

Any actor's career is determined in part by inherent and inescapable physical and intellectual attributes, though these may be extended and developed by training. Judi Dench is short—5 feet 2 inches. There is nothing much she can do about that, as she knows. Russ McDonald, in a substantial study of her work as a Shakespeare actor, writes, 'Having accepted Peter Hall's invitation to do *Antony and Cleopatra* at the National Theatre in 1987, she began the first rehearsal by saying to him "Well, I hope you know what you're doing. You are setting out to direct Cleopatra with a menopausal dwarf."[3] But she has extraordinary transformative powers which enable her to look convincing in an exceptionally wide range of roles. Her features are regular, her eyes large and expressive. In youth she had a delicate, luminous beauty which has mellowed over the years, her face illuminated by her penetrating intelligence and radiant, often mischievous smile. Though she is not gifted with the 'voice beautiful' of the Terry family, she has a wide vocal range of both pitch and volume, along with a huskiness that has been seen as a trademark which is both an asset and a handicap. It is said that a notice appeared outside a theatre in which she was appearing, reading 'Judi Dench does not have a cold, this is her natural speaking voice'. But her vocal delivery in both verse and prose is of exemplary clarity and energy. The voice is fully supported and projected. The vowels are pure, the consonants crisp. Every syllable makes its contribution. She can speak fast if the situation demands it. Her mental agility means that, as her fellow actor Michael Pennington writes, she can 'move from a thought to a related half-thought, complicate it with a burst of feeling and move on to a physical action that incorporates all three, like mercury, at the speed of light'.[4] But even when speaking fast she never gives an impression of unintended haste.

In verse, she is conscious of rhythm, but does not overstress it. She knows where the caesura, the break within the verse line, occurs, and she can use it, perhaps with a scarcely perceptible pause, a little silence, that suggests the working of the character's mind, the thought processes in which meaning and poetry coalesce. She has often stressed the importance of what musicians call *legato*—the carrying over of the tone from one note or syllable to another, producing an apparently seamless flow of sound.

For all the emphasis that she herself, as well as those who write about her acting, has placed on the contribution to her work of her mastery of the speaking of both verse and prose, she is a mistress too of body language. I felt this in her performance of Perdita in Trevor Nunn's 1969 production of *The Winter's Tale* (in which she also played a gravely beautiful Hermione). Her dancing in the pastoral scene was imbued with a kind of innocent eroticism, a rapt enjoyment of the music and of the sensuous movement of her own limbs that fully justified Florizel's praise:

When you do dance, I wish you
A wave o'th'sea, that you might ever do
Nothing but that, move still, still so,
And own no other function.

The seriousness that Judi Dench brings to technical matters of verse speaking is no less apparent in her characterization of roles. She looks for the humanizing touches, the person below the style. This is true even in the filmed musical *Comedy of Errors*. A high spot is the wordless interpolated moment when she appears on a balcony, impatient for her husband Antipholus to come in to dinner, and sees his identical twin brother, of whose existence she is oblivious, in the courtyard below. Drawing herself up to her full height (such as it is) in a wonderfully imperious manner, like a latter-day Sarah Siddons, she glares at the hapless twin, and with a gesture like that of an exasperated traffic policewoman directs him into the house for what can only be going to be an exceedingly uncomfortable confrontation. This is splendid, but the actor knows that farce needs to be grounded in reality, and her performance succeeds in the way in which she underlies the exaggerations required by the production style with touches of true feeling that draw sympathy for Adriana in her plight.

As her success in comedy may suggest, she is a great joker, a giggler, a husky chuckler, and a hearty laugher, famous for the jokes she plays on her fellow actors in rehearsal and even onstage, and for corpsing. She tells of an incident in a performance of *The Merchant of Venice*:

In the casket scene Michael Williams [her husband] was standing in the centre of the stage as Bassanio, about to make his choice. There was the wind band at the back of the stage, Peter Geddis as Gobbo, Polly James waiting to sing 'Tell me where is fancy bred', and my brother Jeff and Bernard Lloyd as monks. I was supposed to say

I speak too long, 'tis but to peize the time,
To eke it, and to draw it out in length,
To stay you from election.

But I said 'erection.' The band just put down their instruments and walked off, as did the monks, leaving Polly James to sing on her own. I have never been in such a state, and the scene had only just started.[5]

This irrepressible sense of fun, the lack of self-importance that it betokens, the ability, even the desire, to laugh at herself, is among the qualities that make her a natural team player—and also the natural leader of any company in which she appears.

The thoughtfulness that she brings to the preparation of a role can result in interesting freshness of interpretation. As Beatrice in John Barton's 1976 *Much Ado About Nothing* she softened the character's asperities by picking up on the suggestions in the text that Beatrice and Benedick had had a love affair in the past. The key line comes in response to Don Pedro's words 'Come, lady, come, you have lost the heart of Signor Benedick.' 'Indeed, my lord,' she replies, 'he lent it me a while, and I gave him use for it, a double heart for his single one. Marry, once before he won it of me, with false dice.' When, talking to her before the production opened, I mentioned that the line was often omitted, she replied that she had agreed to take the role only on condition that it was retained. It was part and parcel of her portrayal of Beatrice as a woman of some maturity, of a wisdom born of not entirely happy experience. There was enormous fun in her performance—the slightly bawdy comedy of the scene (3.4) with her girlfriends, in which she has a cold, was as funny as I have ever seen it— but the ground bass of seriousness had been sounded again at the end of the second deception scene, when she emerges from hiding after hearing herself criticized. 'What fire is in mine ears?' she says. 'Can this be true? | Stand I condemned for pride and scorn so much?' I have heard the speech spoken farcically, but she knew better. Responding to its lyrical style with a tenderness that did not deny an element of self-mockery, she showed that this is a response to a learning experience, that Beatrice is a wiser woman at the end of the scene than she had been at its beginning.

Economy is a keynote of her acting, nowhere better exemplified than in the final scene of *All's Well that Ends Well* when she played the Countess in Gregory Doran's RSC production of 2003. As Doran has written,

The Countess says nothing when Helena returns, as if from the dead, at the end of the play. Her new daughter-in-law turns to the Countess with the line, 'Oh, my dear mother, do I see you living?' There is no reply. There can't be. Judi's choice was for the Countess to stare at Helena, almost unable to move, and finally, slowly turn her outstretched hands palm up to signal silent welcome, acceptance, and profound relief. It was a moment to haunt you with its stillness, and she created it with such economy and truth, the effect was devastating.[6]

Judi Dench had been a great Lady Macbeth in Trevor Nunn's 1976 Other Place production in Stratford, in which, wrote Michael Billington, Ian McKellen's 'study of evil bursting through a mask like a clown through a paper hoop is finely complemented by Judi Dench's Lady Macbeth which is not some painted Gorgon but a portrait of a novice dabbling in Satanic powers ... the cry of remorse she utters in the sleep walking scene apparently drawn from her very soul is guaranteed to haunt one for nights to come'.[7] But the Shakespeare role that gave her the greatest scope for the full range of her talents is one that she had long thought she would never play, Cleopatra. In Peter Hall's 1987 National Theatre production she embraced its challenges and opportunities with joyous acceptance of all it has to offer, extending herself into every aspect of the role, from the sordid to the sublime, while never losing the sense of a unifying self that could encompass the character's 'infinite variety'. From her first appearance this was clearly a woman of volatile passions, physically restless, richly sensual yet with a shrewd, instinctive intelligence that probed suspiciously, vulnerably, behind the appearances with which she was presented. She realized the comedy of the role with perfect timing and brilliant transitions. As she questioned the messenger about Octavia, her self-confidence grew until, as he said 'I do think she's thirty', the smile froze on her face and, gathering her skirts, she swirled abruptly around, ran towards the door, and almost left the stage. The poetry of the role, too, was fully realized, climactically when, her restlessness subdued, she spoke 'I dreamt there was an Emperor Anthony....' with rapt, hushed lyricism to a Dolabella who stood in the auditorium aisle with his back to us, so that she was addressing us as well as him. Our silence was palpable. We were united in a single emotional response. This was great acting achieved through a perfection of vocal technique along with the highest physical economy.

An actor is nothing without an audience. Judi Dench's long love affair with those who come to see her act is reflected in the admiration and affection in which she is held by countless admirers. The generosity of her art reflects and is enabled by the generosity of a great spirit. She is the best-loved English actress since Ellen Terry, and her success onstage, like Ellen Terry's, is indivisible from the personality that enables it.

Derek Jacobi

Figure 34.1. Derek Jacobi as Prospero in *The Tempest*, Royal Shakespeare Theatre, 1982: photograph by Tom Holte. Thos. F. and Mig Holte Theatre Collection © Shakespeare Birthplace Trust

1938– . *Principal Shakespeare roles*: Hamlet, Richard II, Benedick, Prospero, Lear.

Derek Jacobi is one of the many Cambridge-educated actors who have benefited from contact with George Rylands in their early careers. Even as a boy he developed a passion for acting, playing Prince Hal in *Henry IV, Part Two* for the National Youth Theatre and Hamlet at the age of 18 in a school production which went to the Edinburgh Festival. It was, he writes, 'a black-and-white Hamlet, very simplistic, in which I tore several passions to tatters'.[1] Although given on the

Edinburgh Fringe, it attracted favourable critical notice which gave him confidence to embark on acting as a career. He won a scholarship to read English at Cambridge (which, of course, like Oxford, has no drama department) where Ian McKellen and Trevor Nunn were contemporaries. Spending more time onstage than in the study, he played leading roles which included Edward II for the Marlowe Society in 1958, directed by Rylands and John Barton, Prince Hal, and a second Hamlet which toured on the Continent.

Already an experienced actor, he decided to bypass drama school and after graduating started his professional career, like many others before him, with Barry Jackson's Birmingham Repertory Company, for which he played Troilus, Aaron (in *Titus Andronicus*), and, somewhat improbably, Henry VIII—but in Robert Bolt's *A Man for All Seasons*, not the Shakespeare–Fletcher play.

Red-headed and amiable-looking in youth, and with a winning smile, in later years he has become a touch portly and rubicund of countenance. In his gossipy memoir *As Luck Would Have It* (2013) he writes that he has 'a big vocal range, which means that I can do a two-octave jump'.[2] Certainly his voice, musical in tone and flexible in expression, is one of his greatest assets and has helped to determine the roles he has played. He is a lyrical, not a heroic actor; his greatest successes in Shakespeare have been in roles in which Gielgud too excelled: Hamlet—a role that he has played close on 400 times—Richard II, Benedick, Prospero, and Lear. He has won acclaim on television, as Richard II and Hamlet in the BBC Shakespeare series and as the emperor Claudius in an adaptation of Robert Graves's *I, Claudius*, and on film, giving a beautifully controlled and subtly sinister Claudius in Branagh's *Hamlet*.

In 1963, having been turned down by the RSC, he became a founding member of the National Theatre Company, playing Laertes to Peter O'Toole's disastrous Hamlet in their opening production, Cassio to Olivier's Othello (1964), and Don John (later Don Pedro) to Maggie Smith's Beatrice in Zeffirelli's production of *Much Ado About Nothing* (1965–7). Joining the Prospect Theatre Company in 1973, he played Pericles in an innovative production by Toby Robertson set in a transvestite brothel.

His return to Hamlet for the same company in 1977 was however in a traditional, Renaissance staging which toured extensively both in England and overseas, including a rain-sodden Elsinore, and which became the first-ever English Hamlet to be given in China. Irving Wardle wrote that Jacobi 'restores the figure of the renaissance prince,—equipped with all the courtesy, irony, and masterful variations of tempo and weight that traditionally belong to the part'.[3] And J. C. Trewin—who over a period of sixty years, starting in 1922, must have seen more Hamlets than anyone else on the planet— wrote in his book *Five & Eighty Hamlets* (1987) that, 'logical, graceful, possibly the most touching Hamlet since John Neville'—at the Old Vic in 1957—'but fortified always by his fiery spirit, he recharged my faith in the courtier's, soldier's, scholar's eye, tongue, sword. To listen to him was like reading the play in a fresh format.' And there were original touches—for example (though to Trewin's displeasure), he spoke 'To be or not to be . . .' directly to Ophelia. Seeing a revival, Trewin wrote that 'Jacobi's searching performance had been altered, not entirely for the better, to explore Hamlet's "antic disposition" in the context of the King's description of the exterior madness as a turbulent and dangerous lunacy'.[4]

Eventually invited to join the Royal Shakespeare Company in 1982, Jacobi played Benedick in a production directed by Terry Hands with attractive designs by Ralph Koltai which was a great popular success, winning him a Tony award when given on Broadway. Emrys Jones, in *The Times Literary Supplement*, wrote of this as 'a likeable, commanding performance. He makes him a genial, slightly foolish fellow, with not much dignity but a good deal of natural warmth.'[5] Billington too found this 'a highly engaging performance that gets better with every scene'. He 'starts out as a skittish, larky, life-and-soul-of-the-party bachelor who even during the gulling scene is ready to knock Don Pedro's block off; but after the church scene he acquires a steadfast sobriety'.[6]

When I saw Jacobi's Benedick I felt that in the earlier scenes he tended to flirt with the audience in a somewhat self-indulgent manner which has marred other of his performances. But when in 1982 he came to play Prospero, another of the great Gielgud roles, for the same company, he did so with full dignity and high seriousness. James Fenton found him 'more at ease than ever in this role, which gives him unquestioned authority on stage'.[7] His verse-speaking skills came to the fore in a performance that Michael Coveney found 'skilfully and beautifully spoken' and 'interestingly less benevolent than usual'.[8] This was, wrote Robert Cushman, a gripping performance on several levels that took him 'as an actor beyond the skilled charm that got him through Benedict [*sic*] and Peer Gynt; there are deeper tones in his voice, more iron in his soul'.[9] And David Nokes, in the *TLS*, also found this a deeply felt, thoroughly thought-through performance: 'Jacobi's Prospero is a mortal, a scholar whose authority comes from an unassertive humanity; from lines which are meditated rather than declaimed, and sentences that are delivered as much in sorrow as in anger.'[10]

The contrast between Jacobi's Benedick and his Prospero was reflected in 1988–9 when he played Richard II and Richard III in undistinguished productions at the Phoenix Theatre in London—Jim Hiley in *The Listener* went so far as to say that they were of the 'kind that used to put schoolchildren off their national poet by the coach-load'.[11] Richard II—again the Gielgud role—played to Jacobi's strengths. Billington said that he showed 'Richard to be a callous, even brutish tyrant who believes he is rendered inviolable by the mystic power of kingship. He shocks even his courtiers by the blow he aims at the dying John of Gaunt with his gage.' This was

a stirringly unsympathetic reading from an actor whose natural asset is charm. But what Mr Jacobi now possesses, to a greater degree than almost any of his contemporaries, is the Continental actor's ability to change emotional gear in a split second. There is a classic example in the Deposition scene at Westminster. . . . 'Mine eyes are full of tears, I cannot see' is rendered with a heart-wrenching pathos. Within a moment Mr Jacobi turns to a wild, intemperate anger with the treacherous court and then to a moody reflectiveness on his own participation in his downfall.

Even so, Billington discerned 'occasional lapses in taste',[12] and these came by the bucketful in Jacobi's Richard III, in which, wrote Sheridan Morley, he 'celebrates a petulant high-camp villain prepared to give his kingdom if not for a horse then certainly for a laugh'.[13] More than one critic drew comparisons with the outrageously camp comedian Frankie Howerd.

Jacobi likes to be liked. The out-and-out villainy of Richard III did not come naturally to him, and neither did the more nuanced subtleties of Macbeth, which he played for the RSC in 1993. It is, he has written, 'not my most glorious Shakespeare role by any straw (generally reckoned my worst)'.[14] John Gross wrote that 'you become aware that Jacobi can be a very actorish actor: there is a sternness in the part that eludes him'.[15] And to Paul Taylor, the soliloquies sounded 'like a case of someone trying to derive consolation from tuning in to the beauteous flexibilities of his own voice'.[16] But the deficiencies in this performance did not stem from lack of understanding of the role's demands. Jacobi contributed to *Players of Shakespeare 4* a deeply thoughtful and perceptive essay from which anyone aspiring to play Macbeth could learn much.[17]

Late in 2010, directed by Michael Grandage, Jacobi played King Lear at the Donmar and on tour. Michael Coveney, describing him as 'this most exacting and pernickety of actors', spoke of the performance as 'most beautifully spoken and detailed' while finding that, 'terribly polite', it kept 'too many secrets'.[18] But according to Charles Spencer, 'enjoying a blaze of autumnal glory as an actor' Jacobi captured 'the full depth and breadth of the character'.[19] In *The Observer*, Susannah Clapp charted his progress through the role. 'Jacobi begins with twinkling dignity, almost a touch of Santa Claus and a definite echo of Prospero . . . he relinquishes power leaning on a staff. He steps delicately, precisely into madness, his low-level vehemence making evident how full this play is of curses. He creates an electric shock in the storm scene, by seeming to do less than expected: his imprecations to the elements are delivered in a level whisper.' (Sinden, too, had whispered 'Blow, wind, and crack your cheeks . . . ') 'He saves his big roars for the howls of his towering final scene, when he enters carrying the dead Cordelia, then sinks back into a soft register for the closing moments—and a long, expiring sigh.'[20] It was the grand climax of Jacobi's career as a Shakespearian actor.

Ian McKellen

Figure 35.1. Ian McKellen as Macbeth, with Judi Dench as Lady Macbeth, The Other Place, Stratford-upon-Avon, 1976: photograph by Joe Cocks. Joe Cocks Studio Collection © Shakespeare Birthplace Trust

1939– . *Principal Shakespeare roles*: Richard II, Romeo, Macbeth, Iago, Coriolanus, Richard III, Kent, Lear.

It is easy to draw parallels between the careers of Derek Jacobi and Ian McKellen. Almost exact contemporaries, both men come from relatively humble backgrounds with no theatrical antecedents; both developed a passion for acting as schoolboys and won scholarships to Cambridge where they met and, coming under the influence of George

Rylands and John Barton, acted together with the Marlowe Society; both spent more time acting than studying; both went straight into the theatre without going to drama school.

Yet—happily for them and for their careers—there are significant differences. Jacobi is a Londoner, McKellen a northerner whose voice and intonations still reveal traces of his origins. In natural characteristics and—partly as a consequence—in areas of excellence Jacobi invites simplistic comparison with Gielgud, McKellen with Olivier. McKellen, good-looking in a wirily rugged way, is taller and, even in his later years, leaner than Jacobi. Whereas Jacobi is noted for mellifluousness of speech, McKellen has a more clipped, tauter mode of utterance. He is less strong on lyricism—Prospero at the West Yorkshire Playhouse in 1999 was not a happy experience for him. Though he played Romeo at Stratford at the age of 37—by his own account, too old for the role— he said he thought the character was mad and acted frenetically in the attempt to convey youthfulness.

The romantic high comedy of a Berowne, a Benedick, or a Bassanio is not, and never has been, for him. Whereas Jacobi likes to be liked, McKellen is happy to be hated—he can project evil with frightening power. His great strengths lie in the presentation of self-deprecating irony, of emotional complexity, and of a troubled inwardness of soul. Like Michael Redgrave, he is a questing actor with a strong improvisatory streak, liable to experiment with details of a performance even during the course of a play's run.

McKellen played Henry V at school, and in 1963 this became his first major Shakespeare role as a professional actor when he undertook it successfully for a short run in the intimate space of the Arts Theatre, Ipswich. Even here he did not project uncomplicated heroism; he spoke 'Once more unto the breach' quietly to his modest band of followers scattered among the audience in the small auditorium. Later in the same year he joined another, more prestigious provincial theatre company in Nottingham to play the major role of Aufidius in *Coriolanus* under the stimulating direction of Tyrone Guthrie, who, recognizing McKellen's potential, took the young actor under his wing and gave him private coaching. In the new social climate of the sixties Guthrie felt free to explore the homosexuality latent in the relationship between Aufidius and Coriolanus, a theme which may well have appealed especially to McKellen at a time when he still felt compelled to conceal his sexual orientation. A career-defining moment appears to have come when Guthrie succeeded in breaking through the actor's inhibitions to elicit a great cry of grief and remorse as he held the body of the enemy he had both desired and destroyed.

At Nottingham McKellen also undertook the role of Sir Thomas More in a pioneering production of the multi-authored Elizabethan play in which Shakespeare is believed to have had a hand. Some of the events of this play are also dramatized in Robert Bolt's *A Man for All Seasons*, but when once, in South Africa, I saw a production of that followed by a reading of *More* I was struck by how much more vigorous and colourful is the dialogue of the early play. In the episode attributed to Shakespeare More expresses deep compassion for foreigners expelled from London:

> Imagine that you see the wretched strangers,
> Their babies at their backs, with their poor luggage,
> Plodding to th'ports and coasts for transportation,
> And that you sit as king in your desires,
> Authority quite silenced by your brawl,
> And you in ruff of your opinions clothed.   (Add.II.D.83–8)

The speech stuck in McKellen's mind, appealing to his deeply humanitarian instincts. He quoted it many years later in a speech at the Shakespeare Birthday Lunch in Stratford, making of it a plea for compassionate treatment of all homeless and displaced people.

McKellen's first big success in a major Shakespeare role came late in 1968 when he played Richard II with the touring Prospect Theatre Company; later Marlowe's *Edward II* was added to the repertory. Slim, tall, and beautiful, costumed in gold, McKellen found a modern parallel to Richard in the figure of the Dalai Lama, taking encouragement, he writes on his website, 'that there was in the 20th century a living god who was also a suffering man'.[1] His first entry, wrote Irving Wardle, was made 'in the midst of a priest-like procession, palms upraised and face chastely impassive, consciously holding himself as a sacred vessel'.[2] Richard, according to the director, Richard Cottrell, was seen undergoing a spiritual journey, 'shallow and heartless at the beginning',[3] but deepening in humanity with the 'hollow crown' speech in which the deposed Richard says:

> . . . you have but mistook me all this while.
> I live with bread, like you; feel want,
> Taste grief, need friends. Subjected thus,
> How can you say to me I am a king?   (3.3.170–3)

McKellen broke the verse rhythm on the words 'need friends', making it difficult not to hear them as a desperate plea on behalf of all men cut off, for whatever reason—such as their sexuality—from their fellows. Although numerous actors, including Gielgud and Jacobi, who succeeded as Richard II have also been great Hamlets, McKellen's Dane of 1971, also with the Prospect Theatre Company, was not one of his triumphs. Nor was Romeo at Stratford in 1976. J. C. Trewin complained of a 'mannered voice' and 'indulgent changes of tempo'.[4] But later that year another of the tragic heroes, Macbeth, brought out the best in him in a low-budget production of great simplicity at The Other Place—a theatre holding only around 150 people—directed by his Cambridge contemporary Trevor Nunn. Now, wrote J. W. Lambert, 'gone are the physical and vocal flourishes which for me have often spoiled enjoyment of Mr McKellen's powers. Reflective, natural (in, needless to say, a way possible only to a highly-skilled actor) he marvellously achieves that blend of the practical—in, for instance, his briefing of Banquo's murderers—and the introspective, and establishes with his wife a rich relationship full of affection, desire, awe, inspiration, and protectiveness.'[5] Michael Billington was no less impressed, writing of 'Ian McKellen's overwhelming Macbeth, which charts, stage by stage, the character's self-willed disintegration'. And, he wrote, 'if this is not great acting, I don't know what is'.[6]

The Other Place became the scene of another of McKellen's great studies in evil in 1990 when he played Iago, directed again by Trevor Nunn, in an *Othello* updated to the late nineteenth century with strong hints of the American Civil War. I wrote in *Shakespeare Survey* 43 that 'a fully written account of this production', which was packed with social detail, 'would read like a Victorian novel'.[7] As Iago to Willard White's Othello McKellen was a tall, trim figure of military bearing, a non-commissioned officer with a slightly plebeian accent, so professionally disciplined that he was obviously a strong candidate for Cassio's lieutenancy. In Othello's presence he was always under iron control, but his eyes narrowed to slits in intense concentration as he observed any movement or gesture that he might turn to his advantage. He barely attempted to conceal his contempt for Zoë Wanamaker's Emilia, but it was clear why he would have attracted her. His insolent scorn extended even to the audience as he addressed his soliloquies directly to them with a baleful, challenging gaze. After the murder there was a frightening sense of danger as he rushed to escape over the bed in which the dead Desdemona lay; dragged back, captive, he stared fixedly down at her corpse, unresponsive to Lodovico's 'This is thy work', advancing close to the foot of the bed to gaze on his handiwork, still staring in implacable, unflinching fascination as the lights went down.

As Iago, McKellen wore a Hitlerish moustache, and Hitler lay even closer to the surface of his portrayal of Richard III in Richard Eyre's National Theatre production of 1990 (though the moustache was reserved for the 1995 film adaptation, directed by Richard Loncraine.) Several reviewers saw this performance as what Jack Tinker in *The Daily Mail* called 'the hissing cousin to his own celebrated Iago'.[8] The action was updated to a vaguely Edwardian period, becoming what Billington called 'a deeply political study of the fascist instinct' in which Richard 'raises his right hand in an unequivocal Hitlerish salute ... With his slicked-down hair and dry parade ground voice McKellen offers us not a charismatic Richard but a beautifully executed study in the banality of evil.'[9]

In the same season McKellen had loyally undertaken the relatively minor role of Kent to Brian Cox's King Lear, and his own assault on this acting summit came in 2007 in a production directed again by Trevor Nunn as the climax of the Royal Shakespeare Company's fifteen-month long Complete Works Festival. As in Nunn's *Othello* (though to a lesser extent) the text was fleshed out with business that pushed it in the direction of naturalism. McKellen's first entry (perhaps recalling his long-past Richard II) saw him benevolently if bemusedly bestowing blessings on his followers in the manner of a religious patriarch. Nunn left us in no doubt that this was a society with a profound awe of the supernatural. Everyone onstage knelt in fear as Lear invoked 'the operation of the orbs | From whom we do exist and cease to be' in his banishment of Cordelia, and Goneril tottered and collapsed as Lear cursed her.

McKellen's Lear was a complex human being, no austere, rigidly authoritarian patriarch but a self-aware humorist, capable of folly, of acting the role of despot, but also of recognizing his weaknesses. He had clearly prepared his abdication speech in advance; as he delivered it point by point he let drop the cards on which it was written. The idea that Lear would 'crawl toward death' amused him; he spoke jokily, as if it were all part of a premeditated game. By far the most relaxed character onstage, he allowed us entry into the king's personal feelings by ruefully wiping his lips after accepting Regan's hypocritical kiss. Lear was amused by the disguised Kent's bluntness, tolerant of the Fool, very much one of the lads with his knights, but rose to true magnificence on 'I gave you all'. The subsequent 'O reason not the need' was masterly in its pacing, moving in its shifts of emotion. There was comedy but pathos too in Lear's insistence that Edgar's plight, like his own, must have been brought about by filial ingratitude. Lear splayed apart the legs of the prone and nearly naked Edgar as he contemplated 'unaccommodated man', taking down his trousers to reveal his genitals. This aroused prurient criticism, but is surely justified by the play's latent Christian iconography. The first time I saw the play McKellen followed this up by pointing to his genitals on 'every inch a king' as if to suggest exceptional endowment; later this self-indulgence was dropped. He boldly sustained his self-irony in the dialogue with the blind Gloucester, blowing his nose as he said he was 'not ague-proof' and imitating a baby's cries on 'Thou know'st the first time that we smell the air | We waul and cry'. He was tenderly vulnerable in his reunion with Cordelia. In the final scene some actors deliver 'Howl, howl, howl, howl' purely as an internal cry; others treat it as an imperative address to the onlookers. McKellen affectingly did both, speaking the word twice as if to himself as he carried on Cordelia's body, then twice again to the watchers as he displayed her corpse. His speeches over her body flowed with the inevitability of music. The five 'nevers', widely spaced, hung on the air like drops of blood from Lear's heart. This king died as he had lived, every inch a human being.

Janet Suzman

Figure 36.1. Janet Suzman as Cleopatra, Royal Shakespeare Theatre, Stratford-upon-Avon, 1972: photograph by Reg Wilson. Reg Wilson © Royal Shakespeare Company

1939– . *Principal Shakespeare roles*: Joan la Pucelle, Portia, Celia, Katherine, Rosalind, Beatrice, Cleopatra, Volumnia.

Even more than her great forebears Peggy Ashcroft and Sybil Thorndike, Janet Suzman is a political activist whose principles inform her theatrical career as well as her private life. Born in South Africa, niece of the great anti-apartheid campaigner Helen Suzman, she trained for the stage at the London Academy of Music and Dramatic Art (LAMDA) and joined the Royal Shakespeare Company in 1963. She is a woman of vibrant personality and sultry sexuality whose intelligence and strength of character shine through her appearance, fine-featured and strong-voiced with challenging eyes and fluently decisive gestures. She has excelled in passionate, emotionally complex roles, and, especially in the later part of her career, has directed plays as well as acting. Her multiracial, politically informed production of *Othello* at The Market Theatre, Johannesburg, in 1987 before audiences still subject to segregation had inflammatory consequences. In 2006 she directed a mixed-race cast in *Hamlet* for the Baxter Theatre of the University of Cape Town in which John Kani, her Othello in 1976, played Claudius. The young black actor cast as Guildenstern was horrifyingly murdered shortly before the production was to move to Stratford-upon-Avon as part of the RSC's Complete Works season. And in 2010 she directed Kim Cattrall as Cleopatra, her own most famous Shakespeare role, in Liverpool, repeating the production in Chichester in 2012.

In her first Stratford season, of 1963, she made her mark in the small role of Joan la Pucelle in a heavily rewritten version of *Henry VI, Part One* which formed part of the Peter Hall–John Barton *Wars of the Roses*, acting, wrote J. C. Trewin, 'with fanatical vigour'.[1] Barton was to exert a strong influence on her technique and future career. Two years later she undertook the more prominent roles of Rosaline in *Love's Labour's Lost*, Portia, and Ophelia. Of her Rosaline—still not a starring role—an anonymous critic in the *Birmingham Post* wrote presciently that she 'develops a wit and warmth that one day may serve her well as Beatrice'.[2] And in *The Tribune* Mervyn Jones, recalling the 'ferocity' with which she had played Joan la Pucelle, commented that it had 'entitled her to a shot at Lady Macbeth'.[3] Surprisingly, she played this role only on television, with Eric Porter as Macbeth in 1970.

Jones, still playing the casting game, continued that the 'charm and sprightliness' of her Rosaline fitted her for Viola, and, somewhat indiscriminatingly, that she played Portia 'so well that she could reasonably try her hand at anything'. Her originality of approach paid dividends in what Charles Landstone, writing in the *Jewish Chronicle*, described as 'a fascinating Portia. Delightful in repose, it is intriguing to watch her in the casket scenes, her eyes dreading Morocco's choice, her body taut in anticipation of Bassanio's success. She is measured and judicial in the trial scene, beautifully averring that the quality of mercy is not strained.'[4]

Suzman's talent for playing strong women made her natural casting for what Gareth Lloyd Evans described oxymoronically as a 'superbly virile Katherine' to Michael Williams's engaging Petruccio in 1967, though her 'shrewishness is but a cloak for waiting love'.[5] B. A. Young, too, found more than mere stridency in her interpretation: she 'gives a fine performance that stands out amongst the rest as being something more than merely comic'.[6]

From this it was a natural step to Beatrice in *Much Ado About Nothing*, but in Stratford this was the least successful of her comic roles. Lloyd Evans wrote that she seemed 'not altogether to have got over her Katherine'. 'She bounces on the lines, flinging her arms in accompaniment, mistaking emphasis for wit and a coquettish look for grace.'[7] He was not alone. Ronald Bryden, in *The Observer*, while finding that 'she can't be less than enchanting', thought nevertheless that 'her Beatrice is perhaps too level-headedly good-natured—the part needs a sharper, more impatient edge'.[8] Nor was this a purely masculine reaction. Hilary Spurling, in *The Spectator*, found her 'shrewish enough—indeed too shrewish, too close to the obstreperous high spirits of her Katherine' with 'neither Beatrice's subtlety nor her unsentimental hardness'.[9] A moment that has stuck in my mind is her advancing towards the audience from her place of concealment after her overhearing scene with the words 'What fire is in mine ears?' It was comic in its sense of personal affront, but it lacked the sense that Beatrice has undergone a transformational learning experience which can give depth to the role and prepare us for the emotional volte-face in her relationship with Benedick.

When the production transferred to London, however, her performance appears to have matured significantly. 'A new spirit of intelligence seems to have spread through the whole thing,' wrote B. A. Young. 'Janet Suzman's Beatrice, a sour-tongued blue-stocking who has to wear glasses to read Benedict's halting sonnet, is witty and confident, and her lines come sizzling across.'[10] Irving Wardle, too, found that the production had been 'transfigured by its passage from Stratford to the Aldwych' and had 'blossomed into a gorgeous piece of comic ensemble'.[11]

To be cast as Celia to the Rosalind of Dorothy Tutin in David Jones's production of *As You Like It* after playing Portia might have seemed like a downward step, but Suzman's ability to convey emotion in silence, evinced in her playing of the caskets scene in *The Merchant of Venice*, stood her in good stead in this role too. 'In her long silences', wrote Gareth Lloyd Evans, 'the eyes speak and the body declares that here is another Rosalind. When she speaks it is with a mocking affection that suggests envy without rancour.'[12] Irving Wardle found that in her hands the role acquired 'an enchanting combination of self-mocking dignity and sheer fun which redoubles the comic delight of the Rosalind scenes'.[13] She was 'just as gay and hoydenish as her cousin, and never retreating into nonentity as she so easily may'.[14] And Robert Smallwood notes that 'the danger represented by Celia's silent presence to Rosalind's loquacious love-making is very real. If "watch out for your Iago" is famous advice to any actor contemplating the role of

Othello, "watch out for your Celia" is equally pertinent for would-be Rosalinds. It only needs an eyebrow flickered at the audience at the wrong (or the right—according to one's point of view) moment, and tragic hero, or comic heroine, can be sunk.'[15]

In the 1968 revival of this production Suzman did indeed succeed to the role of Rosalind. 'Duly promoted', wrote Michael Billington, 'Miss Suzman vindicates critical acumen by turning in an attractive perform-ance that successfully combines the character's nimbleness of wit and ecstasy of spirit in a way we have not seen since Vanessa Redgrave played the part'[16]—this was in a classic Stratford production of 1961 which had vindicated Olivier's claim (see Chapter 26) that Vanessa's birth heralded the arrival of a great actress. Lloyd Evans, however, in a comparison with Tutin, found that 'trickiness replaces winsomeness, coquetry ousts romance'.[17]

The climax of Suzman's career as a Shakespeare actor came in 1972 when, along with playing Lavinia in *Titus Andronicus*, she undertook Cleopatra to the Antony of Richard Johnson in a production of *Antony and Cleopatra* directed by Trevor Nunn, whom she had married the previous year. Just as Lloyd Evans had discerned virility in her Kather-ine, so B. A. Young found that she gave 'a touch of masculinity' to Cleopatra. 'She is an Egyptian Elizabeth 1.' And he found that she brought 'sharply to life the "infinite variety" Shakespeare wrote into' the character; 'the sudden changes of temper, the intrinsic dignity and the childish dishonesty, the majesty and the trivialities'.[18] Michael Billington too was impressed by her volatility: her 'tawny-fronted Cleopatra begins as skittish, vain and mercurial, moving from deep feeling to bedroom playfulness in an instant. She is also good on tiny details such as her instinctive recoil on seeing Antony paralysed by defeat after Actium.'[19]

It is in the play's final scenes that Shakespeare asks the performer to bring transcendence to the role, and here again Suzman triumphed: Young wrote that she was 'best of all in her speaking of the beautiful lines of the last act'; Trewin that she 'finds some of the ultimate ecstasy of the "lass unparalleled" in the long adagio of the end'; and Billington that 'in death she gains a real dignity, suggesting that she can at last match her dream-image of a superhuman Antony'.[20] Again, too, critics found that her performance gained in strength when they saw a revival in London: here, wrote Frank Marcus, she 'comes as near to success as any Cleopatra that I have seen: her performance has developed wonderfully. She is much lighter and more teasing in the first half, with the streak of masculine determination almost gone. She is alluring and she is majestic.'[21] And Trewin, not easy to please, found that 'she has deepened and extended her Cleopatra, a portrait of persuasive magnificence'.[22] In the following year the production was filmed for television.

Many years later, in 2012, Suzman published a racily written book, *Not Hamlet*,[23] in which she devotes a chapter to Cleopatra. This is, she writes, 'the richest, most varied, most misunderstood part that Shakespeare wrote, and it's quite impossible to get it all'. Doggedly flying in face of the evidence that it was originally played by a boy, she argues that 'a woman with imagination and life experience of all kinds has a decent chance of getting most of it' (p. 73). Echoing, probably unconsciously, B. A. Young's comment that 'She is an Egyptian Elizabeth I', she writes: 'As for her personal involvement in the battle, her motives are resoundingly Elizabethan...shades of Elizabeth at Tilbury' (pp. 93–4). And her concluding comment on the role perceptively compares it to King Lear:

In her turn, when he [Antony] dies in her arms, her poetry too begins an unmatched flight, as if such a man can only be realised once he's melted away. The verse becomes transcendent, elevated, as we watch her reaching for an understanding of herself, and her love, and her loss, and how ordinary that makes her. 'No more but e'en a woman.' She understands, too late, the magnitude of what is gone from her. Just as Lear learns he is a poor, forked animal, merely, a man, before being a king, so does Cleopatra learn she is no more than 'the maid that milks' before she is a queen. (p. 98)

This, the most demanding of all Shakespeare's female roles, formed a fitting climax to Suzman's career as a Shakespeare actor, but thirty-five years later, in 2007, she returned to Stratford to play Volumnia to the Coriolanus of William Houston. It was good casting. In *The Observer*, Clare Fitzsimons wrote that 'Janet Suzman triumphs as Volumnia', finding her 'the perfect cajoling mother pressurizing her son into battle and moulding a monster'.[24] And a critic in the *Daily Telegraph* wrote that she 'gives a thrilling, chilling performance as the mother who has created this killing machine and deformed his personality. The way this old boot rejoices in her son's wounds and calls him to heel is terrifying to behold. But the key scene in which she finally reduces him to tears as he belatedly acknowledges the demands of love and compassion is almost unbearably affecting.'[25]

Antony Sher

Figure 37.1. Antony Sher as Richard III, Royal Shakespeare Theatre, Stratford-upon-Avon, 1984: photograph by Joe Cocks. Joe Cocks Studio Collection © Shakespeare Birthplace Trust

1949– . *Principal Shakespeare roles*: Lear's Fool, Richard III, Shylock, Leontes, Macbeth, Iago, Prospero, Falstaff.

The multi-talented Sir Antony Sher is a writer both of personal memoirs and of novels and plays, a painter, and a theatre director as well as a great actor. South African by birth, and Jewish, he trained at the Webber Douglas Academy of Dramatic Art from 1959 to 1961, and acted with the theatre group Gay Sweatshop and at the Liverpool Everyman Theatre before joining the Royal Shakespeare Company, for which he has performed most of his Shakespeare roles, in 1982.

Relatively short, burly and powerfully built, he is, as was Edmund Kean, a highly physical actor, capable at least in his younger days of daring feats of athleticism, as he showed in his thrilling Tamburlaine of 1994. Like Kean too (whom he has played in Sartre's adaptation of the play by Alexandre Dumas) Sher is both powerful and mellifluous vocally, and his piercing gaze has an almost hypnotic effect. Although he has played Prospero, he is not by nature a lyrical actor—by no means a Romeo, not even a Hamlet or a Richard II. And he prefers to forget his Malvolio.

Like Kean again, Sher is at his best in heroic and tragic roles. Deeply earnest in his approach to his art, skilled in physical transformation—on both stage and film he has convincingly portrayed real people, such as Benjamin Disraeli, Enoch Powell, Stanley Spencer, Ringo Starr in a play about the Beatles which gave him his first West End role, and even Henry Irving in an eightieth birthday tribute to Olivier—he prepares assiduously for his roles and likes to be involved in all stages of the production process.

At Liverpool he played the Fool in *King Lear*, and this became his first part for the RSC, in a spectacular 1982 production by Adrian Noble starring Michael Gambon. Sher's was an eye-catching, elaborately and cleverly contrived performance which drew heavily on traditions of the music hall and other popular entertainment. Billington wrote that 'With his red nose, coxcomb, patch trousers, violin case and deformed, heavily booted feet' he was 'a strange mixture of Grock, Little Titch, Beckett's Didi and Max Wall. But above all he is Lear's alter-ego, the visible mark of his master's insanity as he perches on his lap like a ventriloquist's doll.'[1] And Benedict Nightingale recognized both the virtuosity and the high intelligence that had gone into the performance, finding it 'the most exciting and impressive' that the evening had to offer. He wrote that though it 'could become merely showy, attention-getting', in fact Sher 'makes sense of difficult lines, evolves into a splendidly acidulous character, and is patently a powerful influence on Gambon's Lear'.[2]

A starring role clearly loomed, and Sher tells in his revealing memoir *Year of the King* how, after numerous misgivings and much heart searching, the choice fell on Richard III—boldly in view of the long shadow cast by Olivier's interpretation on both stage and film. Directed by Bill Alexander, Sher played it in a large-scale, picturesque production set mostly in a cathedral which almost took us back to the days of John Philip Kemble at Covent Garden. I vividly recall the thrill of Sher's first entry on opening night as, costumed in black, he emerged from the backstage shadows, swinging menacingly towards us on a pair of adeptly managed elbow crutches, his hump displayed as if in a kind of inverted pride. Short, curly-headed, he looked like a spindle-legged, knock-kneed caricature of Henry Irving. His rapid, jerky movements suggested hyperactive mental activity; he exhibited a capacity to charm and fascinate as well as to repel. His encounters with both Lady Anne and Queen Elizabeth were appropriately erotic, but essentially this was a cerebral character, a satirist who delighted in analysing Anne's weakness—he spoke 'Was ever woman in this humour wooed...' to the audience with aggressive, contemptuous malevolence. Irony rather than emotion governed his actions; the play was treated as an ironic tragedy, not as a first study for *Macbeth*. Comedy verged on farce as, carried on a portable throne, he had himself rapidly turned from one direction to another in response to his mother's rebukes; but he was shaken by her curse, his tongue flicking like a reptile's as he strove to regain his equilibrium.

Irony governed the closing scenes, too. His final soliloquy, true to the style in which it is written, was an intellectual self-exploration, not an emotional revelation: what shook him was his astonished discovery that he was capable of experiencing fear. There was pathos in his final, deformed, dismounted, bloodstained helplessness as Richmond stabbed him from behind through his corslet and the body rocked from side to side before toppling over, sideways, to the ironic sound of a Gloria.

Sher's Jewishness made Shylock an obvious choice for his next RSC role. But he writes in his autobiography *Beside Myself* that as he prepared he found himself thinking more about racism than about anti-Semitism. Nevertheless, Bill Alexander's picturesque production stressed religious issues, opening with the sounds of a Kyrie Eleison in parallel with offstage Jewish chanting. Similarly, a Hebrew prayer and sacrificial ritual matched by anguished chanting of Latin prayers from the Christians were inserted as Shylock prepared to cut into Antonio's flesh.

Sher's dignified but passionate Shylock gained in sympathy because, as in much modern criticism of the play, the Christians were seen as no less morally culpable than the Jews. Submissive in adversity, he was yet immensely exciting in the self-justifying parable of Jacob and the sheep, vigorously and rhythmically slapping one fist into the palm of the other as he illustrated 'the work of generation'. It was Jessica's defection to the Christian party that turned his attitude to the bond from playfulness to vindictiveness, then the eloquent climax of the 'I am a Jew' speech came with the word 'Revenge'. At the end of the scene he sat at the corner of the stage, prayed (in Hebrew), and rocked backwards and forwards muttering obsessively of revenge as the house lights went up for the interval. From being a representative of a wronged race he had become a vindictive individual, but even in court he still made a plea for sympathy which was also a bitter attack on Christian practices as, on

the words 'You have among you many a purchased slave', he dragged
forward a cowering young black from among the onlookers to illus-
trate his point.

It was a political as well as a theatrical move. This was a crucial time
for Sher's native country; feelings ran high in Stratford about the
invitation to a South African representative to attend the annual
Shakespeare Birthday celebrations, and at the Birthday performance
itself Sher explicitly directed this action to the South African representative sitting in the stalls. His political commitment to his native
country showed itself again in 1995 when he played Titus Andronicus
in a multiracial production at The Market Theatre, Johannesburg
which, acclaimed when it came to England, aroused controversy on
its home ground, and also when he played Prospero in 2008 at the
Baxter Theatre, Cape Town, addressing the plea for forgiveness in the
Epilogue directly to Caliban.

In acting, as in musical performance, virtuosity can be the enemy of
spontaneity. The self-consciously studied nature of Sher's art which
reflects the acute intelligence and deep thoughtfulness with which he
prepares his roles means that for some spectators the artifice of his
playing can seem too close to the surface. The original intention
when he undertook Leontes in a 1999 production of *The Winter's
Tale* directed by Gregory Doran was that—even though he admits to
being tone-deaf and consequently unable to sing—he should double
the role with that of the musical tinker Autolycus, a self-conscious feat
of virtuosity which so far as I know had never been attempted. Perhaps
fortunately, the idea was abandoned, though not before the play was
already in rehearsal.

Reviews of his Leontes show an interesting divergence between
those critics who capitulated to his brilliance and others for whom, as
Billington wrote, 'he often seems to be explaining the role rather than
to be demoniacally possessed by it'.[3] John Gross wrote that 'A Sher
performance always involves flashiness as well as intensity'. But, he
continued, 'this time it is the intensity that wins out'.[4] Billington, in
spite of his reservations, found that 'he is at his best when he surrenders
to the emotion of the moment: heartbreakingly so in the final act'.[5]
And John Peter wrote that 'this is one of Sher's most intense, most fully
achieved performances'.[6]

It was quickly followed by a *Macbeth* directed by Doran in the more
confined space of the Swan which evoked admiring comparisons with

Trevor Nunn's famous Other Place production of 1976. The deep intelligence and depth of Sher's understanding of the role, finely matched by Harriet Walter's Lady Macbeth, won general admiration. In the *Independent on Sunday*, to give only one example, Robert Butler wrote, 'Sher's command of the text is absolute . . . again and again he uncovers new colour and meaning in familiar lines, pushing the range of tone within a single speech to exhilarating extremes.'[7] Similarly Ian Shuttleworth wrote that he 'is almost unparalleled at conveying the full nuance of an emotionally complex speech without seeming laboured or actorly'.[8] John Gross found that 'virtually every line is packed with meaning, and the most hackneyed scenes shed their familiarity'.[9] And Susannah Clapp remarked on his 'extraordinary ability for physical transformation' while expressing a minority opinion that 'you're always conscious of what he's doing: being bug-eyed at the weird sisters, fracturing his speeches'.[10]

The racial issues that had been apparent in Sher's interpretations of Shylock and Prospero came to the fore again when he played Iago in Gregory Doran's 2004 production of *Othello*, also in the Swan. Billington wrote that he 'adds an element of racial hatred' and that 'when he describes Othello as an "erring Barbarian" he does a grotesque simian dance'. His relationship with Emilia was bitterly misogynistic: 'he invests Iago with a sexually warped nature that manifests itself in a frozen contempt for his wife and a sexual excitement when he re-imagines his bed-sharing with Cassio'.[11]

In 2014 Sher returned to the challenge of playing a major comic role, this time with great success. His Falstaff in both Parts of *Henry IV* at Stratford, beautifully spoken, finely thought through, was a dignified and unsentimental reading, not shirking any of the character's more unpleasant aspects. 'Sher reminds us', wrote Michael Billington, 'that Falstaff is one of nature's predators. Sher plays down the fatness to emphasize the knight's upper-class origins. That has a double advantage in that it gives weight to his laugh-lines in the Eastcheap tavern scenes and provides a plausible explanation for his ruthless exploitativeness.'[12]

Simon Russell Beale

1961– . *Principal Shakespeare roles*: Thersites, Richard III, Ariel, Edgar, Iago, Hamlet, Macbeth, Malvolio, Benedick, Leontes, Timon, Lear.

Figure 38.1. Simon Russell Beale as Thersites in *Troilus and Cressida*, Royal Shakespeare Theatre, Stratford-upon-Avon, 1990: photograph by Joe Cocks. Joe Cocks Studio Collection © Shakespeare Birthplace Trust

Simon Russell Beale's performing career began at the age of 8 when he became a chorister at St Paul's Cathedral in London. His musical skills and interests have never left him; his singing voice developed into a fine light tenor, which he deployed to great effect when he played Ariel for the RSC in 1993, and he has what amounts to an alternative career as a broadcaster and writer on the history of music.

Moving from St Paul's to Michael Redgrave's old school, Clifton College, Bristol, Beale developed acting skills and, like many others over the past century or so, played leading Shakespeare roles as a boy: Desdemona at the age of 14, Lear at 17. He had a distinguished undergraduate career at Cambridge, where he took first-class honours in English, and went on to study at the Guildhall School of Music and Drama, graduating in 1983. Not simply an instinctive actor, he has written about some of his roles in a manner that demonstrates a high degree of analytical skill, as for instance in an essay on playing Thersites published in *Players of Shakespeare 3.*[1]

As an actor Simon Russell Beale defies classification. He has performed in farce, in musicals, in a wide range of classic and modern plays, even in ballet (as the Duchess in *Alice in Wonderland* at the Royal Opera House in 2011). He has a penchant for the comic-grotesque, witnessed by his performance in outrageously camp roles in Restoration comedy and in modern plays such as Peter Nichols's *Privates on Parade.* This was apparent too in one of his earliest performances for the RSC, as Thersites in 1987, of which Charles Spencer, describing it as the 'chief glory of the evening', wrote in the *Daily Telegraph,* 'Hunchbacked, rheumy-eyed, and limping, and wearing a greasy raincoat, Russell Beale savours every syllable of the character's scabrousness and jibes.'[2] This production, like many others in which he has appeared, was directed by Sam Mendes.

Beale's overall versatility is reflected in his range as a Shakespeare actor. Conforming to no theatrical stereotype, he has already in his early fifties won success in a wider range of Shakespearian roles than perhaps any actor since Richard Burbage. Neither particularly tall nor conventionally handsome, bullet-headed, portly even as a young man, he has (like Charles Laughton) exceptionally mobile features, expressive eyes, and a strong speaking voice with exquisitely flexible diction. Unwieldy in build, he is nevertheless light on his feet. He is not a romantic or a lyrical actor; not a Romeo, or a Richard II, or (so far) a Prospero. Nor is he suited by nature or physique to such heroic roles as Henry V and Coriolanus. He might seem to be most easily classified as a character actor, and indeed he has played roles, including Thersites, Richard III, Iago, Leontes, and (on television) Falstaff that might more or less fit into this somewhat nebulous category. But he has also played major supporting roles, such as Cassius, Ariel, and Edgar; comic leads, including Benedick and Malvolio; and tragic heroes: Hamlet, Macbeth, Timon of Athens, and King Lear.

It is both a strength and a limitation of Beale's acting that he seeks to plumb Shakespeare's words for every conceivable nuance of meaning. His desire to convey interiority of feeling through his handling of the language can give great depth to his characterization of a role, but it can also result in a mannered sacrifice of verse rhythms as he tries to reveal meaning between words and phrases rather than through the longer unit of the line—a practice that is unsuited to the speaking of lyrical verse. He also has a tendency, not uncommon in modern actors, to run sentences together as if in the attempt to convey spontaneity. So, Michael Dobson wrote, his Macbeth of 2005 'was forever watching himself, looking surprised to hear himself say things, registering change in himself, often during long mid-line pauses: at 1.3.138, "My thought, whose murder [shocked to find the word in his mind, thinks for a long time about it, then tries to sound dismissively provisional] yet is but fantastical..."'[3] It is the very opposite of Bernard Shaw's advice that Shakespeare should be played 'on the line and to the line, with the utterance and acting simultaneous, inseparable, and in fact identical'.[4]

I said that Richard III might be considered a 'character' part, and it certainly became this when Beale played it at The Other Place in 1992, again directed by Mendes, as his first starring role. As with his Thersites, external appearance played its part in the actor's success. 'Squat, hairless, and plump with an impressive hump beneath his overcoat, he stumps around on his stick looking every inch the "poisonous, bunch-backed toad"', wrote Charles Spencer.[5] Beale made so much of the role's comic potential that Benedict Nightingale 'laughed more at Russell Beale than at any Richard I have seen'. He went on to ask, 'But where is the terror, the weight, the power?'[6] Other critics, however, found these qualities in good measure. Billington wrote that 'what makes this a fine performance is the revelation that underneath the campy wit lurks a gargantuan appetite for power'.[7] And Charles Spencer considered that 'From the magnificent opening speech, delivered with an irresistible mixture of humour and contempt, Beale makes the part emphatically his own.'[8] There was praise for his technique: 'The timing of his asides is impeccable, his ability to load a single word with a cargo of comic disdain a real wonder.'[9] And, as often in this actor's work, characterful silent business played its part: 'Thrillingly, at the start of the second half, Richard enters through the audience in an ermine cloak and crown to a percussive accompaniment that made this reviewer leap in terror. Just before he reaches the throne, however, he slips and falls and there's an electrifying moment of enraged panic as he angrily rejects any helping hand but that of Stephen Boxer's Buckingham.'[10] Another piece of added business, and one that attracted much attention, was when, as Ariel, he spat contemptuously in Prospero's face as he bade him farewell. (It was dropped later in the run.)

The ability to create a sense of idiosyncratic character both from external detail and from imaginative identification with a role which was apparent in his Thersites and in Richard III found expression too in his Malvolio of 2002, described by Michael Dobson as 'simply the best and most closely observed Malvolio I have ever seen, at once the funniest and the most heart-breaking...He managed to combine prissiness, profound earnestness and an underlying sense of insecurity to a whole range of effects, all of them beautifully highlighted by a visibly cherished Hercule Poirot moustache and an Edward VII beard which struggled in vain to confer an air of distinction on his dumpy chin.'[11]

Beale is an interior actor in the sense that his skills lie rather in imaginative identification with the characters he plays than in the kind of physical transformation at which Antony Sher excels. This is not to say that he declines to try to match the outer to the inner man, as he conspicuously did with both Thersites and Malvolio. But he has a special ability to convey interiority of emotion, an intensity of pent-up feeling that only slowly finds an outlet in action which is all the more devastating for the wait. This was apparent early in his career in what has become a famous climax to his performance of Konstantin in *The Seagull*, when, as Carol Chillington Rutter writes in a substantial essay on the actor, about to commit suicide, 'he stood almost paralysed over his desk, tidying papers, destroying writing, a two-minute silence re-playing a whole damaged life before exiting to suicide'.[12] It was a deeply moving stretch of silent acting.

Somewhat similarly, when he came to play Edgar to Michael Gambon's Lear, traumatized, as Peter Holland wrote in *Shakespeare Survey* 47, 'by the blinding of his father',[13] he attacked Oswald with single-minded ferocity, blinding him with his staff as he killed him, as if, it seemed to me, it was only by a desperate effort of will that he could force himself to commit so uncharacteristic a deed.

Beale has a special skill in effecting swift transitions from one state of mind to another; as Iago in a small-scale production of *Othello* in the Cottesloe Theatre, wrote Robert Smallwood, 'with Othello unconscious on the floor, the shadows from the ceiling fan passing rhythmically across his twitching body, he laughed a brilliant, chilling, contemptuous laugh of satisfaction, which turned into an extraordinary retch, as though the boundaries of destruction and pain that he was treading had made him sick with excitement and fear'.[14]

Though the bulky Beale did not seem obvious casting for Hamlet, his performance in the role in a production directed by John Caird in the Lyttelton auditorium in 2000 won major awards as well as praise from discerning critics. It is finely described in *Shakespeare Survey* 54 by Michael Dobson, who singles out the closet scene as its 'most striking moment. . . . just after "but look, amazement on thy mother sits", when for the briefest moment Hamlet found himself between Gertrude and the Ghost, touching both of them, poised yearningly between this world and the next. For a tiny second this family triad was and was not reunited, and Russell Beale's expression eloquently conveyed his sense of all that had been lost: his frustration that Gertrude could not see the ghost was almost unbearable.'[15] This was creative acting that brings a new light to bear on the play as well as on the character.

In 2012 and 2014, in the wide-open spaces of the Olivier auditorium of the National Theatre, Beale, by this time widely regarded as a national treasure, took on the closely related roles of Timon of Athens, directed by Nicholas Hytner, and King Lear, directed again by Sam Mendes. The action of Timon was updated to reflect current political and social issues, Athens becoming a money-obsessed London, the hinterland to which Timon flees a cardboard city in which Beale's fallen Timon might easily have begged a crust from his earlier incarnation as Thersites. Textual changes deprived him of the withdrawn poetry of Timon's closing moments, but he played the character's two faces with superlative ease, all smooth diplomacy with his sycophants in prosperity, savagely bitter in his disillusioned exile. And Beale's virtuosic ability to combine grotesque humour with profound interiority was well summed up in Michael Billington's account of his Lear:

There is a wild comedy to the moment when Russell Beale's Lear, padding around in his underpants, affects to put Goneril and Regan on trial while staring at an upended tea-urn and a lavatory bowl. But suddenly the deranged Lear takes an iron bar to the Fool and batters him to death. It is truly shocking because it is so brutal, unexpected and without sense given Lear's love for the Fool.[16]

So far Beale has played Falstaff only in an abbreviated version of *Henry IV* on television: the complexities in his portrayal of Lear whet the appetite for a stage realization of this equally but differently complex role, too.

Kenneth Branagh

Figure 39.1. Kenneth Branagh as Henry V, Royal Shakespeare Theatre, Stratford-upon-Avon, 1984: photograph by Joe Cocks. Joe Cocks Studio Collection © Shakespeare Birthplace Trust

1960– . *Principal Shakespeare roles*: Henry V, Hamlet, Romeo, Benedick, Touchstone, Coriolanus, Richard III, Macbeth.

Writing of Ralph Richardson, I quoted James Agate's comment that he played Henry V 'as a human being and not as a mailed fist, eating, sleeping, and thinking in armour' and suggested that this sounded like an anticipation of Branagh rather than of Olivier in the role. The warm and easy likeableness that characterizes this actor derives partly from the comfortableness of his figure—manly but huggable—and especially from the rich warmth of his speaking voice and the impression of relaxed intimacy that it can create. Alastair Macaulay, speaking of his Richard III, said to Branagh's biographer Mark White: 'it was the voice that was the revelation. . . . His voice in the theatre is perfectly focused. It comes from support in the diaphragm and the chest, and the voice is right there in front of the face so he can speak very fast and without any artifice. I don't know that I've ever heard an actor who can project fast

Shakespearean diction without it seeming all period or mannered.'[1] He is a superb speaker of poetry, responsive to verbal inwardness and to subtle rhythmic variation.

Born in Belfast of humble origins, Branagh became stage-struck as a lad and took part in school theatricals after his family moved to England. A schools matinee of *Romeo and Juliet* turned him on to Shakespeare when he was 14, and a few years later he was bowled over by seeing Derek Jacobi, with whom he has often worked in later years, as Hamlet. He played the role himself for the first time while training at the Royal Academy of Dramatic Art, where he won the Bancroft Gold Medal.

Rapidly making his way in the profession by way of a leading role in the West End production of Julian Mitchell's *Another Country* and some film and television appearances, he was recruited by the RSC, still aged only 23, for their 1984 season to play Laertes to Roger Rees's Hamlet (which he understudied), the King of Navarre in *Love's Labour's Lost*, and—the plum role—Henry V.

In his revealingly astute and hilarious memoir *Beginning* (1989), Branagh tells how his intensely conscientious and enthusiastic preparation for this role culminated in a visit to Kensington Palace to talk to the Prince of Wales about the stresses and strains attendant upon the royal office, a meeting which, he writes, 'enormously increased my understanding of many aspects of the role'.[2] His interpretation inevitably reacted with Olivier's in his famous film, as well as provoking rather silly suggestions that Branagh was seeing himself as a second Olivier. There are points of comparison, and they have grown over the years. Both actors have developed successful second careers as film actors and as directors of Shakespeare films starring themselves. Both have played Romeo, Henry V, Hamlet, Coriolanus, Richard III, and Macbeth. But Olivier's acting had a sardonic cutting edge that made him more obviously suited than Branagh to the last three of these roles.

As in his later film, released in 1989, Branagh's stage Henry V was notable for warm humanity, emphasizing, especially in the speech before Harfleur, Henry's understanding of the suffering brought about by war. He already had a relaxed, confident stage presence. Michael Coveney, acknowledging his 'natural authority', wrote, 'He speaks Shakespeare as well as anyone in recent years at Stratford and does so without a trace of verbal or physical mannerism.'[3] For Michael Billington this was 'a performance that betokens a great Shakespearean future for this young actor'.[4] And John Barber wrote in the *Daily*

Telegraph, 'Through it all Mr Branagh impresses with his stern youth, his ferocious anger, his quiet regrets when giving harsh commands and, finally, with a rough country boy charm' in the wooing scene, where brilliant comic timing got him a great laugh on 'Here comes your father'.[5] His stage interpretation is reflected in the film which (following in Olivier's footsteps) he directed himself.

The stage run of *Henry V* was not without its mishaps. Branagh's account in *Beginning* of his frantic efforts to improvise during a performance when the gloves with which he was to tease Fluellen went missing is a classic:

> Fluellen, ... as I do remember me,
> I bethinkst myself that I did have some gloves
> For which it was my full intent
> That thou should'st with them work.
> But see alas they are not here,
> Nor know I when'st they be.

Time passed while a fresh pair of gloves were sought—'I haven't got any more fucking gloves', the Stage Manager whispered frantically, by which time, Branagh writes, 'I had mourned individually over each of the Agincourt dead, and the shuddering shoulders of the English army told me that concentration was at an end.'[6]

In 1986 Branagh played Romeo in Hammersmith in a production that led to his founding (with David Parfitt) of the Renaissance Theatre Company, with which, assembling an immensely talented and loyal group of colleagues, he put on a number of productions of Shakespeare plays in the provinces as well as in London, sometimes with himself in relatively minor roles such as Peter Quince in *A Midsummer Night's Dream*, and as Edgar in *King Lear* (1990) with Richard Briers as the King. In 1988 he imaginatively invited three leading actors to direct plays in which he also appeared, playing Benedick for Judi Dench, and for Geraldine McEwan a hilarious Touchstone in *As You Like It*. Of his Benedick Billington wrote that he 'has the music-hall comic's instinctive sense of timing',[7] and of Touchstone—a notoriously difficult part to bring to comic life for today's audiences—'Mr Branagh, forever hunching his shoulders, shooting out his arms and dancing lightly on the balls of his feet, plays him as an urban spiv who makes no compromise with the spirit of Arden. Shaw said that any self-respecting Eskimo, confronted by Touchstone, would ask for his money back:

Mr Branagh actually makes you wait impatiently for every appearance of Shakespeare's unfunniest clown.'[8] This was a major achievement.

With this company Branagh also had his second shot at Hamlet, directed by Derek Jacobi, but his most successful stage appearance in the role came in 1992 in a beautifully conceived and executed full-length RSC production directed by Adrian Noble. This 'fine Hamlet', wrote Billington, 'stamped with rueful sadness...should still any doubts about Branagh's staying power'.[9] Benedict Nightingale thought it 'the most impressively princely Hamlet I have seen in ages',[10] for Charles Spencer it was 'the finest performance of his career',[11] and Jack Tinker considered it 'undoubtedly the great Hamlet of our time'.[12] Spencer linked it to Branagh's earlier performances, remarking that 'This actor's greatest strength has always been his manifest humanity, his dogged decency. He lets you into his character's mind with a complete absence of guile and showy flamboyance and at almost every stage you feel you know exactly what he is thinking and what he is feeling. As a result many of the play's difficulties seem to dissolve. The soliloquies have a conversational clarity...there is wonderful warmth and humour here, as well as shafts of cruelty, sardonic wit and emotional violence.' And Spencer singled out as the emotional climax of the role the 'spell-binding moment' when 'we watch as weary fatality gives way to a spiritual illumination that seems to light up his whole being'.[13] Branagh's outstanding film of *Hamlet*, boldly using a full text, is indebted to the stage production.

Branagh's warmth of personality, his easy stage presence, the natural lyricism of his speaking, mean that he is more easily attuned by nature to playing sympathetic rather than villainous or violent roles. His strongly cast Chichester *Coriolanus* of 1992 was notable mainly for Judi Dench's Volumnia, Branagh himself finding his role unsympathetic.

After completing the Stratford run of *Hamlet* in 1993, still aged only 32, Branagh abandoned the stage for ten years in favour of screen work as both director and actor. This included his own musical version of *Love's Labour's Lost* (2000) set in an Oxford college with himself as a typically warm-hearted Berowne, which is at its best in the song and dance numbers, and his film of *Hamlet* (1996). He also played Iago in a film of *Othello* directed by Oliver Parker.

His return to the stage came in 2002 when he played Richard III in a relatively modest, mainly modern-dress production directed by Michael Grandage at the Crucible Theatre, Sheffield. Michael Dobson offers a thoughtful analysis of the production in *Shakespeare Survey* 56, finding that though Branagh's performance sometimes seemed low-key, he had 'lost nothing of his touch in the live theatre'; 'though his was a Richard who was less of a satanic practical joker than any I have seen before, he was still in intimate contact with the audience throughout, able to indicate which lines were modulating into half-asides, which were to be heard in a different sense by his confidants in the auditorium than by his onstage interlocutors, with the lightest gestures of face or intonation'. This was 'a nuanced, subtle, close-up, studio-theatre Richard brilliantly communicated to a full-scale house'.[14] The result 'was a *Richard III* which shared a surprising amount of tone and spirit, rather than just structure, with *Macbeth*'. And *Macbeth* is the play in which Branagh returned to Shakespeare again in 2013, co-directing it himself in the setting of a disused church in Manchester. Though it had a run of only two weeks it was transmitted widely in cinemas and at the time of writing is to be presented again in New York—Branagh's first stage appearance in the city. Maybe a film will follow.

Endnotes

INTRODUCTION

1. *On Acting* (London: Weidenfeld and Nicolson, 1986), 246.
2. *Around Theatres* (London: Rupert Hart-Davis, 1953), 36.
3. Quotations are from the Oxford *Complete Works*, ed. Stanley Wells and Gary Taylor (1986 etc.).
4. *On Acting*, 72.
5. Philip Ziegler, *Olivier* (London: Maclehose Press, Quercus, 2013), 66.
6. Cited by Alan S. Downer, *The Eminent Tragedian: William Charles Macready* (Cambridge, Mass.: Harvard University Press, 1966), 32–3.
7. William Dunlap, *The Life of George Frederick Cooke*, i (2nd edn., London: printed for Henry Colburn, 1815), 120, citing 'a German writer of the name of Goede'.
8. Michael Strachan, *Secret Dreams: A Biography of Michael Redgrave* (London: Weidenfeld and Nicolson, 2004), 125.
9. James Agate, *Brief Chronicles* (London: Jonathan Cape, 1943), 71.

PRELUDE

1. Katherine Duncan-Jones, *Shakespeare: Upstart Crow to Sweet Swan 1592–1623* (London: Arden Shakespeare, 2011), 34.
2. *Historia Histrionica* (London: G. Groom, 1699), cxlvii.
3. C. M. Ingleby (ed.), *The Shakspere Allusion-Book: A Collection of Allusions to Shakspere from 1591 to 1700*, ii (London: Humphrey Milford, 1932), 260.
4. Nicholas Rowe, 'Some Account of the Life etc. of Mr William Shakespear', in *The Works of Mr William Shakespear*, ed Nicholas Rowe, vol. i (1709; London: Pickering & Chatto, 1999), vi.
5. Rowe, 'Some Account', vi.
6. George Bernard Shaw, *Shaw on Shakespeare: an Anthology of Bernard Shaw's Writings on the Plays and Production of Shakespeare*, ed. Edwin Wilson (London: Cassell, 1961), 85.
7. *The Plays of William Shakspeare*, ed. Samuel Johnson and George Steevens (1778; repr. London: Routledge, 1995), i. 204.
8. Jonathan Bate, *Soul of the Age: The Life, Mind and World of William Shakespeare* (London: Viking, 2008), 355.

9. Bate, *Soul*, 356.
10. Duncan-Jones, *Shakespeare*, 36.
11. Duncan-Jones, *Shakespeare*, 256.

I. RICHARD BURBAGE

1. Everard Guilpin, from 'Satire V', in *Skialetheia* (1598).
2. Cited by Andrew Gurr, *The Shakespearian Playing Companies* (Oxford: Clarendon Press, 1996), 292.
3. John Manningham, *The Diary of John Manningham of the Middle Temple, 1602–1603*, ed. Robert Parker Sorlien (Hanover, NH: University Press of New England, 1976), 75.
4. Cited by Glynne Wickham, Herbert Berry, and William Ingram (eds.), *English Professional Theatre, 1530–1660* (Cambridge: Cambridge University Press, 2000), 182.
5. Cited by Stanley Wells, *Shakespeare and Co.* (London: Allen Lane, 2006), 241.
6. C. M. Ingleby (ed.), *The Shakspere Allusion-Book: A Collection of Allusions to Shakspere from 1591 to 1700*, i (London: Humphrey Milford, 1932), 234.
7. Cited by Wells, *Shakespeare and Co.*, 242.
8. Cited by Wells, *Shakespeare and Co.*, 47.
9. Ingleby (ed.), *Shakspere Allusion-Book*, 487.

2. WILL KEMP

1. Cited by Stanley Wells, *Shakespeare and Co.* (London: Allen Lane, 2006), 32.
2. Cited by Wells, *Shakespeare and Co.*, 32.
3. Cited by Wells, *Shakespeare and Co.*, 34.
4. Cited by Wells, *Shakespeare and Co.*, 34.

3. ROBERT ARMIN

1. Cited by Stanley Wells, *Shakespeare and Co.* (London: Allen Lane, 2006), 37.

4. THOMAS BETTERTON

1. Cited by David Roberts, *Thomas Betterton: The Greatest Actor of the Restoration Stage* (Cambridge: Cambridge University Press, 2010), 95.
2. Cited by Roberts, *Thomas Betterton*, 1.

3. Samuel Pepys, *The Diary of Samuel Pepys: A New and Complete Transcription*, ed. Robert Latham and William Matthews, viii. *1667* (London: G. Bell & Sons, 1974), 421.

4. Colley Cibber, *An Apology for the Life of Mr. Colley Cibber* (London, 1822), 88.

5. Cibber, *Apology*, 88.

6. Cibber, *Apology*, 97.

7. Antony Aston, 'A Brief Supplement to Colley Cibber Esq. His Lives of the Famous Actors and Actresses' (London, 1747); repr. in Cibber, *Apology*, 109.

8. Cibber, *Apology*, 92.

9. Richard Steele, *Selections from the Tatler, Spectator and Guardian*, ed. Austin Dobson (2nd edn., Oxford: Clarendon Press, 1896), 367.

10. Cibber, *Apology*, 91.

11. Anon., *The Laureat* (1740), cited by Roberts, *Thomas Betterton*, 19.

12. Cited by Westminster Abbey website, 29 March 2014, <www.westminster-abbey.org/our-history/people/thomas-betterton>.

5. CHARLES MACKLIN

1. Cited by William W. Appleton, *Charles Macklin: An Actor's Life* (Cambridge, Mass.: Harvard University Press, 1961), 18.

2. John Hill, *The Actor or, A Treatise on the Art of Playing* (London, 1755; repr. New York: Benjamin Blom, 1972), 239–40.

3. Appleton, *Charles Macklin*, 30.

4. Cited by Appleton, *Charles Macklin*, 46.

5. Cited by Appleton, *Charles Macklin*, 49.

6. Francis Gentleman, *The Dramatic Censor; or, Critical Companion*, i (London, 1770; repr. Farnborough: Gregg, 1969), 292.

7. Georg Christoph Lichtenberg, *Lichtenberg's Visits to England: As Described in His Letters and Diaries*, trans. and annotated by Margaret L. Mare and W. H. Quarrell (New York: Benjamin Blom, 1938), 40.

8. Lichtenberg, *Visits*, 40.

9. Macklin's costumes for *Macbeth* are discussed by Dennis Bartholomeusz, *Macbeth and the Players* (Cambridge: Cambridge University Press, 1969), 83–5.

10. William Cooke, *Memoirs of Charles Macklin Comedian* (London, 1804; repr. New York: Benjamin Blom, 1972), 284.

6. DAVID GARRICK

1. Denis Diderot, *The Paradox of Acting*, trans. Walter H. Pollock (New York: Hill and Wang, 1957), 32–3.

2. Richard Cumberland, *Memoirs of Richard Cumberland Written by Himself*, i (London: Lackington, Allen & Co., 1807), 35 (29 March 2014), <http://hdl.handle.net/2027/uc1.b3295148>.

3. Cumberland, *Memoirs*, 80–1.

4. Cited by Peter Holland, 'David Garrick', in. *Great Shakespeareans*, ii. *Garrick, Kemble, Siddons, Kean*, ed. Peter Holland (London: Continuum, 2010), 29.

5. Cited by W. Clark Russell, *Representative Actors* (London: Frederick Warne & Co., n.d.), 111.

6. *Gentleman's Magazine and Historical Chronicle*, 12 (1742), 527.

7. Georg Christoph Lichtenberg, *Lichtenberg's Visits to England: As Described in His Letters and Diaries*, trans. and annotated by Margaret L. Mare and W. H. Quarrell (New York: Benjamin Blom, 1938), 9–10.

8. John Doran, *Annals of the English Stage from Thomas Betterton to Edmund Kean*, ii (London: John C. Nimmo, 1888), 123.

9. Cited by Stanley Wells, *Shakespeare: For All Time* (London: Macmillan, 2002), 217.

10. Francis Gentleman, *The Dramatic Censor; or, Critical Companion*, i (London, 1770; repr. Farnborough: Gregg, 1969), 108.

11. Cited by Stanley Wells, *Shakespeare: For All Time*, 216.

Who Was the First Great Shakespeare Actress?

1. Francis Gentleman, *The Dramatic Censor* (London, 1770), ii. 167.

2. Cited by W. Clark Russell, *Representative Actors* (London: Frederick Warne, n.d.), 103.

7. SARAH SIDDONS

1. James Boaden, *Memoirs of Mrs. Siddons: Interspersed with Anecdotes of Authors and Actors* (Philadelphia: Carey, Lea and Littel, 1827), 202.

2. Philip H. Highfill, Jr., Kalman A. Burnim, and Edward A. Langhans, *A Biographical Dictionary of Actors, Actresses, Musicians, Dancers, Managers & Other Stage Personnel in London, 1660–1800*, xiv. S. Siddons to Thynne (Carbondale: Southern Illinois University Press, 1991), 26.

3. Cited by Lisa A. Freeman, *Lives of Shakespearian Actors, Part II. Edmund Kean, Sarah Siddons and Harriet Smithson by Their Contemporaries*, ii. *Sarah Siddons* (London: Pickering & Chatto, 2009), 316–17.

4. Boaden, *Memoirs*, 141.

5. Cited by Thomas Campbell, *Life of Mrs Siddons*, i (London: Effingham Wilson, 1834), 245.

6. Cited by Russ McDonald, 'Sarah Siddons', in *Great Shakespeareans*, ii. *Garrick, Kemble, Siddons, Kean*, ed. Peter Holland (London: Continuum, 2010), 114.

7. Cited by McDonald, 'Sarah Siddons', 115.

8. Campbell, *Life*, ii. 35–6.
9. Campbell, *Life*, ii. 11–12.
10. Boaden, *Memoirs*, 333.
11. Cited by James Agate, *The English Dramatic Critics, 1660–1932* (London: Arthur Barker, 1932), 74.
12. Cited in *Eyewitnesses of Shakespeare: First Hand Accounts of Performances, 1590–1890* compiled by Gāmini Salgādo (London: Chatto & Windus, 1975), 325.
13. Cited by Campbell, *Life of Mrs Siddons*, i. 215–16.
14. Cited in Freeman, *Siddons*, 285.
15. Campbell, *Life of Mrs Siddons*, ii. 337.
16. Cited in Freeman, *Siddons*, 340.

8. GEORGE FREDERICK COOKE

1. Cited by Arnold Hare, *George Frederick Cooke: The Actor and the Man* (London: Society for Theatre Research, 1980), 87.
2. Cited by Hare, *George Frederick Cooke*, 210.
3. William Dunlap, *The Life of George Frederick Cooke*, i (2nd edn., London: printed for Henry Colburn, 1815), 49.
4. Dunlap, *Cooke*, i. 12–13.
5. Cited by Hare, *George Frederick Cooke*, 151.
6. Cited by Dunlap, *Cooke*, i. 154.
7. Leigh Hunt, *Dramatic Essays*, ed. William Archer and Robert W. Lowe (London: W. Scott, 1894), 103.
8. James Boaden, *The Life of Mrs Jordan*, ii. (London: Edward Bull, 1831), 74–5.
9. John Taylor, cited by W. Clark Russell, *Representative Actors* (London: Frederick Warne, n.d.), 236.
10. Cited by Dunlap, *Cooke*, i. 156.
11. Leigh Hunt, *Leigh Hunt's Dramatic Criticism 1808–1831*, ed. Lawrence Huston Houtchens and Carolyn Washburn Houtchens (London: Geoffrey Cumberlege, 1950), 114.
12. Charles Mathews, *Memoirs of Charles Mathews, Comedian* (2nd edn.) by Mrs Mathews (London: Richard Bentley, 1839), i. 126.
13. Dunlap, *Cooke*, i. 158.
14. Leigh Hunt's *London Journal*, supplement for part 1, p. lix. Google Books, 1 April 2014. <http://books.google.co.uk/books?id=R_EVAAAAIAAJ>.
15. Dunlap, *Cooke*, ii. 403–4.
16. Dennis Bartholomeusz, *Macbeth and the Players* (Cambridge: Cambridge University Press, 1969), 144.
17. Cited by Charles H. Shattuck, *Shakespeare on the American Stage: From the Hallams to Edwin Booth* (Washington, DC: Folger Shakespeare Library, 1976), 33.

9. JOHN PHILIP KEMBLE

1. Walter Scott, *Critical and Miscellaneous Essays*, iii (Philadelphia: Carey & Hart, 1841), 27. Google Books, 22 March 2014 <http://books.google.co. uk/books?id=jNosAQAAMAAJ>.

2. Scott, *Critical and Miscellaneous Essays*, 27–8.

3. Scott, *Critical and Miscellaneous Essays*, 33.

4. Scott, *Critical and Miscellaneous Essays*, 35.

5. G. C. D. Odell, *Shakespeare: From Betterton to Irving* (New York: Scribner, 1920; repr. London: Constable, 1963), ii. 85.

6. Cited by Wells (ed.), *Shakespeare in the Theatre: An Anthology of Criticism* (Oxford: Clarendon Press, 1997), 37.

7. Cited in *Eyewitnesses of Shakespeare: First Hand Accounts of Performances, 1590–1890*, compiled by Gāmini Salgādo (London: Chatto & Windus, 1975), 323.

8. Cited in *Eyewitnesses of Shakespeare*, compiled by Salgādo, 324.

9. William Hazlitt, 'A View of the English Stage', in *The Collected Works of William Hazlitt*, ed. A. R. Waller and Arnold Glover, viii (London: Dent, 1903), 350.

10. Hazlitt, 'View', 379.

11. Scott, *Critical and Miscellaneous Essays*, 35.

12. William Charles Macready, *Macready's Reminiscences, and Selections from His Diaries and Letters*, ed. Frederick Pollock, i (London: Macmillan,1875), 148.

13. Scott, *Critical and Miscellaneous Essays*, 41.

10. DORA JORDAN

1. Claire Tomalin, *Mrs Jordan's Profession: The Story of a Great Actress and a Future King* (London: Viking, 1994), note to pl. 3 between pp. 72–3.

2. Leigh Hunt, *Leigh Hunt's Dramatic Criticism 1808–1831*, ed. Lawrence Huston Houtchens and Carolyn Washburn Houtchens (London: Geoffrey Cumberlege, 1950), 88.

3. Cited by W. Clark Russell, *Representative Actors* (London: Frederick Warne, n.d.), 273 n. 2.

4. Cited by Tomalin, *Mrs Jordan's Profession*, 20.

5. W. C. Macready, *Macready's Reminiscences, and Selections from His Diaries and Letters*, ed. Frederick Pollock, i. (London: Macmillan, 1875), 63.

6. Cited by Tomalin, *Mrs Jordan's Profession*, 51.

7. Cited by Tomalin, *Mrs Jordan's Profession*, 349 n. 20.

8. Leigh Hunt, *Critical Essays on the Performers of the London Theatres* (London: John Hunt, 1807), 161–2. Google Books, 1 April 2014 <http://books. google.co.uk/books?id=C1QJAAAAQAAJ>.

11. EDMUND KEAN

1. Raymund Fitzsimons, *Edmund Kean: Fire from Heaven* (London: Hamish Hamilton, 1976), 68.
2. Cited by Simon Trussler, *The Cambridge Illustrated History of British Theatre* (Cambridge: Cambridge University Press, 1994), 210.
3. Cited by Peter Thomson, 'Edmund Kean', in *Great Shakespeareans*, ii, ed. Peter Holland, *Garrick, Kemble, Siddons, Kean* (London: Continuum, 2010), 148.
4. Cited by Harold Newcomb Hillebrand, *Edmund Kean* (New York: AMS Press, 1966), 371.
5. Cited by Hillebrand, *Edmund Kean*, 53.
6. Cited by Hillebrand, *Edmund Kean*, 71–2.
7. Cited by Hillebrand, *Edmund Kean*, 76.
8. Cited by Hillebrand, *Edmund Kean*, 111.
9. William Hazlitt, 'A View of the English Stage', in *The Collected Works of William Hazlitt*, ed. A. R. Waller and Arnold Glover, viii (London: Dent, 1903), 179.
10. Hazlitt, 'View', 179.
11. Cited by Hillebrand, *Edmund Kean*, 114.
12. Cited by Hillebrand, *Edmund Kean*, 116.
13. Hazlitt, 'View', 181–2.
14. Hazlitt, 'View', 188.
15. Cited by Hillebrand, *Edmund Kean*, 129.
16. Cited by Hillebrand, *Edmund Kean*, 128.
17. Hazlitt, 'View', 223.
18. Leigh Hunt, *Leigh Hunt's Dramatic Criticism 1808–1831*, ed. Lawrence Huston Houtchens and Carolyn Washburn Houtchens (London: Geoffrey Cumberlege, 1950), 137–8.
19. James Winston, *Drury Lane Journal: Selections from James Winston's Diaries 1819–1827*, ed. Alfred L. Nelson and Gilbert B. Cross (London: Society for Theatre Research, 1974), 107.

12. WILLIAM CHARLES MACREADY

1. Cited by J. C. Trewin, *Mr Macready: A Nineteenth-Century Tragedian and His Theatre* (London: George C. Harrap, 1955), 22.
2. Cited by Trewin, *Mr Macready*, 44.
3. Cited by Stanley Wells (ed.), *Shakespeare in the Theatre: An Anthology of Criticism* (Oxford: Clarendon Press, 1997), 57.
4. Cited by Wells (ed.), *Shakespeare in the Theatre*, 60.
5. Cited by Alan S. Downer, *The Eminent Tragedian: William Charles Macready* (Cambridge, Mass.: Harvard University Press, 1966), 71.
6. Cited by Downer, *Eminent Tragedian*, 32–3.

7. Cited by Downer, *Eminent Tragedian*, 29.

8. Cited by Wells (ed.), *Shakespeare in the Theatre*, 58–9.

9. Cited in *Eyewitnesses of Shakespeare: First Hand Accounts of Performances, 1590–1890*, compiled by Gāmini Salgādo (London: Chatto & Windus, 1975), 326.

10. Cited by Wells (ed.), *Shakespeare in the Theatre*, 61.

11. Cited in *Eyewitnesses*, compiled by Salgādo, 307.

12. John Coleman, *Fifty Years of an Actor's Life*, 2 vols. (London: Hutchinson, 1904), ii. 304.

13. Westland Marston, *Our Recent Actors*, i (London: Sampson, Low, Marston, Searle & Rivington, 1888), 86–7.

14. Cited by Trewin, *Mr Macready*, 239.

15. *Diaries of William Charles Macready*, ed. William Toynbee, 2 vols. (London, Chapman and Hall Ltd, 1912), i. 15.

16. Coleman, *Fifty Years of an Actor's Life*, ii. 34.

17. John Forster and George Henry Lewes, *Dramatic Essays*, ed. William Archer and Robert W. Lowe (London: Walter Scott Ltd, 1896), 52–4.

18. Helena Faucit, Lady Martin, *On Some of Shakespeare's Female Characters* (new edn., Edinburgh: Blackwood, 1891), 389–90.

13. HELEN FAUCIT

1. Helena Faucit, Lady Martin, *On Some of Shakespeare's Female Characters* (new edn., Edinburgh: Blackwood, 1891), 4.

2. Cited by Carol Jones Carlyle, *Helen Faucit: Fire and Ice on the Victorian Stage* (London: Society for Theatre Research, 2000), 53.

3. Archibald Alison, *Essays Political, Historical and Miscellaneous*, iii (Edinburgh: William Blackwood, 1850), 585. Google Books, 1 April 2014 <http://books.google.co.uk/books?id=yBsIAAAAIAAJ>.

4. Cited by Carlyle, *Helen Faucit*, 159.

5. Thomas De Quincey, *The Art of Conversation and Other Papers* (Edinburgh: Adam and Charles Black, 1863), 225–6. Google Books, 1 April 2014 <http://books.google.co.uk/books?id=u4ZKAAAAYAAJ>.

6. Cited by Carlyle, *Helen Faucit*, 29.

7. Cited by Carlyle, *Helen Faucit*, 49.

8. J. W. Flynn, *The Random Recollections of an Old Playgoer* (Cork: Guy & Co., 1890; repr. Forgotten Books, 2012), 17.

9. Faucit, *Female Characters*, 4.

10. Faucit, *Female Characters*, 7–8.

11. Cited in Christy Desmet (ed.), *Lives of Shakespearian Actors* (London, Pickering and Chatto, 2011), 337.

12. John Forster and George Henry Lewes, *Dramatic Essays*, ed. William Archer and Robert W. Lowe (London: Walter Scott Ltd, 1896), 174 n.

Who Was the First Great American Shakespeare Actor?

1. Lawrence Barrett, *Edwin Forrest* (New York: Benjamin Blom, 1881; repr. 1969), 16.
2. Charles H. Shattuck, *Shakespeare on the American Stage: From the Hallams to Edwin Booth* (Washington, DC: Folger Shakespeare Library, 1976), 63.
3. John Forster and George Henry Lewes, *Dramatic Essays*, ed. William Archer and Robert W. Lowe ((London: Walter Scott Ltd, 1896), 25.
4. Forster and Lewes, *Dramatic Essays*, 37.
5. Forster and Lewes, *Dramatic Essays*, 41.

14. IRA ALDRIDGE

1. Cited by Ruth M. Cowhig, 'Ira Aldridge in Manchester', in Bernth Lindfors (ed.), *Ira Aldridge: The African Roscius* (Rochester, NY : University of Rochester Press, 2007), 130–2.
2. *The Dramatic Essays of Charles Lamb*, ed. Brander Matthews (London: Chatto & Windus, 1891), 188.
3. Samuel Taylor Coleridge, *Shakespearean Criticism* (2nd edn.), i, ed. Thomas Middleton Raysor (London: Dent, 1960), 42.
4. Cited by Bernth Lindfors, *Ira Aldridge : The Early Years, 1807–1833* (Rochester, NY : University of Rochester Press, 2011), 229.
5. Cited by Lindfors, *Early Years*, 257.
6. Cited by Lindfors, *Early Years*, 267.
7. Cited by Hazel Waters, 'Ira Aldridge's Fight for Equality', in Lindfors (ed.), *Ira Aldridge: The African Roscius*, 108.
8. Cited by Waters, 'Ira Aldridge's Fight', 108–9.
9. Cited by Waters, 'Ira Aldridge's Fight', 118.
10. See Herbert Marshall, 'Ira Aldridge as Macbeth and King Lear', in Lindfors (ed.), *Ira Aldridge: The African Roscius*, 191–203.
11. Cited by Waters, 'Ira Aldridge's Fight', 115.
12. Cited by Errol Hill, *Shakespeare in Sable: A History of Black Shakespearean Actors* (Amherst, Mass.: University of Massachusetts Press, 1984), 19.
13. Cited by Bernth Lindfors, '"Mislike me not for my complexion . . . ": Ira Aldridge in Whiteface', in Lindfors (ed.), *Ira Aldridge: The African Roscius*, 187–8.
14. Cited by Waters, 'Ira Aldridge's Fight', 202–3.
15. Hill, *Shakespeare in Sable*, 25.

15. CHARLOTTE CUSHMAN

1. Clara Erskine Clement, *Charlotte Cushman* (Boston: Osgood, 1882), 75–6.
2. Cited by Clement, *Charlotte Cushman*, 18.
3. Clement, *Charlotte Cushman*, 78–9.

4. Cited by Clement, *Charlotte Cushman*, 82–3.
5. Cited by Clement, *Charlotte Cushman*, 45.
6. John Coleman, *Fifty Years of an Actor's Life*, 2 vols. (London, Hutchinson, 1904), ii. 363.
7. Coleman, *Fifty Years*, i. 306.
8. Emma Stebbins, *Charlotte Cushman: Her Letters and Memories of Her Life* (Boston: Houghton, Osgood & Co., 1879), 56.
9. Clement, *Charlotte Cushman*, 18.
10. *The Times* (3 April 1854), 10 (issue no. 21705).

16. EDWIN BOOTH

1. Charles H. Shattuck, *Shakespeare on the American Stage: From the Hallams to Edwin Booth* (Washington, DC: Folger Shakespeare Library, 1976), 9.
2. Shattuck, *Shakespeare*, 138.
3. Cited by Shattuck, *Shakespeare*, 142.
4. Cited by Horace Howard Furness, *A New Variorum Edition of Shakespeare: Othello* (12th edn., Philadelphia: J. B. Lippincott, 1886), 214.
5. Cited by Shattuck, *Shakespeare*, 7.
6. Cited by Shattuck, *Shakespeare*, 47–8.
7. Cited by Shattuck, *Shakespeare*, 60–1.
8. Shattuck, *Shakespeare*, 102.

17. HENRY IRVING

1. Arthur Colby Sprague, *Shakespearian Players and Performances* (Cambridge, Mass.: Harvard University Press, 1953), 105.
2. Ellen Terry and George Bernard Shaw, *Ellen Terry and Bernard Shaw: A Correspondence*, ed. Christopher St John (London: Constable, 1931), 56.
3. George Bernard Shaw, *Shaw on Shakespeare: An Anthology of Bernard Shaw's Writings on the Plays and Production of Shakespeare*, ed. Edwin Wilson (London: Cassell, 1961), 52.
4. Sprague, *Shakespearian Players*, 117.
5. Ellen Terry, *The Story of My Life* (London: Hutchinson & Co., 1908), 273–4.
6. Henry James, *The Scenic Art: Notes on Acting and the Drama 1872–1901* (London: Rupert Hart-Davis, 1949), 105.
7. Max Beerbohm, *Around Theatres* (London: Rupert Hart-Davis, 1953), 397.
8. Terry, *Story*, 98–9.
9. Dutton Cook, *Nights at the Play: A View of the English Stage* (London: Chatto & Windus, 1883), 261–3.
10. William Winter, *Shakespeare on the Stage* (London: T. Fisher Unwin, 1912), 362–3.
11. Terry, *Story*, 303.
12. Shaw, *On Shakespeare*, 162.

13. Shaw, *On Shakespeare*, 163.
14. Shaw, *On Shakespeare*, 53–4.
15. Winter, *Shakespeare*, 175.
16. Sprague, *Shakespearian Players*, 113–14.
17. Cited by Sprague, *Shakespearian Players*, 116.
18. Henry Arthur Jones, *The Shadow of Henry Irving* (London: Richards, 1931), 52–3.

18. ELLEN TERRY

1. Ellen Terry, *The Story of My Life* (London: Hutchinson & Co., 1908), 12.
2. Theodor Fontane, *Shakespeare in the London Theatre 1855–1858*, trans. Russell Jackson (London: Society for Theatre Research, 1999), 46.
3. *Queen Victoria Goes to the Theatre*, ed. George Rowell (London: Paul Elek, 1978), 71.
4. Terry, *Story*, 18.
5. *Fraser's* (July 1875), 67; reproduced in *Lives of Shakespearian Actors V*, iii, *Ellen Terry*, ed. Katharine Cockin (Pickering and Chatto, 2012), 23.
6. Terry, *Story*, 105–7.
7. Henry James, *The Scenic Art: Notes on Acting and the Drama 1872–1901*, ed. Allen Wade (London: Rupert Hart-Davis, 1949), 143.
8. Cited by Russ McDonald, *Look to the Lady: Sarah Siddons, Ellen Terry and Judi Dench on the Shakespearean Stage* (Athens, Ga.: University of Georgia Press, 2005), 94.
9. James, *Scenic Art*, 163.
10. Edward Gordon Craig, *Ellen Terry and Her Secret Self* (London: Sampson Low, Marston & Co., n.d.), 158.
11. Cited by Charles Hiatt, *Ellen Terry and Her Impersonations: An Appreciation* (London: George Bell & Sons, 1899), 176–7.
12. Cited by Hiatt, *Ellen Terry*, 177.
13. George Bernard Shaw, *Shaw on Shakespeare: An Anthology of Bernard Shaw's Writings on the Plays and Production of Shakespeare*, ed. Edwin Wilson (London: Cassell, 1961), 41.
14. Shaw, *On Shakespeare*, 47.
15. Shaw, *On Shakespeare*, 50.
16. Shaw, *On Shakespeare*, 55–6.
17. James, *Scenic Art*, 283–5.
18. Max Beerbohm, *More Theatres 1898–1903* (London: Rupert Hart-Davis, 1969), 575.

19. TOMMASO SALVINI

1. Henry James, *The Scenic Art: Notes on Acting and the Drama 1872–1901*, ed. Allen Wade (London: Rupert Hart-Davis, 1949), 169.
2. Max Beerbohm, *Around Theatres* (London: Rupert Hart-Davis, 1953), 80–1.
3. Bartolomeo Galletti, *High Art in a Foreign Tongue*, trans. and ed. Tony Mitchell (Brisbane: Australasian Drama Studies Association, 1995).
4. Cited by George C. D. Odell, *Shakespeare: From Betterton to Irving*, ii (New York: Scribner, 1920), 263.
5. Joseph Knight, *Theatrical Notes* (London: Lawrence & Bullen, 1893), 24.
6. *Century Magazine*, 26, NS 4 (1883), 90.
7. Mary Cowden Clarke, 'Salvini's Othello', *The Athenaeum*, no. 1892 (30 January 1864), 157.
8. Cited by Marvin Carlson, *The Italian Shakespearians: Performances by Ristori, Salvini, and Rossi in England and America* (Washington DC: Folger Shakespeare Library, 1985), 48.
9. James, *Scenic Art*, 183.
10. William Winter, *Shakespeare on the Stage* (London: T. Fisher Unwin, 1912), 288.
11. Winter, *Shakespeare on the Stage*, 411.
12. Cited by Carlson, *Italian Shakespearians*, 51.
13. Cited by Carlson, *Italian Shakespearians*, 97.
14. Cited by Carlson, *Italian Shakespearians*, 98–9.
15. Cited by Carlson, *Italian Shakespearians*, 97.
16. Cited by Carlson, *Italian Shakespearians*, 70.
17. Knight, *Theatrical Notes*, 24.

Times of Change

1. Max Beerbohm, *Around Theatres* (London: Rupert Hart-Davis, 1953), 63.
2. Cited by Stanley Wells (ed.), *Shakespeare in the Theatre: An Anthology of Criticism* (Oxford: Clarendon Press, 1997), 170.
3. Cited by George C. D. Odell, *Shakespeare: From Betterton to Irving*, ii (New York: Scribner, 1920), 413.
4. *Shaw on Shakespeare: An Anthology of Bernard Shaw's Writings on the Plays and Production of Shakespeare*, ed. Edwin Wilson (London: Cassell, 1961), 83–7.
5. Dennis Kennedy, *Looking at Shakespeare: A Visual History of Twentieth-Century Performance* (2nd edn., Cambridge: Cambridge University Press, 2001), 46.
6. Max Beerbohm, *More Theatres 1898–1903* (London: Rupert Hart-Davis, 1969), 574.
7. James Agate, *Brief Chronicles* (London: Jonathan Cape, 1943), 249.

8. Michael A. Morrison, *John Barrymore, Shakespearean Actor* (Cambridge: Cambridge University Press, 1997), 140.
9. Cited by Jonathan Croall, *Gielgud: A Theatrical Life* (London: Methuen, 2001), 125.
10. Laurence Olivier, *On Acting* (London: Weidenfeld and Nicolson, 1986), 36.

20. EDITH EVANS

1. James Agate, *The Contemporary Theatre, 1924* (London: Chapman & Hall, 1925), 84.
2. Kenneth Tynan, *A View of the English Stage 1944–1963* (London: Davis Poynter, 1975), 50.
3. J. C. Trewin, *Edith Evans* (2nd edn., London: Rockliff, 1954), 90.
4. Herbert Farjeon, *The Shakespearean Scene: Dramatic Criticisms* (London: Hutchinson & Co., n.d.), 21.
5. James Agate, *Brief Chronicles* (London: Jonathan Cape, 1943), 59.
6. Farjeon, *Shakespearean Scene*, 57.
7. Sybil and Russell Thorndike, *Lilian Baylis* (London: Chapman and Hall, 1938), 88.
8. Cited by Alan Strachan, *Secret Dreams: A Biography of Michael Redgrave* (London: Weidenfeld and Nicolson, 2004), 125.
9. Laurence Kitchin, *Mid-Century Drama* (London: Faber & Faber, 1960), 45.
10. Agate, *Brief Chronicles*, 208–12.
11. Quoted in James Agate, *The Selective Ego*, ed. Tim Beaumont (London, Harrap, 1976), 36.
12. *Shaw on Shakespeare: An Anthology of Bernard Shaw's Writings on the Plays and Production of Shakespeare*, ed. Edwin Wilson (London: Cassell, 1961), 10.

21. SYBIL THORNDIKE

1. Jonathan Croall, *Sybil Thorndike: A Star of Life* (London: Haus Books, 2008), 133.
2. Sybil and Russell Thorndike, *Lilian Baylis* (London: Chapman and Hall, 1938), 48, 56.
3. Gordon Crosse, *Shakespearean Playgoing, 1890–1952* (London: A. R. Mowbray & Co., 1953), 51.
4. Crosse, *Shakespearean Playgoing*, 51.
5. Sybil and Russell Thorndike, *Lilian Baylis*, 57.
6. Crosse, *Shakespearean Playgoing*, 52.
7. Crosse, *Shakespearean Playgoing*, 53.
8. Cited by Croall, *Sybil Thorndike*, 192.
9. Cited by Croall, *Sybil Thorndike*, 192.

10. James Agate, *Brief Chronicles* (London: Jonathan Cape, 1943), 124.
11. Cited by Croall, *Sybil Thorndike*, 201.
12. Cited by Croall, *Sybil Thorndike*, 201.
13. Cited by Croall, *Sybil Thorndike*, 238.
14. Agate, *Brief Chronicles*, 288.
15. Cited by Croall, *Sybil Thorndike*, 238.
16. Tyrone Guthrie, *On Acting* (London: Studio Vista, 1971), 74.
17. Cited by Croall, *Sybil Thorndike*, 143.
18. Agate, *Brief Chronicles*, 168.
19. Croall, *Sybil Thorndike*, 291.
20. Audrey Williamson, *Old Vic Drama: A Twelve Years' Study of Plays and Players* (London: Rockliff, 1948), 176.
21. Sybil and Russell Thorndike, *Lilian Baylis*, 33–5.
22. Sybil and Russell Thorndike, *Lilian Baylis*, 38.
23. Cited by Croall, *Sybil Thorndike*, 202.
24. Agate, *Brief Chronicles*, 220.
25. Sybil and Russell Thorndike, *Lilian Baylis*, 35.
26. Croall, *Sybil Thorndike*, 310.

22. CHARLES LAUGHTON

1. Cited by Simon Callow, *Charles Laughton: A Difficult Actor* (London: Methuen, 1987), 41.
2. Callow, *Charles Laughton*, 66.
3. James Agate, *Brief Chronicles* (London: Jonathan Cape, 1943), 127.
4. Gordon Crosse, *Shakespearean Playgoing, 1890–1952* (London: A. R. Mowbray & Co., 1953), 101.
5. Agate, *Brief Chronicles*, 19.
6. Cited by Callow, *Charles Laughton*, 70.
7. Agate, *Brief Chronicles*, 231.
8. Cited by Callow, *Charles Laughton*, 73.
9. Agate, *Brief Chronicles*, 231.
10. Callow, *Charles Laughton*, 67–8.
11. Cited by Callow, *Charles Laughton*, 68.
12. Cited by Callow, *Charles Laughton*, 68.
13. Cited by Callow, *Charles Laughton*, 42.
14. Kenneth Tynan, *Tynan on Theatre* (Harmondsworth: Penguin, 1964), 93.
15. *The Spectator* (20 August 1959), 15.

23. DONALD WOLFIT

1. Cited by Ronald Harwood, *Sir Donald Wolfit C.B.E.: His Life and Work in the Unfashionable Theatre* (London: Secker & Warburg, 1971), 100.
2. Cited by Harwood, *Sir Donald Wolfit*, 100.

3. Cited by Harwood, *Sir Donald Wolfit*, 100.
4. Cited by Harwood, *Sir Donald Wolfit*, 98.
5. Donald Wolfit, *First Interval: The Autobiography of Donald Wolfit* (London: Odhams, 1954), 136.
6. Wolfit, *First Interval*, 165.
7. Wolfit, *First Interval*, 168.
8. Wolfit, *First Interval*, 169.
9. Cited by Wolfit, *First Interval*, 169.
10. Cited by Wolfit, *First Interval*, 169.
11. Cited by Wolfit, *First Interval*, 171.
12. Wolfit, *First Interval*, 178.
13. James Agate, *Brief Chronicles* (London: Jonathan Cape, 1943), 121–2.
14. Cited by Harwood, *Sir Donald Wolfit*, 154.
15. Cited by Harwood, *Sir Donald Wolfit*, 165–6.
16. Cited by Harwood, *Sir Donald Wolfit*, 167.
17. Harwood, *Sir Donald Wolfit*, 199.
18. Harwood, *Sir Donald Wolfit*, 199.
19. Cited by Harwood, *Sir Donald Wolfit*, 199.
20. Cited by Harwood, *Sir Donald Wolfit*, 274.

24. RALPH RICHARDSON

1. Lord Blake and C. S. Nicholls (eds.), *Dictionary of National Biography 1981–1985* (Oxford: Oxford University Press, 1990), 340.
2. James Agate, *Brief Chronicles* (London: Jonathan Cape, 1943), 89.
3. Cited by Trevor R. Griffiths, 'Introduction', in William Shakespeare, *A Midsummer Night's Dream*, ed. Griffiths (Cambridge: Cambridge University Press, 1996), 53.
4. Griffiths, 'Introduction', 60.
5. Audrey Williamson, *Old Vic Drama: A Twelve Years' Study of Plays and Players* (London: Rockliff, 1948), 80.
6. Agate, *Brief Chronicles*, 113.
7. Agate, *Brief Chronicles*, 291.
8. Herbert Farjeon, *The Shakespearean Scene: Dramatic Criticisms* (London: Hutchinson & Co., n.d.), 167.
9. Cited by Marvin Rosenberg, *The Masks of Othello: The Search for the Identity of Othello, Iago, and Desdemona by Three Centuries of Actors and Critics* (Berkeley and Los Angeles: University of California Press, 1961), 157.
10. Agate, *Brief Chronicles*, 299.
11. Cited by Rosenberg, *Masks*, 145.
12. Williamson, *Old Vic*, 96.
13. Kenneth Tynan, *He That Plays the King: A View of the Theatre* (London: Longmans, Green & Co., 1950), 49.

14. Gordon Crosse, *Shakespearean Playgoing, 1890–1952* (London: A. R. Mowbray & Co., 1953), 128.
15. Williamson, *Old Vic*, 185.
16. *Manchester Guardian Weekly* (19 June 1952).
17. Kenneth Tynan, *Tynan on Theatre* (Harmondsworth: Penguin, 1964), 107.

25. JOHN GIELGUD

1. Jonathan Croall, *Gielgud: A Theatrical Life* (London: Methuen, 2001), 31.
2. Cited by Croall, *Gielgud: A Theatrical Life*, 55.
3. Cited by Croall, *Gielgud: A Theatrical Life*, 209.
4. James Agate, *Brief Chronicles* (London: Jonathan Cape, 1943), 211.
5. Agate, *Brief Chronicles*, 214.
6. Gordon Crosse, *Shakespearean Playgoing, 1890–1952* (London: A. R. Mowbray & Co., 1953), 142.
7. Cited by Croall, *Gielgud: A Theatrical Life*, 243.
8. Cited by Croall, *Gielgud: A Theatrical Life*, 243.
9. Cited by Croall, *Gielgud: A Theatrical Life*, 123.
10. Cited by Croall, *Gielgud: A Theatrical Life*, 129.
11. Croall, *Gielgud: A Theatrical Life*, 135.
12. John Gielgud, *An Actor and His Time* (London: Sidgwick & Jackson, 1979), 94.
13. Cited by Croall, *Gielgud: A Theatrical Life*, 138.
14. Gielgud, *An Actor*, 202.
15. Kenneth Rothwell, *A History of Shakespeare on Screen: A Century of Film and Television* (Cambridge: Cambridge University Press, 1999), 211.
16. Gielgud, *An Actor*, 131–4.
17. Cited by Jonathan Croall, *John Gielgud: Matinee Idol to Movie Star* (London: Methuen, 2011), 413.
18. Cited by Croall, *Gielgud: A Theatrical Life*, 357.
19. Rothwell, *Shakespeare on Screen*, 47.
20. Croall, *John Gielgud: Matinee Idol*, 378.
21. Cited by Croall, *Gielgud: A Theatrical Life*, 420.
22. Cited by Croall, *Gielgud: A Theatrical Life*, 422.

26. LAURENCE OLIVIER

1. *Oxford Dictionary of National Biography*, entry for Olivier, xli. 772.
2. John Cottrell, *Laurence Olivier* (Englewood Cliffs, NJ: Prentice Hall, 1975), 19.
3. Cottrell, *Laurence Olivier*, 20.
4. Laurence Olivier, *On Acting* (London: Weidenfeld and Nicolson, 1986), 79.
5. Olivier, *On Acting*, 57.
6. Cited in Cottrell, *Laurence Olivier*, 123.

7. Philip Ziegler, *Olivier* (London: Maclehose Press, Quercus, 2013), 66.
8. Olivier, *On Acting*, 72.
9. Cited by Ziegler, *Olivier*, 66.
10. Laurence Olivier, *Confessions of an Actor* (London: Weidenfeld and Nicolson, 1982), 82.
11. James Agate, *Brief Chronicles* (London: Jonathan Cape, 1943), 299–301.
12. Olivier, *On Acting*, 101.
13. Olivier, *On Acting*, 93.
14. Alan Dent, *Nocturnes and Rhapsodies* (London: Hamish Hamilton, 1950), 59.
15. Kenneth Tynan, *He That Plays the King: A View of the Theatre* (London: Longmans, Green & Co., 1950), 59.
16. Tynan, *He That Plays the King*, 59.
17. Tynan, *He That Plays the King*, 34.
18. Kenneth Tynan, *Theatre Writings*, selected and ed. Dominic Shellard (London: Nick Hern Books, 2007), 59.
19. Olivier, *On Acting*, 76.
20. T. C. Worsley, *New Statesman* (18 June 1955).
21. J. C. Trewin, *Shakespeare on the English Stage 1900–1964* (London: Barrie and Rockliff, 1964), 235.
22. Trewin, *Shakespeare on the English Stage*, 236.
23. Stanley Wells, *Royal Shakespeare: Four Major Productions at Stratford-upon-Avon* (Manchester: Manchester University Press, 1977).
24. *Oxford Dictionary of National Biography*, entry for Olivier, xli. 779.

27. PEGGY ASHCROFT

1. Cited by Michael Billington, *Peggy Ashcroft* (London: John Murray, 1988), 18.
2. Billington, *Peggy Ashcroft*, 19.
3. Cited by Billington, *Peggy Ashcroft*, 40.
4. Herbert Farjeon, *The Shakespearean Scene: Dramatic Criticisms* (London: Hutchinson & Co., n.d.), 54.
5. Billington, *Peggy Ashcroft*, 64.
6. Laurence Kitchin, *Mid-Century Drama* (London: Faber & Faber, 1960), 41.
7. Cited by Billington, *Peggy Ashcroft*, 78.
8. T. C. Worsley, *The Fugitive Art: Dramatic Commentaries 1947–1951* (London: John Lehmann, 1952), 149.
9. Cited by Billington, *Peggy Ashcroft*, 128.
10. Billington, *Peggy Ashcroft*, 144–5.
11. Cited by Billington, *Peggy Ashcroft*, 145.
12. *New Statesman* (9 May 1953).
13. Laurence Kitchin, *Drama in the Sixties: Form and Interpretation* (London: Faber & Faber, 1966), 172.

14. *Sunday Times* (25 August 1963).
15. Cited by Billington, *Peggy Ashcroft*, 203.
16. *Queen* (29 October 1969).
17. Stanley Wells, 'All's Well That Ends Well', *TLS* (1981), 1392.

28. MICHAEL REDGRAVE

1. Cited by Alan Strachan, *Secret Dreams: A Biography of Michael Redgrave* (London: Weidenfeld and Nicolson, 2004), 52.
2. Cited by Strachan, *Secret Dreams*, 74.
3. Strachan, *Secret Dreams*, 95.
4. Michael Redgrave, *An Actor's Ways and Means* (London: William Heinemann Ltd, 1953), 13–14.
5. Redgrave, *Actor's Ways*, 22–3.
6. Audrey Williamson, *Old Vic Drama: A Twelve Years' Study of Plays and Players* (London: Rockliff, 1948), 64.
7. Strachan, *Secret Dreams*, 249.
8. Strachan, *Secret Dreams*, 250.
9. Cited in Dennis Bartholomeusz, *Macbeth and the Players* (Cambridge: Cambridge University Press, 1969), 249.
10. Cited in Bartholomeusz, *Macbeth and the Players*, 249.
11. Kenneth Tynan, *He That Plays the King: A View of the Theatre* (London: Longmans, Green & Co., 1950), 81.
12. T. C. Worsley, *The Fugitive Art: Dramatic Commentaries 1947–1951* (London: John Lehmann, 1952), 21–2.
13. Audrey Williamson, *Old Vic Drama*, ii. *1947–1957* (London: Rockliff, 1957), 45.
14. Worsley, *The Fugitive Art*, 122.
15. Cited by Strachan, *Secret Dreams*, 262.
16. Strachan, *Secret Dreams*, 269.
17. Richard David, *Shakespeare in the Theatre* (Cambridge: Cambridge University Press, 1978), 201.
18. Worsley, *The Fugitive Art*, 229.
19. *Sunday Times* (29 March 1953).
20. Strachan, *Secret Dreams*, 291.
21. *The Observer* (19 May 1953).
22. Strachan, *Secret Dreams*, 293.
23. *The Observer* (19 July 1953).
24. Cited by Strachan, *Secret Dreams*, 294.

29. PAUL SCOFIELD

1. J. C. Trewin, *Paul Scofield* (London: Rockliff, 1956), 11.
2. Trewin, *Paul Scofield*, 12.
3. Trewin, *Paul Scofield*, 17.
4. Trewin, *Paul Scofield*, 12.

5. *Birmingham Post* (24 April 1946).
6. Trewin, *Paul Scofield*, 37.
7. *Time and Tide* (6 September 1946).
8. *News Chronicle* (30 August 1946).
9. J. C. Trewin, *John O'London's Weekly* (4 October 1946), 4.
10. Cited in Kenneth Tynan, *He That Plays the King: A View of the Theatre* (London: Longmans, Green & Co., 1950), dust jacket.
11. Tynan, *He That Plays the King*, 83.
12. Trewin, *Paul Scofield*, 45.
13. 'G.P.' in the *Manchester Guardian* (15 August 1947).
14. *News Chronicle* (12 June 1948).
15. C. L. Marock, *Daily Herald* (24 April 1948).
16. Worsley, *The Fugitive Art*, 38.
17. Tynan, *He That Plays the King*, 112.
18. Jonathan Croall, *Gielgud: A Theatrical Life* (London: Methuen, 2000), 373.
19. Cited by Croall, *Gielgud*, 99.
20. Kenneth Tynan, *Tynan on Theatre* (Harmondsworth: Penguin, 1964), 121.
21. Kenneth Tynan, *The Observer* (11 November 1962).

30. DONALD SINDEN

1. Donald Sinden, *A Touch of the Memoirs* (London: Hodder and Stoughton, 1982), 94.
2. *Birmingham Post* (16 April 1963).
3. *Financial Times* (18 July 1963).
4. *Birmingham Post* (19 July 1963).
5. Donald Sinden, 'Malvolio in *Twelfth Night*', in *Players of Shakespeare 1: Essays in Shakespearean Performance by Twelve Players with the Royal Shakespeare Company*, ed. Philip Brockbank (Cambridge: Cambridge University Press, 1985), 44–7.
6. 'Theory and Practice: Stratford 1976', *Shakespeare Survey*, 30 (1977), 172.
7. 'The Darkness at the Heart of *Much Ado About Nothing*', *The Guardian* (17 June 2011).
8. *Sunday Times* (24 August 1969).
9. *Birmingham Post* (1 December 1976).
10. *The Times* (1 December 1976).
11. *Birmingham Post* (1 December 1976).
12. *The Guardian* (1 December 1976).
13. *The Guardian* (15 August 1980).

31. RICHARD PASCO

1. *Illustrated London News* (10 April 1965).
2. *Birmingham Post* (16 May 1969).

3. *The Guardian* (10 October 1969).
4. *Coventry Evening Telegraph* (9 April 1971).
5. *Shakespeare Survey* 25 (1972), 266.
6. *The Times* (11 April 1973).
7. *The Guardian* (11 April 1973).
8. *Birmingham Post* (11 April 1973).
9. *Birmingham Post* (13 April 1973).
10. *Daily Telegraph* (13 June 1973).
11. *The Guardian* (13 June 1973).
12. *Sunday Times* (17 June 1973).
13. *The Guardian* (12 September 1980).
14. *The Times* (12 September 1980).

32. IAN RICHARDSON

1. Peter Thomson, 'A Necessary Theatre: The Royal Shakespeare Season 1970', *Shakespeare Survey*, 24 (1971), 117–26, at 119.
2. *Sunday Times* (16 April 1967).
3. *Sunday Telegraph* (16 April 1967).
4. *Birmingham Post* (6 April 1960).
5. *Birmingham Post* (6 June 1962).
6. *Punch* (27 April 1960).
7. *Financial Times*, 3 May 1964.
8. Thomson, 'A Necessary Theatre', 120–1.
9. Peter Thomson, 'Shakespeare Straight and Crooked: A Review of the 1973 Season at Stratford', *Shakespeare Survey* 27 (1974), 143–54, at 146–7.
10. Richard David, *Shakespeare in the Theatre* (Cambridge: Cambridge University Press, 1978), 168–72.

33. JUDI DENCH

1. Cited by Russ McDonald, *Look to the Lady: Sarah Siddons, Ellen Terry, and Judi Dench on the Shakespearean Stage* (Athens, Ga.: University of Georgia Press, 2005), 109.
2. *The Observer* (9 October 1960).
3. Cited by McDonald, *Look to the Lady*, 110–11.
4. 'A Lass Unparallel'd', in John Miller (ed.), *Darling Judi: A Celebration of Judi Dench* (London: Weidenfeld and Nicolson, 2004), 54–62, at 60.
5. Judi Dench, 'A Career in Shakespeare', in Jonathan Bate and Russell Jackson (eds.), *Shakespeare: An Illustrated Stage History* (Oxford: Oxford University Press, 1996), 204–5.
6. 'Dench-olatry', in Miller (ed.), *Darling Judi*, 170–7, at 177.
7. *The Guardian* (11 September 1976).

34. DEREK JACOBI

1. Derek Jacobi, *As Luck Would Have It: My Seven Ages* (London: Harper-Collins, 2013), 69.
2. Jacobi, *As Luck Would Have It*, 290.
3. *The Times*, 31 May 1977.
4. J. C. Trewin, *Five & Eighty Hamlets* (London: Hutchinson, 1987), 165–6.
5. *TLS* (7 May 1982).
6. *The Guardian* (22 April 1982).
7. *Sunday Times* (15 August 1982).
8. *Financial Times* (13 August 1982).
9. *The Observer* (15 August 1982).
10. *TLS* (3 September 1982).
11. *The Listener* (8 December 1989).
12. *The Guardian* (30 November 1988).
13. *Herald Tribune* (15 February 1989).
14. Jacobi, *As Luck Would Have It*, 299.
15. *Sunday Telegraph* (19 December 1993).
16. *The Independent* (18 December 1993).
17. Derek Jacobi, 'Macbeth', in Robert Smallwood (ed.), *Players of Shakespeare 4: Further Essays in Shakespearian Performance by Players with the Royal Shakespeare Company* (Cambridge: Cambridge University Press, 1998), 193–210.
18. *The Independent* (8 December 2010).
19. *Daily Telegraph* (8 December 2010).
20. *The Observer* (12 December 2010).

35. IAN MCKELLEN

1. <http://www.mckellen.com/>.
2. *The Times* (30 August 1969).
3. Cited in M. Shewring, *Richard II* (Manchester: Shakespeare in Performance, Manchester University Press, 1996), 85.
4. *Birmingham Post* (2 April 1976).
5. *Sunday Times* (12 September 1976).
6. *The Guardian* (11 September 1976).
7. Stanley Wells, 'Shakespeare Productions in England in 1989', *Shakespeare Survey* 43 (1991), 183–203, at 192.
8. *Daily Mail* (26 July 1990).
9. *The Guardian* (27 July 1996).

36. JANET SUZMAN

1. *Birmingham Post* (18 July 1963).
2. *Birmingham Post* (9 April 1965).

3. Undated newspaper cutting, Shakespeare Centre Library.
4. *Jewish Chronicle* (23 April 1965).
5. *The Guardian* (6 April 1967).
6. *Financial Times* (6 April 1967).
7. *The Guardian* (15 October 1968).
8. *The Observer* (20 October 1968).
9. *The Spectator* (25 October 1968).
10. *Financial Times* (30 July 1969).
11. *The Times* (30 July 1969).
12. *The Guardian* (16 June 1967).
13. *The Times* (16 June 1967).
14. B. A. Young, *Financial Times* (16 June 1967).
15. *As You Like It: Shakespeare at Stratford* (London: Thomson Learning, 2003), 81.
16. *The Times* (22 May 1968).
17. *The Guardian* (22 May 1968).
18. *Financial Times* (16 August 1972).
19. *The Guardian* (16 August 1972).
20. *Birmingham Post* (16 August 1972).
21. *Sunday Telegraph* (28 October 1973).
22. *The Lady* (8 November 1973).
23. (London: Oberon Books, 2012). Page references to this book will be given in parentheses in the text.
24. *The Observer* (15 March 2007).
25. *Daily Telegraph* (8 March 2007).

37. ANTONY SHER

1. *The Guardian* (30 June 1982).
2. *New Statesman* (2 July 1982).
3. *The Guardian* (9 January 1999).
4. *The Observer* (21 November 1999).
5. *The Guardian* (9 January 1999).
6. *Sunday Times* (10 January 1999).
7. *Independent on Sunday* (21 November 1999).
8. *Financial Times* (18 November 1999).
9. *Sunday Telegraph* (21 November 1999).
10. *The Observer* (21 November 1999).
11. *The Guardian* (19 February 2004).
12. *The Guardian* (17 April 2014).

38. SIMON RUSSELL BEALE

1. Simon Russell Beale, 'Thersites in *Troilus and Cressida*', in Russell Jackson and Robert Smallwood (eds.), *Players of Shakespeare 3: Further Essays in*

Shakespearian Performance by Players with the Royal Shakespeare Company
(Cambridge: Cambridge University Press, 1993), 160–73.
2. *Daily Telegraph* (28 April 1990).
3. Michael Dobson, 'Shakespeare Performances in England, 2005', *Shakespeare Survey* 59 (2006), 298–337, at 332.
4. George Bernard Shaw, *Shaw on Shakespeare: an Anthology of Bernard Shaw's Writings on the Plays and Production of Shakespeare*, ed. Edwin Wilson (London: Cassell, 1961), 87.
5. *Daily Telegraph* (13 August 1992).
6. *The Times* (13 August 1992).
7. *The Guardian* (14 August 1992).
8. *Daily Telegraph* (13 August 1992).
9. *Daily Telegraph* (13 August 1992).
10. Paul Taylor, *The Independent* (13 August 1992).
11. Michael Dobson, 'Shakespeare Performances in England, 2002', *Shakespeare Survey*, 56 (2003), 256–86, at 261.
12. Carol Chillington Rutter, 'Simon Russell Beale', in John Russell Brown (ed.), *The Routledge Companion to Actors' Shakespeare* (London: Routledge, 2012), 4.
13. Peter Holland, 'Shakespeare Performances in England, 1992–1993', *Shakespeare Survey* 47 (1994), 181–207, at 202.
14. Robert Smallwood, 'Shakespeare Performances in England', *Shakespeare Survey* 51 (1998), 254.
15. Michael Dobson, 'Shakespeare Performances in England, 2000', *Shakespeare Survey* 54 (2001), 246–82, at 260.
16. *The Guardian* (24 January 2014).

39. KENNETH BRANAGH

1. Mark White, *Kenneth Branagh* (London: Faber and Faber, 2005), 270.
2. Kenneth Branagh, *Beginning* (London: Chatto & Windus, 1989), 144.
3. *Financial Times* (29 March 1984).
4. *The Guardian* (29 March 1984).
5. *Daily Telegraph* (29 March 1984).
6. Branagh, *Beginning*, 146–7.
7. *The Guardian* (5 May 1988).
8. *The Guardian* (7 May 1988).
9. *The Guardian* (27 May 1988).
10. *The Times* (21 December 1992).
11. *Daily Telegraph* (21 December 1992).
12. *Daily Mail* (19 December 1992).
13. *Daily Telegraph* (21 December 1992).
14. Michael Dobson, 'Shakespeare Performances in England, 2002', *Shakespeare Survey* 56 (2003), 256–86, at 277–8.

Select Bibliography and Further Reading

THEATRE CRITICISM

Agate, James, *Brief Chronicles* (London: Jonathan Cape, 1943).

Beerbohm, Max, *Around Theatres* (London: Rupert Hart-Davis, 1953).

Beerbohm, Max, *More Theatres 1898–1903* (London: Rupert Hart-Davis, 1969).

Beerbohm, Max, *Last Theatres* (London: Rupert Hart-Davis, 1970).

Billington, Michael, *One Night Stands: A Critic's View of Modern British Theatre* (London: Nick Hern Books, 1993).

Brown, Ivor, *Theatre: 1954–1955* (London: Max Reinhardt, 1955).

Clapp, Henry Austin, *Reminiscences of a Dramatic Critic* (Boston and New York: Houghton, Mifflin and Co., 1902).

Cook, Dutton, *Nights at the Play: A View of the English Stage* (London: Chatto & Windus, 1883).

Crosse, Gordon, *Shakespearean Playgoing, 1890–1952* (London: A. R. Mowbray & Co., 1953).

Darlington, W. A., *Six Thousand and One Nights: 40 Years a Dramatic Critic* (London: George G. Harrap & Co., 1960).

David, Richard, *Shakespeare in the Theatre* (Cambridge: Cambridge University Press, 1978).

Farjeon, Herbert, *The Shakespearean Scene: Dramatic Criticisms* (London: Hutchinson & Co., n.d.).

Forster, John, and Lewes, George Henry, *Dramatic Essays by John Forster and George Henry Lewes*, ed. William Archer and Robert W. Lowe (London: Walter Scott Ltd, 1896).

Hazlitt, William, *Dramatic Essays by William Hazlitt*, ed. William Archer and Robert W. Lowe (London: Walter Scott Ltd, 1895).

Hobson, Harold, *Verdict at Midnight* (London: Longmans, Green & Co., 1952).

Holland, Peter, *English Shakespeares: Shakespeare on the English Stage in the 1990s* (Cambridge: Cambridge University Press, 1997).

Hunt, Leigh, *Leigh Hunt's Dramatic Criticism, 1808–1831*, ed. Lawrence Huston Houtchens and Carolyn Washburn Houtchens (London: Geoffrey Cumberlege, 1950).

James, Henry, *The Scenic Art: Notes on Acting and the Drama 1872–1901*, ed. Allan Wade (London: Rupert Hart-Davis, 1949).

Kitchin, Laurence, *Mid-Century Drama* (London: Faber & Faber, 1960).

Kitchin, Laurence, *Drama in the Sixties: Form and Interpretation* (London: Faber & Faber, 1966).

Knight, Joseph, *Theatrical Notes* (London: Lawrence & Bullen, 1893).

Lamb, Charles, *The Dramatic Essays of Charles Lamb*, ed. Brander Matthews (London: Chatto & Windus, 1891).

Lewes, George Henry, *On Actors and the Art of Acting* (New York: Henry Holt and Co. 1880; repr. Forgotten Books, 2012).

MacCarthy, Desmond, *Drama* (London: Putnam, 1940).

Montague, C. E., *Dramatic Values* (London: Methuen, 1911).

Morley, Henry, *Journal of a London Playgoer 1851–1866* (London: George Routledge and Sons Ltd, 1891).

Robertson, W. Graham, *Time Was* (London: Hamish Hamilton, 1931).

Rowell, George (ed.), *Victorian Dramatic Criticism* (London: Methuen, 1971).

Russell, W. Clark, *Representative Actors* (London: Frederick Warne and Co, n.d.).

Scott, Clement, *The Drama of Yesterday and Today*, 2 vols. in 1 (London: Macmillan & Co, 1899).

Shaw, George Bernard, *Our Theatres in the Nineties*, 3 vols. (London: Constable & Co., 1932).

Speaight, Robert, *The Property Basket: Recollections of a Divided Life* (London: Collins and Harvill Press, 1970).

Trewin, J. C., *Going to Shakespeare* (London: George Allen & Unwin, 1978).

Tynan, Kenneth, *He That Plays the King: A View of the Theatre* (London: Longmans, Green & Co., 1950).

Tynan, Kenneth, *Theatre Writings*, selected and ed. Dominic Shellard (London: Nick Hern Books, 2007).

Wells, Stanley (ed.), *Shakespeare in the Theatre: An Anthology of Criticism* (Oxford: Clarendon Press, 1997).

Wilson, A. E., *Playgoer's Pilgrimage* (London: Stanley Paul & Co., n.d.).

Winston, James, *Drury Lane Journal: Selections from James Winston's Diaries 1819–1827*, ed. Alfred L. Nelson and Gilbert B. Cross (London: Society for Theatre Research, 1974).

Winter, William, *Shakespeare on the Stage* (London: T. Fisher Unwin, 1912).

Worsley, T. C., *The Fugitive Art: Dramatic Commentaries 1947–1951* (London: John Lehmann, 1952).

Young, B. A., *The Mirror up to Nature: A Review of the Theatre, 1964–1982* (London: William Kimber & Co., 1982).

LIFE WRITINGS

Ira Aldridge

Lindfors, Bernth (ed.), *Ira Aldridge: The African Roscius* (Rochester, NY: University of Rochester Press, 2007).

Peggy Ashcroft

Billington, Michael, *Peggy Ashcroft* (London: John Murray, 1988).
Keown, Eric, *Peggy Ashcroft* (London: Rockliff, 1955).

John Barrymore

Morrison, Michael A., *John Barrymore: Shakespearean Actor* (Cambridge: Cambridge University Press, 1997).

Lilian Baylis

Thorndike, Sybil and Russell, *Lilian Baylis* (London: Chapman and Hall, 1938).
Schafer, Elizabeth, *Lilian Baylis, A Biography* (London, University of Hertfordshire Press/Society for Theatre Research, 2006).

Thomas Betterton

Roberts, David, *Thomas Betterton: The Greatest Actor of the Restoration Stage* (Cambridge: Cambridge University Press, 2010).

Edwin Booth

Ruggles, Eleanor, *Prince of Players Edwin Booth* (New York: Norton and Co., 1953).

George Frederick Cooke

Hare, Arnold, *George Frederick Cooke: The Actor and the Man* (London: Society for Theatre Research, 1980).

Charlotte Cushman

Leach, Joseph, *Bright Particular Star: The Life and Times of Charlotte Cushman* (New Haven and London: Yale University Press, 1970).

Judi Dench

McDonald, Russ, *Look to the Lady: Sarah Siddons, Ellen Terry, and Judi Dench on the Shakespearean Stage* (Athens, Ga.: University of Georgia Press, 2005).

Edith Evans

Trewin, J. C., *Edith Evans* (2nd edn., London: Rockliff, 1954).

Helen Faucit

Carlyle, Carol Jones, *Helen Faucit: Fire and Ice on the Victorian Stage* (London: Society for Theatre Research, 2000).

John Gielgud

Croall, Jonathan, *John Gielgud: Matinee Idol to Movie Star* (London: Methuen Drama, 2011).

Gielgud, Kate Terry, *An Autobiography* (London: Max Reinhardt, 1953).

Henry Irving

Holroyd, Michael, *A Strange Eventful History: The Dramatic Lives of Ellen Terry, Henry Irving, and Their Remarkable Families* (London: Chatto & Windus, 2008).

Hughes, Alan, *Henry Irving, Shakespearean* (Cambridge: Cambridge University Press, 1981).

Derek Jacobi

Jacobi, Derek, *As Luck Would Have It* (London: HarperCollins, 2013).

Dora Jordan

Boaden, James, *The Life of Mrs Jordan* (London: Edward Bull, 1831; repr. Cambridge: Cambridge University Press, 2012).

Tomalin, Claire, *Mrs Jordan's Profession: The Story of a Great Actress and a Future King* (London: Viking, 1994).

Edmund Kean

Fitzsimons, Raymund, *Edmund Kean: Fire from Heaven* (London: Hamish Hamilton, 1976).

Kemble family

Kelly, Linda, *The Kemble Era: John Philip Kemble, Sarah Siddons, and the London Stage* (London: Bodley Head, 1980).

Charles Laughton

Callow, Simon, *Charles Laughton: A Difficult Actor* (London: Methuen, 1987; Vintage Books, 2012).

W. C. Macready

The Diaries of William Charles Macready, ed. William Toynbee, 2 vols. (London: Chapman and Hall, Ltd, 1912).

Downer, Alan S., *The Eminent Tragedian: William Charles Macready* (Cambridge, Mass.: Harvard University Press, 1966).

Trewin, J. C., *Mr Macready: A Nineteenth Century Tragedian and His Theatre* (London: George Harrap and Co., 1955).

Ian McKellen

Barrett, Mark, *Ian McKellen: An Unauthorised Biography* (London: Virgin Books, 2005).

Laurence Olivier

Cottrell, John, *Laurence Olivier* (Englewood Cliffs, NJ: Prentice Hall, 1975).
Olivier, Laurence, *On Acting* (London: Weidenfeld and Nicolson, 1986).
Ziegler, Philip, *Olivier* (London: Maclehose Press, Quercus, 2013).

Michael Redgrave

Redgrave, Michael, *An Actor's Ways and Means* (London: William Heinemann Ltd, 1953).
Strachan, Michael, *Secret Dreams: A Biography of Michael Redgrave* (London: Weidenfeld & Nicolson, 2004).

Tommaso Salvini

Carlson, Marvin, *The Italian Shakespearians: Performances by Ristori, Salvini, and Rossi in England and America* (Washington, DC: Folger Shakespeare Library, 1985).

Sarah Siddons

French, Yvonne, *Mrs Siddons: Tragic Actress* (London, Derek Verschoyle, 1936; rev. 1954).
McDonald, Russ, *Look to the Lady: Sarah Siddons, Ellen Terry, and Judi Dench on the Shakespearean Stage* (Athens, Ga.: University of Georgia Press, 2005).

Antony Sher

Sher, Antony, *Beside Myself: An Autobiography* (London: Hutchinson, 2001).
Sher, Antony, *Year of the King: An Actor's Diary and Sketchbook* (London: Chatto & Windus, 1985; repr. with a new introd., Nick Hern Books, 2004).

Donald Sinden

Sinden, Donald, *A Touch of the Memoirs* (London: Hodder and Stoughton, 1982).

Ellen Terry

Edgar-Pemberton, T., *Ellen Terry and Her Sisters* (London: C. Arthur Pearson Ltd, 1902).
Hiatt, Charles, *Ellen Terry and Her Impersonations: An Appreciation* (London: George Bell & Sons, 1899).
Holroyd, Michael, *A Strange Eventful History: The Dramatic Lives of Ellen Terry, Henry Irving, and Their Remarkable Families* (London: Chatto & Windus, 2008).
McDonald, Russ, *Look to the Lady: Sarah Siddons, Ellen Terry, and Judi Dench on the Shakespearean Stage* (Athens, Ga.: University of Georgia Press, 2005).
Manvell, Roger, *Ellen Terry* (London: Heron Books, 1968).
Terry, Ellen, *The Story of My Life* (London: Hutchinson & Co., 1908).
Terry, Ellen, *Ellen Terry's Memoirs*, ed. Edith Craig and Christopher St John (London, Victor Gollancz Ltd, 1933).

Terry, Ellen, and Shaw, George Bernard, *Ellen Terry and Bernard Shaw: A Correspondence*, ed. Christopher St John (London: Constable, 1931).

Donald Wolfit

Harwood, Ronald, *Sir Donald Wolfit C.B.E.: His Life and Work in the Unfashionable Theatre* (London: Secker & Warburg, 1971).

OTHER WORKS

Astington, John H., *Actors and Acting in Shakespeare's Time* (Cambridge: Cambridge University Press, 2010).

Bartholomeusz, Dennis, *Macbeth and the Players* (Cambridge: Cambridge University Press, 1969).

Drake, Fabia, *Blind Fortune* (London: William Kimber, 1978).

Honigmann, E. A. J., and Susan Brock (eds.), *Playhouse Wills 1558–1642* (Manchester: Manchester University Press, 1993).

Lelyveld, Toby, *Shylock on the Stage* (London: Routledge and Kegan Paul Ltd, 1961).

Odell, G. C. D., *Shakespeare: From Betterton to Irving*, 2 vols. (New York: Scribner, 1920; repr. London: Constable, 1963).

Pickering, David (ed.), *International Directory of Theatre 3: Actors, Directors, and Designers* (Detroit: St James Press, 1996).

Schoch, Richard W., *Queen Victoria and the Theatre of Her Age* (London: Palgrave Macmillan, 2004).

Shattuck, Charles H., *Shakespeare on the American Stage: From the Hallams to Edwin Booth* (Washington, DC: Folger Shakespeare Library, 1976).

Sprague, Arthur Colby, *Shakespearian Players and Performances* (Cambridge, Mass.: Harvard University Press, 1953).

Wiles, David, *Shakespeare's Clown: Actor and Text in the Elizabethan Playhouse* (Cambridge: Cambridge University Press, 1987).

Index

Numbers in bold indicate chapters; those in italics indicate illustrations.